£2

Andrew Wingate is Canon Theologian of Leicester Cathedral and a Chaplain to The Queen. In 2009, he was awarded the OBE for his work in interfaith relations. He has been a theological teacher for long periods in Madurai, Tamil Nadu, and at Queen's College in Birmingham. He was Principal of the international College of the Ascension at Selly Oak, Birmingham, before moving to Leicester in 2000, where he founded the St Philip's Centre for Study and Engagement in a Multi Faith Society, a local, national and international project. He has been immersed both in Islam and in Hinduism, and is an honorary lecturer now at De Montfort University. This book comes out of 30 years of experience with Hindus in India and in the West. He studied in Oxford and Birmingham Universities, and his doctorate in Birmingham was on issues of interreligious conversion in South India, published by ISPCK/SPCK. He has written six books, including the much-used, and now in its fourth printing, *Celebrating Difference, Staying Faithful: How to Live in a Multi-Faith World* (Darton, Longman & Todd, 2005).

THE MEETING OF OPPOSITES?

Hindus and Christians in the West

ANDREW WINGATE

17/4/15

To Liza and Mike,

With many thanks for a happy visit to your welcoming home on the occasion of Alison Cozens Induction to Dunfermline – from the very Hindu heartland of Leicester!

Andrew

First published in Great Britain in 2014

Society for Promoting Christian Knowledge
36 Causton Street
London SW1P 4ST
www.spckpublishing.co.uk

British Library Cataloguing-in-Publication Data
A catalogue record for this book is available from the British Library

ISBN 978–0–281–06675–9
eBook ISBN 978–0–281–06676–6

Typeset by Graphicraft Limited, Hong Kong
First printed in Great Britain by Ashford Colour Press
Subsequently digitally printed in Great Britain

eBook by Graphicraft Limited, Hong Kong

Produced on paper from sustainable forests

For
my family – my three grown-up children Joanna, Jenny and Matthew, and my wife Angela – with thanks for their sharing the Indian journey with me, and hence my involvement with Hindus

Contents

Foreword

To engage seriously in interfaith dialogue is a complex matter. Too often it has been reduced to one of two distorted forms: 'arguing for victory', scoring points over a partner in conversation; or dismissing all serious points of tension in a search for convergence at all costs. Doing it seriously entails something uncomfortably like a spiritual discipline of looking beyond the obvious dualities; which means moving beyond both the aggressive 'yes or no' stance of argument and the search for some comfortable consensus that challenges neither party. And if we can't get beyond these shrivelled versions of dialogue, then, as Andrew Wingate clearly implies, our world will be poorer – poorer in the presence of people willing to be transformed by staying with the challenge of the other, patiently and lovingly. As Scripture suggests, *staying with* is near the heart of wisdom.

Andrew brings to this issue a really unusual depth of engagement at ground level both in Asia and the UK, in addition to the depth of his knowledge of diverse traditions. He has for decades painstakingly and lovingly created environments where real difference can be faced and thought through together in a transforming way; and in this book we have a digest of what he has learned and taught in the diverse contexts of a devoted and exceptional ministry. Those of us – among whom I count myself – who have learned more than they can easily say from his example and reflection will be delighted to have this work of witness from him; those who have not had the good fortune to sit at his feet will have a deeply valuable and enlarging experience ahead in reading these pages.

Dr Rowan Williams, former Archbishop of Canterbury
Master of Magdalene College, Cambridge

Acknowledgements

Thanks to SPCK staff, for their working together with the author in the production of this book, and especially to Ruth McCurry, recently retired, for accepting the book proposal and for showing enthusiastic support all the way through.

1

Today Islam, tomorrow Hinduism? Challenges for Christians in the West

The main theme of this book is the place and potential of Hindus, and their religious base, to become a challenge to other religions and communities, and in particular that of Christianity, as a faith, world view and way of life. Can there be a long-term and deep encounter, a positive interaction between Christianity and Hinduism, between Christians and Hindus, or are they to develop in different worlds? Can there be, potentially and in practice, a theologically and spiritually rich engagement? I believe there can be, hence this book. And we have a chance in the West to help this to happen, where there are not the same political agendas that arise in India. Can there be a true meeting between these two faiths here, or are they so different, so much opposites, that the most that can happen is that they remain at peace, but keep themselves at a distance, as inevitably opposites at all kinds of levels – spiritual, theological, missiological?

There is an obvious contemporary starting point: the growing economic power of India. This can be symbolized by its demand to be a permanent member of the UN Security Council, in the way that China is. Its population is now over one billion, so why should it not be at the top table? It is a nuclear power, having successfully defied the West without losing its respectability as a negotiating partner. Its nuclear bomb became known as the Hindu bomb, as a counter to the Muslim bomb in nearby Pakistan. The USA even agreed, in 2012, to allow export of vast amounts of nuclear technology, and India offered around £97 billion of contracts to foreign investment in nuclear power. Like China, it resisted the pressures of the economic collapse, and its growth continued seemingly uninterrupted, though with the occasional blip, as in 2013. Like China, it has resisted the pressure to take enforceable steps about the environment and global warming, arguing that it is in the process of 'catch-up' and its per capita use of the world's resources remains low compared with either the USA or Europe. Its poverty remains widespread and often extreme, but claims are made that this is reducing both through proactive government and through the trickle-down effect of the growing middle class, around the urban centres in particular.

At the same time, the Indian diaspora has spread throughout the world, and Indians are marked by their high level of educational, technological and economic achievement. They are the most educated community in the UK, and have incomes not far off that of Chinese and Koreans as the highest earners in the USA (see Chapter 8 on the USA). In some ways, they are everyone's favourite immigrants, with their reputation for hard work, cultural identity, family coherence, colourful artistic achievement and culinary excellence. Eighty per cent of Indians are classified as Hindus, and this religion has consequently had a good press wherever the diaspora has gone. It is known for its colour, music, festivals, joyfulness, and for its lack of ideology and aggressive rhetoric, or missionary zeal. It is inclusive of women and the family. It is not feared like Islam, but welcomed into the cultural map of the places where it has gone. It appears not to want to impose itself, but to adjust to context. Its seeming inclusiveness makes it attractive to the Western way of thinking and to postmodernism. You can take this or that from it, and nothing is required. It also seems to hold its communities together, with very little crime or indiscipline among its young people, and lower rates of marriage breakdown than elsewhere.

Nor does it seem to be a threat to Christianity. With few exceptions, it does not wish to convert others; indeed the concept of conversion has little meaning in the Western sense as found in the Abrahamic faiths. It is a question of 'live and let live'. It is not credal or dogmatic, and the seeming absence of a Church, central structures, a hierarchy, is deeply attractive to those who have rejected these within their own faith tradition. Its seeming spiritual focus on meditation and yoga, and its world view that seems to emphasize history less, and the spirit more, also provides an attraction to those who have rejected the faith of Christianity and especially of the church in which they have been brought up. Its willingness to accept Jesus as an incarnation of God also allows an inclusiveness of the central part of Christian faith – and the belief that there are many other incarnations than Jesus of Nazareth, born 2,000 years ago in a remote province of the Roman Empire, seems to have considerable attraction.

Hence the theme of this introduction. How far can we envisage the challenge of Hinduism in the coming decades? Can it to any degree replace the challenge of Islam, or become any kind of rival in terms of influence and importance? Would it want to be this? The answer to this question bears on the main chapters of the book, a study of Hindu–Christian encounter in the Indian diaspora in general, and in the UK in particular. Where have we come from, and where are we going? Little has been written on this theme, and Islam or Judaism has been dominant in the literature in recent decades. The aim of this book is to fill some of this gap, and this chapter is an introduction to what gap is to be filled.

One thing that is clear is that Hinduism cannot in any real sense be understood without considering its roots in India. Whatever it is, it is a religion of the soil, and in that sense it can be compared with Judaism, a religion of the land. This is hard to understand, and to feel, for those following global religions. Origins in Palestine or Arabia do not dominate Christianity or Islam, though the Arabic language has much greater importance for Islam than Greek for Christianity.

In many ways, Hinduism appears to differ from the Abrahamic faiths. They are seen as the religions of Moses, Jesus and Muhammad respectively. There are named founders. There are confined scriptures – the Torah, the New Testament, the Qur'an. And there are required beliefs, however interpreted – in the Ten Commandments; the nature and work of Jesus, and of God as Trinity; the Qur'an, Allah, and Muhammad as the last prophet. There are clear requirements in each case, in terms of ethical or legal demands. And there are norms of prayer and worship to be followed, and boundaries as to what makes one a Jew, a Christian or a Muslim. There is a firm view of the place of history, and the way that God has worked through that history. There is an eschatology of what is to happen in the end times, as well as an explanation of origins in Creation. There are markers in the history of these faiths – the call of Abraham, Moses on Mount Sinai receiving the commandments, the exodus from Egypt; the life, death and resurrection of Jesus, and the formation of the Church at Pentecost; the calling of the Prophet Muhammad, the revelation of the Qur'an and the formation of the new Islamic community.

In apparent contrast with this, the traditions behind Hinduism go back an unspecified number of years – 5,000 years is often referred to loosely. There is no one and agreed founder, no one official scripture recognized as mandatory for the believer. There is no authorized creed, no organization to be compared with church, no hierarchy that is immediately recognizable. There are of course rich traditions and ancestors to whom Hindus look, such as Shankara and Ramunuja, and there are a range of scriptures central to different groups, as well as the Vedas, traditionally acknowledged by all. The Upanishads and Vedanta are also so recognized, and the countless stories (Puranas), and epics. The Bhagavadgita (or simply 'the Gita') has become almost *the* scripture in the West, as it was for Gandhi.

But of course there are organizations and hierarchies within different Hindu groups; and there is the caste organization, with Brahmins at the top of a very powerful hierarchy. There is the Sanskrit language, unifying across higher-caste Hindus. There are immense regional variations. There is no common understanding of what it means to be a Hindu. It may have little to do with temple attendance or religious practice or knowledge; it has a great deal to do with seemingly hard-to-define questions such as ethos, culture, tradition, heritage, Indianness, regional feel.

To go on to consider the engagement between indigenous Christians and incoming Hindus in the UK, the USA and elsewhere, it is necessary to go back to the beginning of the encounter at the Indian end, and our next chapter looks at the churches in India within the Hindu context where they were born and developed. There is a fundamental difference here. Incoming Christian missionaries came as a tiny minority with a primary purpose of creating Christian churches in a new land. In no sense did Hindus come to the West, or to British imperial territories in Africa, the Caribbean, and other parts of the East, to create new Hindu communities. They brought those communities with them as they came for other purposes – trade, employment, education or as bonded labourers. Of course, in the colonial era, Christians came to India as administrators, soldiers, engineers, tea planters, educators, doctors, traders, adventurers. The colonial administrators and traders not only adjusted to Hinduism as they found it, but often used it for their own purpose, encouraging the highest-caste Brahmins to help them to divide and rule.

But there was a particular group who came to spread Christianity, following an expansionist ideology, 'to make disciples of all nations' (Matthew 28.19), which included Indians of all varieties. Here they met the challenge of Hinduism in all its complexity, as we shall be considering in this book, a challenge that has only come directly to UK churches and those in other Western countries in the last few decades. Until then, encounter with Hinduism was always 'over there' and was encounter with 'the exotic' or 'the demonic', to be read about, to be heard about in missionary talks, but to be kept safely at a distance. As such there was a fascination with Hinduism as it was gradually discovered and engaged with. Geoff Oddie, in his recent book *Reimagining Hinduism*,[1] has shown through a study of missionary journals and literature that in the nineteenth century it was Hinduism rather than Islam that received most of the attention. It was an exciting journey of discovery, with the early emphasis being on the horrific, and later the challenge of a religion to be taken very seriously as a rival for Indian minds and communities.

There can be no dispute that the present (early twenty-first-century) perceived challenge to Christians, and to churches, lies in the profile of Islam. How to respond to the post-1989 dominance of agendas related to

Islam? September 11, 2001 is the tip of the iceberg, the moment when this became most apparent. But this date does not represent an isolated event, coming from nowhere. The Huntington Thesis, about the inevitability of the Clash of Civilizations between Islam and the West, became highlighted at this point, and gained considerable credibility – and indeed notoriety.[2] But this was because it was the most dramatic of a series of such incidents, and was followed also by further terrorist events, such as the London Bombings of 7 July 2005, and the bombings of 2004 in Madrid, and in Boston and a Nairobi shopping centre in 2013. These were only the most striking of the events happening in the West. Meanwhile, there were endless terrorist events going on in countries in Africa and Asia, involving Islamist rhetoric, and the vast number of deaths in Iraq and Afghanistan, precipitated by the invasions of these countries in response to September 11. Huntington could claim at least a prima facie case for this thesis, and popular rhetoric and the media fed itself on belief in this. The clash between capitalism and Marxist communism had been replaced decisively by that between Christianity and Islam.

This was not just about violence. It was also about world view, philosophy and way of life; it was about cultural difference. It was about the law, rationalism, the place of women, moral values, materialism, freedom, democracy. Emotionally, *sharia*, and all it symbolized, was as important a part of this clash as the seemingly endless acts of violence in the name of Allah. Huntington wrote memorably:

> Islam's borders are bloody and so are its innards. The underlying problem for the West is not Islamic fundamentalism. It is Islam, a different civilization whose people are convinced of the superiority of their culture, and are obsessed with the inferiority of their power.[3]

He was also conscious of what he felt were the inherent weaknesses in the West, and in the USA in particular. The American dream had become fragmented, not least by Hispanic immigration. Christianity was fragmented also, and in Europe in steep decline. An ideologically coherent Islam posed a real threat, not just in terms of global presence, but also in the heartlands of the USA and Europe.

There are many flaws in Huntington's often oversimplistic generalizations, and painting things as black and white, with little grey. I will quote just two critiques. The first is from a leading younger Muslim academic practitioner in the UK:

> Muslims are now part of the West, so the discussion is not really between 'them' and 'us' but between 'us' and 'us', amongst ourselves, with our common

> humanity. Talk of 'clash of civilisations' in this context is not only dangerous and irresponsible (for the fault lines it perpetuates), it is also foolish ... Muslims living in the West may not agree with certain material motivations in the West or the way the family is being neglected, and on these issues they may stand together with many of their fellow citizens of Christian and other faiths, and non-faith backgrounds. Muslims living in the West may take issue with the current state of social and international justice, and they would again stand with the majority of fellow citizens.[4]

The other is from the leading prophet of Islamic reform, Tariq Ramadan. He writes in the powerful summary he has compiled of his thinking, *What I Believe*:

> I mean to build bridges between two universes of reference, between two (highly debatable) constructions termed Western and Islamic 'civilizations' (as if those were closed, monolithic entities), and between citizens within Western societies themselves. My aim is to show, in theory and in practice, that one can be both fully Muslim and Western and that beyond our different affiliations we share many common principles and values through which it is possible to 'live together' within contemporary pluralistic, multicultural societies where various religions coexist.[5]

Less prominent in the discussion have been Samuel Huntington's other 'civilizations' – they are Latin, Japanese, Sinic, Hindu, Orthodox and African. Even since Huntington wrote 15 years or more ago, the growing importance of the Chinese presence in the world has been endorsed by its population numbers, its enormous economic growth and its centrality to the world economy, with its vital contribution to stabilization after the great banking crisis of 2008–9. It has now overtaken Japan as the second largest economy in the world. Brazil has been leading South America economically, while Venezuela resisted the power of the USA with the demagogic leadership and socialist rhetoric of its now late President Chavez. The Hispanic population grows in proportion rapidly within the USA. Africa has the potential to become less of a basket case, and more assertive of its place in the world. Here we have witnessed the symbolism of the football World Cup taking place in South Africa, and the potential growth in several countries, once stability is shown to be sustaining, and natural resources come to the fore. David Smith, in *The Observer* in July 2010, described how what had been dubbed the 'hopeless' continent, ten years before, was now experiencing a spectacular recovery from the global recession thanks to decades of market reform and strong trade ties with China.

Outline of the book

I wish in this Introduction to say from the outset that this is not primarily an academic book, but one to encourage practitioners, and would-be practitioners from both faiths, to develop their competence and confidence in the field of Hindu–Christian relations. As such, it is written mainly in broad-brush colours rather than narrowly argued academic reasoning. This does not mean that it is merely popular in its feel, but though chapters vary in this way, it is a book written with a mission: to encourage a wider interest in its subject across the churches, clergy, theological students and lay people, and Hindus who wish to go deeper in their engagement with Christians.

After the chapter on Christians in India and their engagement with Hindus, there follow three chapters which consist of three lectures I gave in India in several colleges, in autumn 2011. They are constructed around three *bhakti* movements in the West, primarily the UK. These are ISKCON, a very promising movement for Christians to interact with; South Indian *bhakti* movements and their temples; and examples of conversion to Christianity, where *bhakti* has been to the fore, including an example of someone who calls himself a *Jesu Bhakter* (someone devoted to Jesus). There follows a short chapter on the Swaminarayan movement, a very important movement found wherever Gujaratis have settled, which means throughout the diaspora. Next there are three case-study chapters. Two are major studies: on the city of Leicester, where I live and which is seen as the Hindu heart within the UK; and on the USA, with a considerable and wealthy Hindu population. The third case study is a smaller one, from Sweden, where I have spent some time. It is hoped that these three chapters can give a feel for our topic throughout the diaspora. Next there is a chapter on Hindu–Christian forums in the UK that I have been involved in. The final chapter, before the concluding comments on the question about how far this is a 'meeting of opposites', is a discussion of the major theological, spiritual, dialogical and mission issues arising out of the encounter between Christians and Hindus in the West.

There are many interviews in this book, and these were conducted mainly in 2011 and 2012, and some in 2013 and 2014. These were recorded accurately at the time, and checked where possible.

2

Christian–Hindu encounter in India: From the beginnings of Christianity in Kerala to the present day

A key to understanding Indian Christianity is that it is the faith of a minority, and indeed a tiny minority. Just 2.3 per cent of Indians registered as Christians in the last census, and this number was down from 2.6 per cent in 1971. In numbers this is over 24 million people, a large proportion practising. Some estimates are that the figure is now around 30 million. There are, of course, enormous regional variations, with Christianity by far the majority faith in certain small north-eastern states, and comprising around a quarter of the population in the highly educated state of Kerala. Southern states also have percentages well above the average, as do certain urban areas. But other states vast in population such as the Hindi belt of North India have tiny numbers of Christians. There are less than 0.3 per cent in the largest state by population, Uttar Pradesh, and no more in the rest of the northern areas outside the cities or tribal areas. This means that Christians are, and always have been, surrounded by a vast ocean of people of other faiths; they are so often indeed just a drop in that ocean.

Of course, the nature of the ocean around them will vary; in most areas it is Hinduism in a broad sense, but the make-up of that population varies enormously in terms of caste, main theological and philosophical traditions, deities worshipped in rural contexts and city temples, and manifestations of Hindu practice in terms of festivals and customs. Among these factors, the Dalit questions have come to the fore in recent decades, and whether Dalits see themselves as Hindu at all; and the variety of tribal belief systems and practices varies enormously regionally and locally.[1]

It is therefore impossible for Christians to live uninfluenced by these contexts. How far have expressions of Christianity changed within this environment? At the same time, what is surprising is how much influence Christianity has had on those around them, particularly Hindus. A question is how to measure this relationship – is it by the number of Hindus who have become Christians, or by the changes found in Hinduism as a result of living alongside this minority? This influence has been both upon the individuals concerned and also in the thinking and practice of the faith or faiths that make up Hinduism.

In terms of relationships, a key question is whether Christianity is an Indian religion or not. Ambedkar was clear it was not.[2] He admired it greatly for the strength of its social gospel, but felt he could never join it, because it would mean joining a 'foreign' religion, just as much as Islam was. The Hindutva movement of recent decades has also had, as a major platform, that only Hindus can be truly Indian, and neither Christians nor Muslims can be fully trusted for their Indianness because their ultimate loyalties lie elsewhere. A diametrically opposed view was taken by India's first prime minister, Nehru, who in Parliament in 1955, around the question of conversion and the constitution, affirmed strongly that Christianity was an Indian religion as were others. He said, vividly, 'Christianity is as old in India as Christianity itself. Christianity found its roots in India before it went to countries like England, Portugal and Spain. Christianity is as much a religion of the Indian soil as any other religion of India.'

I now look at the history of the major churches, in terms of their relationship with people of other faiths, especially the 80 per cent who are Hindus.

The churches in India and their interaction with Hinduism

Orthodox (St Thomas) Christians and other faiths

Nehru was calling attention to the very early advent of Christianity to southern India, through the agency of St Thomas or those associated with this apostle in the first two centuries of Christianity. Christianity in Kerala was not the introduction of Western colonial mission; it came from Syria, and it has always remained independent of such missions. Its history was a remarkable example of survival without help from outside for more than a thousand years. The change came with the coming of the Portuguese in the sixteenth century, when parts of this Church became part of the Roman Catholic Church. But many were allowed to keep the Syrian rite and customs. Others remained within the Syrian Orthodox traditions completely. They have survived all these centuries surrounded by Hinduism, and in some areas by Islam, by becoming a kind of high caste, and being accepted by other high Hindu castes as equals. Their relationship was one of mutual respect, with strict rules against intermarriage with those 'lower' than themselves. They were also clear they were not to evangelize other faiths around them. These were ways of survival, and this led to fossilizing of life and liturgy.

In the nineteenth century, some of these St Thomas Christians felt this fossilization. They felt there should be a sense of mission and theological development. They asked the Anglican Church Missionary Society (CMS) to send missionaries to help them. The result was not what they expected. The vigour of the two missionaries sent led to a split in the Church. The Mar Thoma Church was formed, which still maintained the Syrian rite, but engaged actively in mission and evangelism to Hindus. It believed in a vigorous relationship with those around, and became a major Christian Church in terms of influence up to the present day. It holds the largest annual evangelistic convention in the world. At the same time, another mission – that which later became the Church of South India in Kerala – worked with the low caste, and formed the Diocese of Madhya Kerala. Hinduism indirectly or directly was the reason for these church divisions. If mission was to be successful, in practice it seems it had to live within the caste system. By this route, casteism became endemic in the Kerala Church, as it was to become within all the main churches, by various routes.

The Roman Catholic Church

Meanwhile, the major Roman Catholic missionary engagement had come further up the coast, beginning from Goa and spreading at speed around all of coastal southern India. The intrepid missionary Francis Xavier converted so many that individual baptism was impossible, as crowds of fishermen and their families sought the protection of the Portuguese navy and their religion. The relationship with the Hindu communities around was that of conquest, and the creation of little Portugals in southern and western India, centred on Goa. Baptism meant in some ways deculturization, and the adoption of a new way of life, as well as obedience to a foreign ruler. Churches were built according to Portuguese architecture, and Hindu festivals were replaced by Christian festivals, with statues of Mary and the saints replacing Hindu deities as they were carried round the streets in procession.

The Roman Catholic missions penetrated inland from the coasts, and the challenge of how to do mission was at its sharpest in Madurai, in what is today Tamil Nadu. Here the well-known Jesuit mission of Di Nobili (1577–1656) followed a model of indigenization that ring-fenced the high-caste status of Brahmin converts or potential converts.[3] Himself of noble birth, he felt that in the interests of spreading the gospel it was legitimate to develop a community that lived by caste rules, and enabled new converts to remain unpolluted by close contact with Christians from lower castes. In particular, he employed Brahmin cooks to serve pure Brahmin food.

Marriage was strictly within the caste. He himself learned Sanskrit, as well as Tamil, and wore the saffron robes of a Hindu holy man. At the same time, other missionaries worked among the lower castes and so-called untouchables, where they were more successful numerically. But he argued that only by beginning at the top could Christianity penetrate deeply into Indian life. He engaged also in dialogue with Hindu *pandits* (scholars), looked for commonalities and differences, and coined new words in Tamil to explain Christian concepts such as grace, church, Bible, mass and so on. In the end, he went too far for Rome, and his mission was derecognized.

It can be argued that any attempt to enshrine caste distinctions in the Church, even for the best of motives, has disastrous consequences, since it is a denial of the essence of the body of Christ where there should be no hierarchical social distinctions. Moreover, such one-caste communities tend not to last. A similar attempt was made to create a Brahmin Christian community in Tiruchi, Tamil Nadu, in the early part of the twentieth century. Again, there was some success, but before long the need for marriages outside the closed community led to its breakdown. One negative consequence of these experiments was that, until comparatively recently, there were separate graveyards for different castes within some Catholic cemeteries, divided beyond death. Moreover, in Tiruchi itself, as late as the 1920s, a new bishop refused to take up his place unless a wall was removed in the cathedral, separating high and low caste. Worshippers could see the same altar when mass was celebrated, but could not mix when coming forward to receive the sacrament of unity!

A British anthropologist, David Mosse, studied one large village in Tamil Nadu in the 1990s.[4] It is half Catholic and half Hindu. He found that the arrangements for the annual festival for the female deity, and for Mother Mary, were remarkably similar. Who does what were in both cases organized on caste lines. And adherents of both faiths participated in both festivals, though some Christians would not do so. I myself visited a similar village in Tamil Nadu, and here the Roman Catholic Christians were keen to emphasize that their statue and festive cart were bigger than those of their Hindu counterparts!

At the same time, the most effective and creative examples of indigenization have also been within the Roman Catholic Church. The National Biblical and Catechetical Centre in Bangalore has been in the forefront of movements in music, liturgy, art and dancing. It has had some effect on the wider Church, enabled through the networks of religious orders, as well as dioceses. Nearby has also developed the ashram of Jyoti Sahi. He is the Indian artist best known in the West, and his painting has developed stylistically. His earlier work was influenced by classical work, then by the mandalas of Buddhism. In recent decades his style has centred on Dalit and tribal cultures. His art is seen in churches, as well as murals and paintings. He also taught many sisters, from North India in particular, to develop their own style of art coming out of interaction with tribal religion.

The wider ashram movement has featured both Anglican and Roman Catholic communities. The Christ Seva Ashram in Poona is a protestant example, though this has now ceased to exist as an ashram. Two prominent examples of Catholic ashrams have been the Kurisumala Ashram in Kerala, with a Syriac rite, founded by Francis Acharya and Bede Griffiths in 1958, and Shantivanam in Tamil Nadu, to where Bede moved in 1968 and where he died in 1993. He began as an associate of the founder of Shantivanam, which I know well, Father Le Saux, and developed a thoroughly Catholic ashram in a thoroughly indigenous style. In so doing, he attracted many Westerners who were on a spiritual search in India, and led them back to Christianity. The ashram follows the architecture of a Hindu temple. The worship practices within the mass are evocative of Hindu *puja* practices, with much symbolism introduced, including the offering of flowers and *arati* over the bread and cup. Moreover, a reading from Hindu scripture is included before the Bible readings. *Bhajans* are sung in a range of languages, particularly Sanskrit.

Meanwhile, Le Saux had gone much further, as he took the name Abhishiktananda, and journeyed to Rishikesh, in North India, after a long period in the Hindu ashram in Tiruvanamalai, Tamil Nadu.[5] Here he struggled to integrate Christianity and Vedantic Hinduism, and went as far as anyone ever has in this, achieving what he defined as the ultimate Vedantic experience of unity. By its nature, such an example could never become popular, but it provides an important symbol of the possibilities of integration between the two faiths. Bede never went this far, though he encouraged the teaching of yoga in his ashram, and led many courses on meditation within the two traditions.

Protestant and Anglican churches

These entered India along with colonialism, from the eighteenth century. They came with a reformation zeal, and mission commitment, to save people from what was seen as the darkness of Hindu practices and the demonic idol worship. It seemed to be self-evident that Christianity was superior in all respects, and that Hinduism would fall down like a pack of cards when it encountered the preaching of the gospel. But gradually, there was the discovery of the depth of spirituality and philosophical traditions found in the best of Hindu scriptures that the oriental movement revealed to the West. Moreover, it became clear that Hinduism did sustain people in their daily lives, and was not as vulnerable to the missionary movement as people had expected.

A vigorous discussion ensued in these missions, in the nineteenth century, about questions of caste and its relationship to conversion. The general missionary view was that caste was evil in its nature and its effects. As Bishop Wilson of Calcutta said in 1833, caste 'must be abandoned decidedly, immediately, finally' within the Church itself and on conversion to Christian faith. There could be no compromise here with an egalitarian gospel. This was shown most dramatically within the American Madura Mission. New converts had to eat a meal cooked by Dalit cooks, before baptism. This was extended to existing Christians, and the mission lost a good proportion of its higher-caste catechists, who reverted, or joined another church, rather than agree to such an *agape* meal before the Eucharist.

The Lutheran churches took a more relaxed attitude, quoting the 'two kingdoms' theology of Luther. A casteless world would only happen in the kingdom beyond this world! Higher-caste Anglican converts argued that caste was no worse than the social divisions found in Western countries, and they stood out against the lead of Bishop Wilson. In the end, these discussions made little difference. Marriage customs, above all, continued as before, and the arranged-marriage system enabled caste divisions to continue. The Hindu-linked casteism penetrated the Church at all levels, and this has continued to the present day. The difference is that often the members of the higher castes now claim to be marginalized, as more and more bishoprics and other powerful positions have fallen into the hands of Dalit-background Christians. One of the saddest Hindu influences on the churches lies in this apparent inability or unwillingness to set aside community politics within the church, where it is often little better than outside.

Many missionaries gave their life to India for decades, and some died there. A sample can be included here for the enormous contribution they made to the development of the Indian Church, and local cultures. The first of these were Ziegenbalg (1663–1719) and Plutschau, Danish pioneers deeply identified with Tamil culture, who first came to Tranquebar. William Carey went from Leicester to Serampore, to begin the Baptist mission in 1799. Alexander Duff made a major educational contribution, coming from the Scottish Presbyterian tradition. G. U. Pope and Bishop Caldwell, two Anglican missionaries with the Society for the Propagation of the Gospel in Foreign Parts (SPG) in the nineteenth century, were so honoured for their contribution to Tamil language and culture that their statues were erected on Madras Marina, by the Tamil Dravidian governing party, the Dravida Munettra Kalagam (DMK), in the 1960s. Bishop Lesslie Newbigin, whose birth anniversary was in 2009, was a giant figure in the world ecumenical movement, but above all was a missionary who gave his all to India. Rather different were C. F. Andrews, Anglican priest, the close companion of Gandhi; Verrier Elwin, Anglican priest, who ended being Nehru's adviser on tribal affairs; and Dick Kaitahn, who was twice sent out of India, back to the USA, because of his espousing of the nationalist cause, and ended by establishing an ashram in the Tamil hill station of Kodiakanal, in post-independence India.

I make mention here of two remarkable North Indian converts who both became Anglicans, and then moved to a post-denominational Christianity, since they could not tolerate the divisions they found in the churches in Europe which had then been exported to India. I make no apology for giving an account of them in detail. Sadhu Sunder Singh (1889–1929) was a convert from a high Sikh family. As a Christian, he put on the robes of a *sannyasi*, and became a wandering and evocative preacher and mystic, who travelled to many countries abroad, as well as in India, dying somewhere in the Himalayas on his way to Tibet. He describes himself as not worthy to follow in the steps of Jesus, except by sharing in his wandering life, without home or possessions, relying on those who give him food and shelter, an evangelist simply speaking of the love of God that he had experienced himself.

Pandita Ramabai (1858–1922), probably because she was a woman, is less well known, but no less remarkable. She came from a Brahmin family, losing most of her family from cholera. She married, and her husband also died young, leaving her with a child. She was taken in by missionaries in Calcutta, and there studied the Bible and also Sanskrit. She was converted when teaching at Cheltenham Ladies' College in England. She was deeply impressed by the care shown by a Christian mission in London for 'fallen' women, following the example of Jesus and the Samaritan woman in John 4. She returned to North India and worked tirelessly for the women of her country, to provide literacy, shelter and hope for the downtrodden, particularly child widows. She founded the Pandita Ramabai Mukti Mission, which has continued to this day. She refused to be submissive to clergy members who questioned her orthodoxy. She believed that true religion was the love of God and love of one's neighbour, and that she should live by this creed was all that anyone could ask of her. She was named Pandita by Hindus, who recognized her wisdom and learning more than her own fellow Christian leaders.

To end this section, mention should be made of the achievement of the formation of the Church of South India in 1947, and the Church of North India in 1970. These two Churches have often not fulfilled the high promise under which they were born. But to join churches across the main Anglican and Protestant divisions into one structural unity was remarkable, as is the fact that they have largely remained together. One of the reasons for the move to unity was the fierce criticism that came from Hindu thinkers about church divisions which made their mission ineffective. Bishop Azariah, the first Indian bishop in South India, famously said that what Indians need is a common Christ in the face of the Hindu masses, not the divisions he encountered when he walked down an English high street and saw all the different churches.

Another special creation of the Indian churches were indigenous missionary societies. The earliest and best known of these were the Indian Missionary Society (1903) and the National Missionary Society (1905). Both are still very active and, though based in the south, work all over India and beyond, supporting large numbers of workers, particularly in tribal areas.

Interfaith dialogue and the Indian churches

Interfaith dialogue has been a necessity of life for Indian Christians, long before it was defined by this technical phrase. As has been seen, they have lived with their neighbours for 20 centuries, and dialogue was necessary to survive. The Roman Catholics have called this the *dialogue of life*. Theologies may be incompatible, but life is lived together. Christians have faced the same struggles as their fellow villagers, or fellow migrants to the cities, fellow slum dwellers, or fellow students or high fliers in the new dynamic metropolitan India. They share common passions such as those for cricket, Bollywood, common political adherences (it is noteworthy that most vote across faiths, for common parties), common concerns for their neighbourhood, health, education. So also in the sharing in 'bad' and 'good things' of life – births, marriages, illness, death.

A second level is that of *theological dialogue* or *dialogue of discourse*. This is normally informal, as talk turns to faith and belief. This can happen on the train, in the village coffee shop, beside the well. It can happen more formally, as seminars on dialogue are held on common themes. For example, the Tamil Nadu Theological Seminary, in Madurai, held two significant three-day seminars, one on justice and one on grace, which were then published as books, and included contributions from the major faiths as well as a variety of Christian traditions. They looked at theology, scriptures and the application of these themes to life. The aim has been to become aware of similarities but also of differences. Some dialogues are bilateral, some trilateral, some multilateral, and there are examples of all in India. Meetings, for example, were convened by the Roman Catholic Church, on word and silence (in Bangalore), on working for harmony in the contemporary world (in New Delhi), and in Pune on Hindu and Christian cosmology and anthropology. There has also been a Religious Friends Circle in Madurai, based in the seminary, lasting for many years, involving Hindu, Muslim and Christian leaders, teachers and theological students. Also in Madurai there was a sustained dialogue on Saivism and Christianity, with Drs Gangatharan, Thomas Thangaraj and Israel Selvanayagam. They developed this, building on the work of Dayanandan Francis, who contributed much to the Christian understanding of Sikhism.

Scriptural dialogue has also taken place, if in a fitful way. There have been Christian commentaries on the Bhagavadgita (such as that by Bede Griffiths) and Hindu books focusing on Christian Scripture, such as Radhakrishnan's major book *Eastern Religion and Western Thought*.[6] Here there is a strong emphasis on John's Gospel as the essence of Christianity and on the Synoptic Gospels as the Jewish takeover of the original Jesus. There have been many other initiatives, but sustained dialogue at a scriptural level is difficult between a faith centred on one book and one person, and a diffuse faith with countless scriptures and a whole range of systems and deities.

This interaction between two very different faiths and world views has also meant that sustained theological dialogue has not been easy. Similar terms are found to have very different meanings. For example, *avatar* seems a fitting concept to describe the Incarnation of Jesus. But, as Parrinder has shown in his classic work *Avatar and Incarnation*,[7] the differences in use of the term are vast. Jesus can never be one among many *avatars* (incarnations) alongside Krishna, Rama and so on. His humanity was complete, his footprint on the earth was real, his suffering and death were real. The docetic Christ was heretical for good reasons.[8] So also the theology of the cross. Gandhi loved the cross as a deep inspiration of self-giving love. His favourite hymn was 'When I Survey the Wondrous Cross'. He himself was to suffer in a similar way, at the hands of a Hindu extremist. But Gandhi had no truck with the historical uniqueness of Jesus and the cross, and its saving quality, beyond viewing Jesus as a special exemplar of love. The future principal of Madras Christian College, Alfred Hogg, brings out these sharp differences in considering the cross, in his book *Karma and Redemption* (first published in 1909).

A third area is *dialogue of action*. This is dialogue for liberation, development, social justice. Here it is a question of joining together across faiths to face issues locally, community-wise, within particular states, nationally and internationally. Action for the oppressed has included working together for the betterment of those with leprosy, for exploited women, against child labour, for Dalit liberation, and so on. There are examples of all of these taking place in association with others, particularly in recent years. My own involvement in work with prisoners and their families was another example, the prisoners mostly coming from the lowest social strata. Work with HIV/AIDS victims is another recent example. By far the majority of those helped in all these cases are Hindus. Action has included advocacy for excluded groups, alongside Christians, who have been the object of Rashtriya Seva Sangh (RSS)[9] opposition. There have been specific campaigns related to reservation policy, or about anti-conversion bills. These have all been ecumenical from a Christian church perspective. There were massive interfaith relief works in the period after the 2004 tsunami.

The fourth category is that of *religious experience*. This has included acts of common solidarity involving prayer alongside each other, from the same platform, in the face of a common issue or disaster, or national celebration, and this seems natural within multi-religious India. Prayers are offered before meetings or formal dialogues. In ashrams, such as Shantivanam above, people from different faiths enter into the experience of the other. As Bede Griffiths said, 'Hinduism and Christianity are poles apart in terms of doctrine; but they can meet in their spiritual depths, in the heart of the lotus – there is Christ.' There are also the simple acts of prayer in a village or when someone is sick. A Christian pastor will be asked to pray in Hindu homes quite naturally. I remember visiting a group of villages where, every full-moon night, the pastor and his team visited all the homes in a village, mostly Hindu, and offered to pray in each house. They were accepted in most.

The *bhakti* devotional experience is common across all faiths, whatever it is called. It will be seen at the tombs of saints in Sufi Islam. It is seen in the major Sikh temples on their holy days. It will be found on new-moon days within Buddhism. It will be seen in popular Hindu festivals, when thousands of devotees are taken out of themselves in prayer and enthusiasm.

It is seen in a shrine such as Velanganni in Tamil Nadu, which now hosts the biggest annual religious festival. It is a shrine in honour of Mary, and her appearances there. Hindus are by far the majority of the devotees, but also Christians of all backgrounds come to this Catholic shrine by the Indian Ocean, at all times of year. The annual festival time in September has become an official holiday for those from the neighbouring districts of Tamil Nadu. Prayers are to fulfil vows, or for healing, and practices of popular religiosity are seen such as going towards the shrine on the knees, or walking there with a full pot of water on the head and avoiding spilling. Such can be seen also in the Tamil shrines to Murugan, the second son of Siva, and the most popular deity here, as he is worshipped in temples on six hills around the state. The Christmas festival is both a Christian celebration and a time for Hindus to attend churches, and to welcome the Christ child, born as an *avatar*.

An area of creative spiritual dialogue has been that of music and hymnody. Early hymns were those brought from Europe, translated into regional languages or Hindi. But as the decades went by, there grew up a rich tradition of *bhajan* singing, and lyrics. These were very much in the Hindu *bhakti* and poetic tradition, but clearly Christ-centred. They included a style of dialogue between the lead singer and the congregation, as they go back and forth in expressing their part. There also developed the *kalachebbam*, a style of narrating a story involving a dialogue with the audience. Indian instruments normally associated with temples were introduced, especially various forms of drums, combining with the harmonium adapted from Europe. Attempts to introduce the Indian flute largely failed, because it is the instrument traditionally associated with Krishna. Dance in worship was never widespread, because of the association of dancing with temples and ritual prostitution. But the Roman Catholic Church has encouraged the development of highly trained groups in Bangalore and in Tiruchi. They have very beautifully adapted classical dances, usually found in Hindu culture, to tell Gospel stories such as that of the Samaritan woman at the well, as shown at the World Mission Conference in Edinburgh in 2010. They are a direct way in which Indian Christianity, adapting Hindu-style art, has made an impact in the West, through regular tours, particularly to Germany and the UK. I was external examiner for a doctoral thesis on Indian Dance and the Catholic Church, by Jessica Sinniah, and she received this degree from Birmingham University in December 2013. She was the leading dancer and choreographer at Edinburgh.

A study of village Christians in Andhra Pradesh, by P. Luke and J. Carman, nearly all of them from one of two Dalit communities,[10] shows how many of these villagers lived across two religions, in terms of religious practice. To differing degrees, they shared in the majority religious life of Hindus, particularly around festivals, and for marriages and funerals. They could technically be named 'syncretists', but they were clear about their Christian identity. They just did not see this as incompatible with sharing in the spiritual highs and lows of the lives of their neighbours. This is a kind of grass-roots inclusivism.

Indian Christian theology

There is a long history of Indian Christian theology, and this has been at its most creative when it has been born out of deep interaction with Hinduism or another Indian faith. It has been largely from the work of converts from higher castes, or their descendants in such communities. Many examples are found in Robin Boyd's much reprinted book, *Introduction to Indian Christian Theology*.[11] These pioneers struggled with the great themes of Christian theology – God, Trinity, above all Christology, atonement, sacramental theology – and produced inspiring books of faith-centred theology, as they worked to find meeting points between their former religion and their new-found, salvific, Christ-centred faith. Some focused upon what has become thought of in the West as the highest forms of Hindu philosophy, known as Advaita, where God is essentially impersonal. This has as its aim the realization of the oneness of God and the human soul, and the absorption of that soul into the divine. Those following this way usually centre upon John's Gospel, and texts such as 'I and the Father are one' (John 10.30). They look too to the Logos concept, the self-expression of the divine, with parallels in the *Om* in Hinduism as the primeval voice of Brahman, the divine.

Others focused upon the *bhakti* devotional traditional, where God is intensely personal. An example is Bishop Appaswamy. Another initiative is that of relating to Saivism. This is seen in the work of Israel Selvanayagam, who engages deeply with *Saiva Siddhanta*, a Tamil philosophical tradition. More recently, there has come a focus on the Spirit, largely absent in earlier writings, and this can be found in a recent doctoral thesis of Christine Manohar, published as *Spirit Christology*.[12] As an Indian Christian she builds on the earlier recent work of Kirsteen Kim, *Mission in the Spirit*, on the Spirit in Indian traditions.[13]

Another recent work of significance is that of Thomas Thangaraj, *The Crucified Guru*,[14] which takes the Hindu concept of teacher, so often seen in Hindu leaders, who become the objects of personal devotion, not least by Westerners, and shows how Jesus could be seen in this way. The guru is voice of God to the devotee, and can easily be seen as a god. Clearly there can be seen to be links with developments in Christology, though Christ as servant is very different in its implication. Links can be seen here with the key concept of the guru in Sikhism (see later in this chapter).

There has been much discussion about sacramental theology, particularly related to baptism. The challenge was raised, most notably by the Mar Thoma church theologian M. M. Thomas, whether baptism was strictly to be insisted upon within the Indian context. He engaged in a vigorous controversy with his friend Lesslie Newbigin.[15] Thomas was deeply disturbed with what seemed like the de-indianization, or deculturation of a convert, symbolized by baptism into what was seen as a Western organization, the Church. A challenge came from Russell Chandran, then principal of the United Theological College, in Bangalore, who held that baptism is not about separation from the original family or community, or about bringing disunity, but about separation from sin.

Newbigin held strongly to the traditional understanding of baptism, and if there was pain in separation, that had to come – conversion, obedience to new norms and joining a new community (the Church) are not three different things but are all aspects of the same thing. He held that the Church was a sign of the new humanity, which must include the capacity to embrace people of varying cultural backgrounds in one fellowship. This would of necessity in India include people of all castes and communities. This was a mark of the kingdom. Better a smaller church of quality than a large church which followed caste divisions. Newbigin fought against a tendency to look to higher numbers of converts by following the mission strategy of the 'church growth' school of Donald McGavran, where leaders considered how churches would grow best and followed that strategy – the homogenous growth principle. Baptism, believed Newbigin, was often divisive, but so was it in New Testament times. Being part of the visible Church was to be a Christian. M. M. Thomas defined the new humanity as 'that which responds in faith and receives the liberation of Jesus Christ as Lord and Saviour'. This did not require baptism.

All this was part of a wider discussion about what it means to be Indian and Christian. There have been a number of initiatives to establish Indian Christian fellowships or churches independent of Western churches. Examples of these were the Indian Church of the Only Saviour (Nattu Sabai). This was formed as the 'Hindu Church of the Lord Jesus' in Tinnevelly in 1858, and consisted of Christians of the Nadar community who kept their caste distinctions, and abandoned baptism.[16] Another was the movement in Andhra Pradesh of Subba Rao. He was virulently anti-baptism, and called himself a Hindu devotee of Christ. The Old

Testament was abandoned, as he responded to a direct vision of Christ in 1942. Again it was a one-caste movement. These are just two of several such groups, none of which has been sustainable long term in any numbers. Moreover, such is the power of Hinduism, and its inclusiveness, that adherents are soon absorbed back into their former fold.

The same applies to so-called secret Christians. These are many and are of two types. Some have been secretly baptized, and are single-minded in their Christianity, usually conservative in their theology and negative to their Hindu background. But social circumstances and family realities mean they keep their baptism secret. The most famous group of these were women in Sivakasi, Tamil Nadu, whose faith was sustained often for two or three generations, until they 'came out' as part of the Church. The other group are the large numbers who follow Jesus through prayer, Bible reading, radio programmes, attending meetings, but are part of family Hinduism otherwise. Research shows that in Chennai there are as many such Christians as there are full members of the Church.[17] Again, sustaining such a position over a period of years is difficult if not impossible.

Theological parameters have changed rapidly, under the impact of the Dalit movement, and the growing importance of other excluded groups as they have gained a voice, such as women and tribals. Dalit theology has become increasingly dominant and has led to a suspicion of all other forms of theology, including Indian Christian theology, as above, being labelled Brahminic. The studious work of K. P. Aleaz, for example, on Christianity and Advaita has, in recent years, been dismissed by such voices. The high volume of Dalit theology has been varied in its quality, but represents a strong voice of protest, about being silenced for generations. Its most famous voices include James Massey, A. P. Nirmal and M. Prabakhar. Much of it rejects all association with Hinduism in any form. But other writers, most notably Abraham Ayrookuziel, were able to bring out the creative and liberative strains within village Hinduism and its traditions, including its songs, poems and oral traditions.[18] Satthinathan Clarke, not himself a Dalit, has written one of the most creative works, coming out of his doctoral thesis, where he compares Christ with the drum. This is the village instrument which a particular Dalit caste is required to play at the funerals of the high caste. He shows how this can become a symbol of liberation rather than of slavery. Recent feminist writings have talked of Dalit Christian women as being threefold discriminated against – as women, Christians and Dalits. There have been attempts to find liberating themes in the persons of goddesses in popular Hinduism, and also in figures such as Sita.

In the Dalit movement some of the distinctions across faiths can fall away, as the emphasis falls on a common identity as the excluded ones, rather than on barriers between faiths. Clearly the Christian movement as a whole has also been a factor in the reform of at least some Hindus' attitudes to Dalits. The need to treat former untouchables with humanity and dignity has not just come out of a defensive attitude, lest they all convert to other faiths. It has also unearthed the better traditions within Hinduism, as it works at showing that such distinctions are not of the true nature of Hinduism, any more than slavery was of the nature of Christianity. But such changes were necessary for apologetic reasons also. The strong stance taken by Ram Mohan Roy against caste divisions and untouchability was an important step forward. Gandhi himself was not uninfluenced by Jesus' teaching, particularly in the Sermon on the Mount, in many of the progressive stances he took. He would not enter any temple if it was not also open to those he had named Harijans (a name they later rejected as patronizing – those 'blessed by God' – as they took on their own designation, Dalit, meaning 'crushed ones'; see note 1). Both the Arya Samaj and the Brahmo Samaj claimed at least to be inclusive of all castes, as did the Ramakrishna Mission. The Ramakrishna Mission has a strong emphasis on social work with the poor. Ramakrishna himself had a strong vision of Jesus, as one of the influences behind his formation of the mission.

Questions of mission, evangelism and conversion

Theology and practice of mission has depended in an integral way on theology of religions. The prime motivation for Christian mission in India for centuries was to save souls, and convert communities and individuals to the gospel and to membership of the Church. Whether they lived under what was seen as the tyranny of Islam, or the demonic possession of Hinduism, the task was to rescue them for the sake of their eternal destiny. This exclusivist theology was the norm among the sending agencies, of whatever faith. Numbers of believers were critical in terms of measuring the success of a mission. Tactics might change, between converting the high caste so that there would be a trickle-down effect, or converting the poor and oppressed, as this is where the numbers lay. By far the majority of Indian converts came through mass or community movements. They came by families, villages or castes. This movement was at its peak in the period from 1800 until the 1930s, but has continued at a lesser level since. It was studied very effectively by J. Pickett in his major work *Christian*

Mass Movements in India.[19] He reckoned that 50 per cent of Roman Catholics were products of such movements, and 80 per cent of Protestants, throughout India. He showed that motives are always mixed, with religious and spiritual reasons going alongside the desire to gain respect, material support and liberation from caste oppression. Duncan Forrester, in his definitive book *Caste and Christianity*, wisely comments on motives:

> The search for material improvement or enhancement of status is seldom, if ever, the sole or even dominant motive in a mass movement. Dignity, self-respect, patrons who will treat me as an equal, and the ability to choose one's own destiny – all these are powerful incentives to conversion.[20]

My own doctoral thesis, published as *The Church and Conversion*, would suggest the same in later movements also. Now, since Indian independence in 1947, the benefits system discriminates heavily against the Christian convert, and especially their children. Only Hindus, and later Sikhs (from 1950) and Buddhists (from 1990), could receive the benefits accorded to the scheduled castes (Dalits and tribals). Converts became 'backward caste' (a category between scheduled castes/Dalits and forward castes). And those from the backward castes, if they converted, were treated as forward caste.

Individuals made their own decision as to whether to take baptism within a people's movement, usually following the lead of their family leader. But in most villages, some converted and built a church; others remained in Hinduism. The evangelistic activity of the missionaries, whether a minority from overseas, or by far the majority, Indian, was usually combined with educational and medical work, and often development work and advocacy. The theological motivation was exclusive, that people could be saved from darkness; but the nature of the darkness was complex – ignorance, illness, hopelessness, oppression, as well as the worshipping of false gods, or the chains of Islam.

But such is the fear of conversion movements that there was a major backlash in recent years from politically powerful Hindu forces. This fear may be irrational – all the statistics show that the Christian percentage in India is static – but stems from the fact that conversion is a political and demographic issue, as well as a religious, spiritual and psychological question. It has often been said that Hinduism in India is a majority faith with a minority complex. Some of this may be nothing to do with Christians, but stem from the much larger minority of Muslims, fear of foreign influence and terrorism, and nearby neighbour Pakistan. Anxiety is projected onto the much weaker Christian communities. It has been focused upon charismatic and fundamentalist movements who since the 1960s have come in significant numbers, from outside and from within India.

It should be noted that when there are conversions to Buddhism this is much less of a threat, and usually passes almost unnoticed. But there were the famous conversions to Islam from Hinduism in Meenaakshipuram, Tamil Nadu, in 1980, which became a national sensation. I studied these, but also conversions from two Christian villages to Islam some time after this. The government was primarily concerned with the Hindu–Muslim conversions, and it led to the village leaders being summoned to Delhi to explain themselves. The story of the two Christian villages showed how effective was Muslim evangelism. The Muslims made clear that there was no caste in their faith and they would be accepted by old Muslims immediately. There would be an imam chosen from their village, to provide local leadership. This was not the case with these Christian congregations, which were looked after by pastors who came and went from the towns or cities. I visited these villages ten years later, and found them satisfied that they were accepted, and their low-caste status had been put behind them. Of course, there are divisions in Islam, but it is sad that the degree of these divisions seems to be less, at least in South India.

The Hindutva movement of recent decades has attempted to claim India for Hinduism, and to eliminate the secular nature of the constitution established in 1949. This made clear that, as a Fundamental Right, subject to public order, morality and health, all persons are equally entitled to freedom of conscience and the right freely to *profess, practise and propagate* religion. As early as the mid-1950s, the Nyogi Commission was established to consider the work of foreign missionaries in Madhya Pradesh, and its report focused largely on questions of conversion. One witness commented that the aim was to create a Hindu state, with existing minorities 'integrated into Hindu culture'. The tug of war has continued since then, with various individual states bringing in anti-conversion bills, covered over under the title 'Freedom of Religion' and highlighted as bills to protect poor, vulnerable scheduled castes and tribes from the onslaught of Christian missionaries, from home or abroad. Political parties were formed around this issue, and eventually the Bharatiya Janata Party (BJP) led the coalition government in Delhi in 1998. It had a Hindutva ideology, and had been behind the destruction of the Babri mosque in Ayodya in 1992. Ayodya is considered the birthplace of Rama. It has led coalition governments twice in Delhi, and it won a landslide victory in May 2014, under the strong and controversial leadership of Narendra Modi, the chief minister of the Hindutva-influenced state of Gujarat. The Congress was seen as tired and unable to deal with corruption. We shall see how important Gujaratis are in the Indian diaspora.

Earlier, the BJP was never able to implement more partial Hindutva demands, such as the building of a temple at Ayodya, and eventually lost power to Congress in 2004. Minorities breathed a sigh of relief. But this did not prevent strong opposition to Christian mission, continuing in BJP-ruled states such as Gujarat, Karnataka and Orissa. In Gujarat it also led to more than 1,000 people being killed, mainly Muslims, in riots in 2002. The activist wing of the BJP, the RSS, was accused of attacks on Christian worship, buildings and occasionally, most notably in Orissa in 2008–9, on village Christians themselves. Arguments centred upon 'inducements' leading to conversions, and for the dedicated Hindu nationalist, Christian education or medical work could be seen as an inducement. So also exploitation of the economic weakness of the lower castes, or their psychological or mental vulnerability. The suggestion was that they were not capable of making spiritual or rational choices.

The result of this struggle over decades has been to strengthen Christian exclusivism as a missionary and theological stance. It has also led to a movement that can only be called evangelistic, to reconvert Indian Christians to Hinduism. The process of reconversion is known as *suddhi*. Certain *mutts* (spiritual centres) are dedicated to such a mission, and there is a liturgical reconversion ceremony where the pollution is removed from the candidate, ash is placed on his or her forehead, and the person readopts a Hindu name, which is then published in the local gazette. For some, this is a genuine reconversion; for others it is a deliberate plan to regain lost benefits. Relief aid is also sometimes used for conversion purposes. It is said that in Gujarat, after the earthquake in 2002, those who were suffering had to chant *Ram, Ram*, before receiving relief. Of course counter-claims were made about certain Christian missions, both then and in the post-tsunami period.

Another factor in reconversion at the village level has been pastoral neglect. In some mass movement areas there was a failure of ministry. Villages were rarely visited by pastors. I have documented this in the Madurai/Tiruchi area. Gradually, villages fall back, not out of belief, but lack of follow-up and teaching, and through lack of creative leadership. Eventually, they end up only celebrating Christmas and New Year, and then even that ceases. They become Hindu in all but name, and eventually in name also.

It should be emphasized that the majority of Hindus remained as they had always been, on good terms with their Christian neighbours. They attended Christian mission schools and went to Christian hospitals, without fear that they would be forced to convert, and sure they were entering institutions of quality where spiritual values were upheld. It is not surprising that, with a few regional exceptions, the Hindu majority has normally joined with the minorities in returning governments of the centre, implicitly rejecting Hindutva as an ideology.

A book by M. M. Thomas, *The Acknowledged Christ of the Indian Renaissance*,[21] is an important record of Hindus who remained Hindus but were deeply influenced by Jesus. Examples include Ram Mohan Roy (from Bengal), Keshab Sen (from Maharashtra) and Gandhi himself.

Apart from exclusivism, other theologies of religion developed through the nineteenth and twentieth centuries. The impact of working closely with Hindus was to lead to awareness that this faith could not just be written off as all bad. There were so many aspects to Hindus, and to Hindu practice. How could these be seen as bad in a world God created as good? The World Mission Conference in Edinburgh in 1910 was a watershed in some ways. It reaffirmed the necessity of evangelizing the world in one generation. At the same time, it studied in detail, with a vast amount of evidence, what was happening in mission around various themes. Commission IV was on Christianity and Other Faiths. Sixty missionaries working predominantly among Hindus in India responded to a detailed questionnaire.

These responses have been studied in detail by a range of modern theologians – Wesley Ariarajah, Kenneth Cracknell, Brian Stanley, among others. This shows the quality of the responses. Kenneth Cracknell's book is entitled, *Justice, Courtesy and Love*,[22] and he shows how missionaries, particularly to India, came up with this description of how to commend the gospel. The predominant theology revealed is that which became known as Fulfilment Theology. Christ can fulfil the longings and spiritual quest found in Hindu traditions. We see the beginnings of a theology of dialogue. To summarize the 70 pages of analysis of the 1910 missionary responses, Cracknell found here answers which reaffirm both a commitment to the finality of the Christian revelation, and the centrality of Christ, with a generous and humble attitude to other religious traditions as encountered in India. This theology was articulated most prominently in J. Farquhar's work *The Crown of Hinduism*.[23] There were two major deficiencies in the work of this commission, as I see it. The movement seen from exclusivism to inclusivism is very selective. The responses are in relationship to the so-called 'higher' Hinduism, particularly Vedanta, and this could later be dismissed as Brahminic. And these were the answers of missionaries. The commission never asked for responses from Indian Christians. Four Indian Christians were present, most notably the future Bishop V. S. Azariah. But they did not give written evidence on their attitude to Hinduism.

However, as the twentieth century advanced, there were further developments in the theology of religions. The major mission conference at Tambaram, Madras, in 1938 moved in an exclusive direction, led by Hendrik Kraemer, whose theology of religions followed from his Barthian background and was published as *Christian Message in a Non-Christian World*.[24] Here there can be no bridge between a human religion like Hinduism and the revelation of the Word of God in Christ.

At the same time, a group of Tamil Christians had been meeting in the same city, and they produced an important study, entitled *Rethinking Christianity*. They were higher-caste converts, usually lay people, and they were looking for bridges between their former faith and Christianity. Examples were P. Chenchaiah and P. Chakkarai. Chenchaiah (1886–1959) was blunt in his stance:

> Christianity took a wrong gradient when it left the Kingdom of God for the Church. Christianity is a failure because we have made a new religion of it instead of a new creation . . . The Hindu will slowly and in different degrees come under the influence of the Spirit of Christ, without change of labels or nomenclature.[25]

Chakkarai (1880–1958) writes memorably, 'What moves a person is not that his old country is bad, but that he has to obey the heavenly call . . . the Church is not just to be for cultus, but communion with the Living Lord, for social action.'

In the post-Vatican II period (after the epoch-making Vatican II document *Nostra Aetate* (1965)), there developed the idea, from Karl Rahner, of 'anonymous Christianity', to explain the evident goodness and spirituality found in people of other faiths, and this could be recognized as salvific. We are here wrestling with a theology that needs people to be part of the Church to be saved, and this must therefore be so anonymously. This was highly relevant to India. Most creatively in India, there was the inclusive theology of Raymond Panikkar, *The Unknown Christ of Hinduism*.[26] Having mixed Catholic and Hindu parents, he finds here a depth of truth in Hindu scriptures that he can only attribute to Christ the Word. Also from the Roman Catholic tradition came the beautiful book by K. Klostermaier, about in-depth encounter in the birthplace of Krishna, *Hindu and Christian in Vrindaban*.[27]

From the Protestant point of view, Stanley Samartha, who wrote from Bangalore when working with the World Council of Churches (WCC), produced a number of very significant books.[28] An evaluation of his contribution to dialogue comes perceptibly from Israel Selvanayagam, in a chapter in *Christian Theology in Asia* where he focuses on Samartha's defining of dialogue as being about the Spirit, and about love and respect for neighbour. Samartha believes it is about mood and lifestyle, about partners as persons and not statistics.

A steady stream of articles relating theology to praxis came out of the Centre for the Study of Religion and Society (CISRS), established in Bangalore by P. D. Devanandan, with M. M. Thomas as his successor as director. From the beginning, they took seriously the need to engage with the faiths of India, as well as the society around. They took seriously the diversity of Hinduism, and also the imperative to hold mission and dialogue together. In the end, they got overtaken by an imperative to be seen to be active, rather than just reflective, and rather lost their way academically. But the contribution of CISRS, through its journal and its publications, has been immense, and paralleled in few other countries.

It should be noted that Hinduism itself has a variety of theologies of religions, though not defined systematically. There are implicit strands of exclusivism, inclusivism and pluralism. There is the easy pluralism that is traditionally associated with Hinduism: let each find his or her own way – that is the way that is right for each. There is the assumption of superiority in Advaita, that this is the only true way of finding truth and unity with God. And there is the kind of inclusivism found in the slogan 'One truth, many religions'. Some of this has come out of encounter with Christianity.

Final reflections

It is perhaps strange that while India was the cradle of the multi-religious world, and much was achieved historically, nevertheless at the present time many of the most dynamic contributions to interfaith relations and dialogue are taking place elsewhere. This is partly because religion has become more and more political in India, and minorities have been tempted to withdraw into themselves. It is partly because of the growing success of evangelical movements, and of Pentecostalism in India, as elsewhere, where the barriers between truth and falsehood are emphasized, and the need to 'save' has become the imperative. It is partly because of deficiencies within the priorities of the leadership in the Indian mainline Churches.

It is noteworthy that while every diocese in the Church of England has an Inter Faith Adviser, if mainly on a part-time basis, there are no such appointments in the Church of South India or the Church of North India. An exception was when Bishop Selvamony of Kanyakumari initiated a Department of Inter Faith Dialogue about 30 years ago, but this did not last. The Roman Catholic dioceses, on the other hand, usually have such an officer in each diocese. Another factor is the dearth of outstanding teachers of theology of religions in Indian theological institutions. This is partly because outstanding persons in this field are serving in the West. It may also be partly because this field of study is not as valued as it used to be.

Nevertheless, as we wrote at the beginning of this chapter, day to day, Indian Christians are living out their lives in faithfulness to their Lord, just as they ever were. Such a minority witness will never be easy. But it remains the greatest inspiration for us from more tired so-called Christian countries, when we visit, or live for periods with, Indian Christians. For such Christians, interfaith relations are never just academic, or detached; they are a matter of life and death. The Church in the rest of the world needs to be ever thankful for their story, and also for how they live in harmony with their Hindu neighbours over the years.

3

Three *bhakti* movements in the UK, and Christianity: 1. ISKCON[1] (Hare Krishna movement)

We now turn to our main theme of Hindus and Christians in the West. There follow three chapters based upon the Teape lectures that I gave in Calcutta, Delhi, Hyderabad and Bangalore in November 2011.[2] The general theme of these lectures was Christian engagement with *bhakti* movements. This was mainly in the UK, but there will be clear links to what I write later about the USA. This applies to all three themes – ISKCON, South Indian *bhakti*, and South Asian conversions, including *Jesu Bhakters*. Readers in the USA are therefore encouraged to read these chapters.

For most Westerners, their image of Hinduism can be stereotyped around yoga, idol worship, festivals, caste and India – some key concepts. Like most generalizations, these associations are both true and not true. Actual contact with Hinduism may have begun with a journey to India, as a student backpacker or a searcher for spirituality, or on a luxury package tour of discovering the exotic. For those who have never made such a visit, their contact in the West may first have been to witness the chanting and preaching of a Hare Krishna group in a high street of their local city. The distinctive saffron clothes and the musical instruments mark them out. The devotion to Krishna is easy to pick out within their much-repeated and rhythmic mantra: *Hare Krishna, Hare Krishna, Krishna Krishna, Hare Hare, Hare Rama, Hare Rama, Rama Rama, Hare Hare*. If onlookers have shown much interest and lingered, they may well have been given a copy of the Bhagavadgita, and perhaps they have glanced into this scripture, as they may have looked at the Bible on their shelves at home from time to time. They may have noticed that the devotees are a mixture of Western and Indian, and there will probably be some curiosity about why their fellow Europeans or Americans have got caught up in this. Have they been brainwashed? Are they free to come and go? Is this movement a cult? Is it to be feared, to be welcomed, or to be ignored?

There may be some other half-remembered connections in the mind of the onlooker – the involvement of George Harrison and other Beatles for a time; the song of Boy George, 'Karma Chameleon'; stories from the USA about residential schools and cases of abuse, something also perhaps about cow worship being taken to excess, where cows can appear to become more important than people.

Overall, there may well be some admiration for the apparent commitment and evangelistic enthusiasm of these groups, a feeling that they are probably harmless, and genuine in their spiritual search. It is not difficult to see this as a *bhakti* movement, if we know the word – a charismatic, spirit-filled devotional movement. Let us then search further, into the history of the movement, its origins in India, its development in the West, its theology and praxis, and whether there has been or could be engagement with Christians in a positive direction. Could this movement be a way into understanding what is the third religion of the world, after Christianity and Islam? For whatever else it is, this movement comes deeply from within Hinduism, and remains so. It is not like, for example, the Brahma Kumaris, also attractive to Westerners, but assertively not Hindu, though from India. Nor Jainism or Sikhism or Buddhism, all stemming from a Hindu background, but again clearly other faiths, sometimes called Indic faiths. We should also clarify at the beginning that Hare Krishna is a popular name, derived from the beginning of their distinctive mantra, while the official name is ISKCON, the International Society for Krishna Consciousness, the Hare Krishna movement. Put simply, this is a Krishna-orientated *bhakti* movement.

Origins and history

As we may know, Hinduism as a concept, as a religion, was only named in the colonial period. But its traditions go back thousands of years, often estimated at 5,000 years. ISKCON's origin is much clearer. It began in Bengal, where its centre remains, though Vrindavan, the birthplace of Krishna, has become equally important, and Puri in Orissa. It centres on Gaudiya Maths – ashrams, spiritual, missionary and educational in intent. And its founder was named Chaitanya. He was a highly charismatic devotee of Krishna, with what has been called a 'theistic intimacy' with God as the beloved. He is from the Vaishnavite tradition, a tradition where the Supreme has personal attributes, expressed in the *avatars* of that tradition, who include Krishna, always associated with his consort Radha, his *Shakti*, who is worshipped passionately and lovingly by devotees. He is seen as a divine child, divine lover, a charioteer who helps those in need who turn to him. He is both cowherd and divine lover. The Gita centres on him. The greatest intimacy with Krishna is called *rasa lila*, the dance of divine love, and the flute symbolizes God's beauty. It calls the worshipper back to Krishna, who is the God of Love, who meets the eternal longing within the human heart. We can compare here the place of the reed, the Sufi flute, as found in Rumi's poems. Here Krishna is both one of the incarnations of Vishnu, and also the intimate supreme deity, beyond Vishnu.

Chaitanya lived from 1486 to 1543. He personified the above *bhakti* so strongly, moved so closely with God, that he became seen as God in his lifetime, not just after his death. He began to chant the mantra, *Hare Krishna, Hare Krishna, Krishna Krishna, Hare Hare, Hare Rama, Hare Rama, Rama Rama, Hare Hare,* which means 'O Lord, O energy of the Lord, please engage me in your ceaseless service.' A Christian theologian, John Moffitt, has written, 'If I were asked to choose one man in Indian religious history who best represents the spirit of devotional self-giving, I would choose . . . Chaitanya.'[3] He attracted a strong personal following, and this became a movement, as he went round the above places preaching and teaching, and above all chanting and dancing. The movement was open to all, across castes, including women. It was known as Gaudiya Vaishnavism. Chaitanya's guidance for chanting was: 'Be as humble as a blade of grass, and tolerant as a tree; demand no respect from others, and give respect to all.' At first it was free and unorganized. As time went by, as usual in India, Brahminic hierarchical tendencies came in. But the founder, and his writings, remained the inspiration in the following centuries.

The movement came to the West from 1965, when it came to the USA through the missionary leadership and spiritual guidance of the founder of ISKCON, Bhaktivedanta Swami Prabhupada. He came for the first time to London in 1969. Interviewed on TV then, he said, 'My mission is to teach how to love God. People have forgotten God, and I am come to remind them.' And 'I am speaking of the same God as the Christian God. There is one God whom we all worship, Christians and Hindus alike, and he has many names. One of his names is Krishna.' 'I have come to teach anyone how to see God. It is possible to talk with God. Just as we are talking to each other now, you can talk with God.' He went on to initiate, called 'taking *diksha*', 300 men and women in the UK. The story of the early years of the movement in the UK is found in a major book, *When the Sun Shines: The Dawn of Hare Krishna in Britain*, by Ranchor Prime.[4] In a very readable way, the author takes the account through to Prabhupada's death in 1977. Martin Palmer writes of the book, on the back cover:

> I can't remember when I saw my first chanting, dancing Hare Krishnas. They were simply there in the late '60s and early '70s, like the pied pipers

> of the alternative worlds, drawing us away from what we thought we knew. Ranchor Prime tells how those who danced and thought and developed made this country a different and better place.

The book tells the story of Prabhupada's meeting with a nun, Sister Mary, who asked him, 'How do we know who is a lover of God?' He quoted Chaitanya describing his love for Krishna: 'Every moment is like 12 years. I am crying torrents of rain. I find everything vacant without God.' Prabhupada went on to the sister, 'Like Jesus Christ, Sri Chaitanya sacrificed everything. That is the love of God. You may follow any religious path – it does not matter. The method is simple: chant the holy name of God. We don't say you chant Krishna. If you have any name, God's name, then chant that. I chant, *Hare Krishna, Hare Krishna, Krishna Krishna, Hare Hare, Hare Rama, Hare Rama, Rama Rama, Hare Hare*.' Prabhupada asked her about her prayer. She replied, 'Lord Jesus Christ, Son of God, have mercy upon us.' He commented, 'That's nice, very good', particularly when she explained that the mercy of God is the love of God. To another Christian he said, 'Jesus said, "Hallowed be thy name, my Father." We are hallowing the name of the Lord. We don't even ask you to say Krishna. You can say Jehovah or Yahweh. Just chant the names of God, purify your heart, and develop love of God. Then you will stop killing and slaughtering each other.'[5] Here we see the centrality of non-violence – both between human beings, and also of animals. Vegetarianism is a central tenet of ISKCON. It is there to varying degrees in Hinduism, but absolute in ISKCON.

In the USA, in the meantime, there was a rapid expansion of the movement, and at the same time acute problems of leadership, and major issues in residential schools, which gave the movement a bad name. There was a real fear of a family member getting involved with what was seen as a potentially dangerous cult. Selling of products, books, CDs and so on had been the main way of financing the movement, but profits dropped greatly as devotees were no longer welcome to chant publicly in city centres, and they were largely confined to marketing in airports. The crisis of leadership came with the death of Prabhupada. He had established a Governing Board Commission (GBC), but few on it were reliable. There were also splits in the movement. A major question was the authority of Prabhupada after his death. There has now been a recovery, and essentially, ISKCON has become a congregational movement, rather than one based on the monks living in temples and seen on the streets. It has settled down to become a denomination (see the case study on the USA (Chapter 8) and the section on ISKCON in the USA today; see also Chapter 9, on Sweden).

In the UK, the history has been much less stormy. The undisputed centre since Prabhupada's time is Bhaktivedanta Manor, near Watford. This is residential, and registered as a kind of theological college. There are then centres around the country, including one in Leicester. The majority of members are now married. Many have been celibate monks for some time, and then moved out of community. Some remain in the community and are married there. There is a relaxed feel about this. Sex is expected to be primarily for the procreation of children, necessary for the future of the movement, and indeed of the human race!

Study is important in ISKCON and in particular the study of the Gita and of the writings of Chaitanya – the Chaitanya Bhagavata – and those of Prabhupada and others. Chanting is compulsory, whether privately or in congregation (*kirtana*). This should be done using beads, a 108-bead rosary given at initiation (*diksha*). Sixteen rounds should be chanted each day. The small book describing its use says: 'Chant and be happy.' It is done to evoke transcendental consciousness and ecstasy, in love of God. It is to anticipate not only release from the material suffering of rebirth, but also an eternal life of bliss and devotion to Krishna.

Two important developments for our purposes are involvement in schools, and interfaith dialogue. There has been a fee-paying school at Bhaktivedanta Manor. But now there are two state-aided schools. One, in Harrow, was established some years ago and has had a very good early record. The aim is to have a Hindu ethos, and food served is always vegetarian. But it has an open atmosphere, and others are welcome. There is now opened in Leicester, since September 2011, a Free School, one of the first of such schools in the UK, and I record here some dialogue I have had there with its founding inspiration, Pradip Gajjar. The aim here is eventually to have 50 per cent of children from non-Hindu families. It is being developed in a former Roman Catholic school premises, next to a Roman Catholic secondary school. It has a chapel room there, and this is being kept by the Hindu school undisturbed, as a place that Christians can use, from within the school or the community. The Bishop of Leicester has given support from the beginning, and the Archdeacon of Leicester was a trustee. It has been developed quite transparently, with cooperation from the city council and careful nurture of other faith leaders through the Faith Leaders Forum, talks and visits (see Chapter 7, on Leicester, for latest developments).

ISKCON's record in interfaith dialogue, especially with Christians, has been long and fruitful. Its members are significant participants in councils of faiths throughout the country, and not just nominally. An example is in Hertsmere, the area around Bhaktivedanta Manor. The clergy chair of the Council spoke to me very highly of their participation. They put on a drama in Inter Faith Week, and visited schools then. They took part, along with Christians and Jews, in Mitzvah Day, and in joint service, *seva*. This has been about clearing up scrubland and cleaning areas of litter. They have taken part in the Armed Forces Day, when a flag is raised. They participate in the annual town festival in Borehamwood, taking a lead which used to include their bringing bullocks. At the same time, from the Christian side, the parish has given support to the Manor when there have been difficult incidents. An example is the famous cow incident, when the RSPCA wanted to take a sickly cow away to be slaughtered. The Christians joined in, writing to the minister Hilary Benn, and a new pregnant cow was presented instead. A recent problem relates to their erecting a large marquee for weddings, and the Letchmore Heath Council making objection and winning both initially and on appeal. The church gave support, as in the famous dispute about the construction of a new road to the Manor, a battle that ISKCON did win. It is these kinds of engagements that matter locally.

They have also played a significant role in the development of the Hindu–Christian Forum UK, which has been struggling to find its way since 2004.[6] Most notable has been the participation of two individuals, Bimal Krishna Das, until he transferred to India, and Gauri Das in more recent years. They have been notable for the wish to reflect theologically and spiritually, and that this should be at the heart of the dialogue.

At this theological level, there has been much engagement at a semi-academic level, much of it recorded in the movement's journal, *ISKCON Communications Journal*.[7] Notable was the position booklet, reproduced there, a group production led by Shaunaka Rishi Das, entitled *ISKCON and Inter Faith: ISKCON in Relation to People of God* (2004). It was authorized by ISKCON's Governing Body Commission and so has a high status. Significant scholars of other faiths were involved in its production. It is a remarkable booklet, unprecedented in any other faith, except Christianity, and even there it is difficult to find something so succinct. The document is just 13 pages long. It has a two-page opening statement, and then sections dedicated to mission, to dialogue and to theology. It ends with guidelines for approaching 'people of faith in God'. There are then responses from around ten key voices from those in official positions across churches and the Jewish community.

There is no space to comment on the whole document here. Throughout, the emphasis is on the supreme personal God, and that no individual or organization has a monopoly on the Lord. By opening ourselves to dialogue with the other, we open ourselves more to that one God. Journeying with those who do not share this monotheist faith is also enjoined, as we work together for humanitarian, ethical and moral standards in society. Mutual respect is at the heart of the document. Affirmed too is the missionary nature of this kind of Hinduism – it will welcome converts with open arms, but does not have an exclusivist ideology. 'We work not at conversion but at spiritual development.' Theistic people are to encourage each other to be more true to their own spiritual practice, and to care for their neighbours.

The document begins with a most helpful statement defining ISKCON, which I reproduce in full:

> ISKCON belongs to the Gaudiya Vaisnava tradition, a monotheistic tradition within Vedic or Hindu culture. Hindu culture is vast, and the term 'Hinduism' encompasses numerous theologies, philosophies, religious traditions and spiritual cultures. Thus, dialogue with Hindu traditions is often difficult. There are no official representatives of Hinduism, as the term Hinduism does not imply a single spiritual tradition. This statement is therefore representative of Hindu culture and religion as it is manifest in ISKCON, a Vedantic, monotheistic Vaisnava tradition.

I refer to two articles in the ISKCON journal, one by a Christian and one by an ex-Christian, now ISKCON devotee. The first is by Kenneth Cracknell (June 2000), entitled 'ISKCON and Inter Faith Dialogue'. He points to the domination of dialogue with Advaita Vedanta, the monistic school of Sankara, reckoned to be, especially by Roman Catholic scholars and monks, 'the essence or highest development of Hinduism'.[8] This is something I would echo, as I think most teaching about Hinduism centres on this philosophy, as though it is the only one, when most encounters with Hinduism are at the *bhakti* level. Abhishiktananda and Bede Griffiths are seen as indicating that such *bhakti* movements prepare the way for higher forms. Protestants have indicated their horror of the 'incurably idolatrous and sensuous' Krishna worship, lacking a content of revelation. Yet others went in a different direction, such as Otto, who sees a real and saving God and his grace experienced in Bhakti Hinduism, and Stanley Jones, the great American missionary, who practised both 'bhajana' and 'kirtana', and felt God is very near, and Bishop Appaswamy, in the 1920s, writing of Bhaktars, who speak of God, adore his goodness, worship him with bowed heads and clasped hands as seeking in all possible ways to establish a relation with him which will grow into mystical Union. Cracknell rejoices in relating to ISKCON after unfruitful Hindu–Christian relations for so long.[9] He feels deeply the willingness of the other party to join in, and their expertise in their own faith. Michael Barnes said that he felt, in dialogue with ISKCON, a rare experience of head and heart being united. We learn about the other, but also with the other, as friendly trust develops. When dealing with others who are dedicated to worship and spirituality, dialogue takes place for the sake of the wider world and deep friendships develop. These include the hardest theological questions, and he lists 16 such questions in the eschatological area coming out of a weekend in Wales: death, resurrection, reincarnation, suffering, the nature of time, pastoral approaches on the approach of death.

The second article is by Ranchor Dasa, and is entitled, 'Looking for the Dearest Friend' (1994). He is a former Roman Catholic, and he describes his conversion as building on the faith he already had as a Catholic: 'A Christian church to me is still a holy place where I intuitively feel at home.' A converting experience for him was to begin chanting, as he had seen on TV. He felt a personal relationship with God for the first time, as he chanted for two hours, using the names of Krishna, Rama and Hare (Hare represents the mercy of God, personified as Radha, the embodiment of pure love and mercy). He became a missionary, following his guru, a missionary to the Western world to teach Krishna consciousness. He was told by Prabhupada, 'Somehow or other, preach.' He teaches that God is our dearest Friend. We should preach about love, and not fear. When his father discovered he was about to move to a Krishna temple, he sent him to Worth Abbey, and his friends held a vigil to win him back to Christ. But the wise abbot at Worth said, 'If I were your age, I would do exactly as you', when he explained his story. 'May God bless you', he added, and Ranchor Dasa ends his article, 'I began my life as a devotee of Krishna with his blessings, and I felt in my heart, the blessings of Jesus Christ.'

Three ISKCON devotees

I now give the substance of three interviews with devotees whom I felt very privileged to have talked to, and received their trust.

Like many in the movement, my first respondent, **Ferdinando**, was a Roman Catholic. Italian, he was a faithful mass attender in Italy and a kind of *bhakti* devotee of Mother Mary, and was very close to his Catholic family. He was active in the boy scouts, and got on well with both priests and nuns. There was no negative push factor. He also felt close to Jesus, but had little understanding of the nature and character of God. He discovered in the Vaishnavite tradition the experience of joy in worship, and of the love of God. What he found new was warmth and joy, and this was the pull factor to the Vaishnavite faith. He feels he is a devotee of God first, and then of ISKCON. He does not like to be too restricted. He discovered this wider tradition when visiting Vrindavan on a spiritual search in India. He was attracted too to Gandhism. ISKCON came into his life when he met a group casually in west London. He visited ashrams, and decided to become a monk, which took him around Europe. Then, like he estimates 90 per cent of monks, he got married, as in Buddhism, his monk period over. Since then he has done a doctorate in the field of Vaishnava research, and become an academic. Where does he see the links between Christianity and what he prefers to call Vaishnavism? The strength of the theist tradition in both, with God both infinite and highly personal, has led him to study Catholic personalist philosophy, as well as finding this in Vaishnavism. 'Krishna' is another name for God, and the manifestation of God in Jesus is no problem. He can see also strong links between *bhakti* worship in his tradition with that of Catholicism (see Chapter 9, on Sweden, for further encounter with Ferdinando).

My second interviewee is **Pradip**. Like the majority of devotees and initiates now – a big change in the last 20 years – he is British Indian Hindu, and was born in Birmingham. He was brought up to attend *pujas* and festivals in the Handsworth Temple, and his father was president of their caste association, which provides security, culture and order for its members. Learned visitors used to come from Gujarat, but he could not understand their religious teaching. As a secondary school student, he began to discover the Gita in English, and also to read the Gideon Bible. The change in his life came when John Lennon died. He went into the history of the Beatles and their connections with India. The song 'Goddess of Fortune' on an old record affected him, as did Hare Krishna chanting, produced by George Harrison. He found the sound 'awesome'. He discussed all this with a school friend, who introduced him to ISKCON, and he used to attend the Hare Krishna gathering every Saturday in a rented hall in the city centre. They also read Prabhupada, and his theological reflection that every person can have a personal relationship with God. He was impressed with his selfless character, his devotion and commitment to service. He valued the teaching that we are spiritual beings, beyond any designation of religion, label or caste.

His parents accepted his becoming a strict vegetarian and his taking up chanting. But they were wary of an organization they felt was being led by white people converting to Hindu practice. He was taken by his uncle to the Manor, in the hope that he would be put off. This failed, as he was impressed with the discipline and clarity of the movement, and the feeling of access to God. Even the Gandhian uncle was impressed, and only said that he should not bow to a white person, a seemingly racist remark.

At 18, he went to London, and after graduation moved to the Manor, and spent ten years as a monk. His goal was not status but life in the spirit, serving and educating others. He eventually left there to get married, and to do an MBA, from which he became a manager within the movement, working alongside the Governing Body Commissioner for the UK. It was a vital area of service where there had been a deficiency, supporting ten temples and many small groups throughout the country. Meanwhile, his father became reconciled to his involvement and even proud of him. After a visit to the Manor, his father heard someone say, 'There is a young man there from our community here, and he speaks well.' His father replied, 'Yes, he is my son.'

He became a temporary leader of a struggling and divided community in Leicester in 2004, and moved with his wife to that city in 2006. He became one of the key persons in establishing the I Foundation, which opened the first state-supported school in Harrow, and since coming to Leicester he has worked towards such a school there, opened in September 2011 (see above, and in Chapter 7 on Leicester). He also is very ready to offer teaching to Christian groups, including future clergy, and has a real gift in explaining the basic parameters of Hinduism, and his own movement, in a way that is clear and engaging.

The third interviewee is **Gauri Das**, a leading person at the Manor, Scottish, and again a former Roman Catholic. He told me how his father had died shortly before the interview, a very devout person, as is his sister. She relates how her father had told her, when near to death, 'Don't worry about the boys; they know God.' This represented, he feels, his father's endorsement. He has had a visionary encounter with his father after his death, which meant a great deal to him. He is convinced that the two faiths use different languages but represent the same spiritual experience.

He is quite a free thinker, and feels the use of Prabhupada in an absolute way is very recent. He feels that a fundamentalist approach to scripture is dangerous. He finds the way the ISKCON leadership went was worrying, as the Governing Body Commissioners just chose themselves. He spent ten years in Vrindavan, and had an arranged marriage with an Indian South African. As he reflects on the movement now, he feels it is brilliant for the Indian diaspora, working out how to be Hindus in the West. But he wonders whether it has the language any more to talk to Westerners, and talking of *karma*, reincarnation etc. is no longer enough. We are in a post-colonial religious time, when spirituality is more important than church attendance. The movement should spend less time trying to convert, and more in affirming people where they are and building on this. The five principles of ISKCON are no longer enough: 'Dream on, if you think Western people will accept all this.' It will just lead them to neuroses. We need to be less judgemental. It is not surprising that he joined the School of Oriental and African Studies in London (SOAS), and studied religion for three years, the last year without wearing his ISKCON clothes. He is devoted to the garden in the Manor, and showed me with reverence that which had been designed by John Lennon's widow, a meditation garden.

Gauri introduced me to Sruti, the current president of the Manor, and a Ugandan Asian. He was another who was influenced by hearing George Harrison on *Top of the Pops* and then saw a Hare Krishna group outside in London. He found them very attractive, and visited the Manor when Prabhupada came in 1977 for the opening. Sruti was 18, and was deeply impressed by his charisma and purity, and determined, after he finished his master's degree, to join the Manor. He did not receive enthusiastic support from his family, thinking it was like Swaminarayan, and also because most residents at that time were foreigners; ten only from India out of 100 in the late 1970s. Now there are 50 residents, 60 per cent of Indian origin. Congregation figures for today are that there are around 10,000 members, 80 per cent from London, and 80 per cent being Indians. Half are committed; the rest are eclectic searchers. He remained a celibate monk for 20 years, and then married through the ISKCON marriage board.

As leader, he has been very committed to interfaith relations, and is very proud of having recited Sanskrit prayers in the church in Harrow when he became a chaplain to the Hindu mayor. He prayed for 'wisdom, strength and love'. The local church support to the Manor has been very important and helped to remove the stigma that ISKCON is a cult.

He appreciates that there are no philosophical blocks between some aspects of Christianity, and Hinduism. He sees Chaitanya as being of the personalist school, and opening up the faith across caste, creed and colour. Chaitanya, he believes, was predicted to come in the Vedas. But he quotes Prabhupada, who said that anyone who claims to be God is God spelt backwards! There were 108 centres in the world when Prabhu died, and now there are 690, 200 in the south and 10,000 devotees in Russia, with groups also in Ukraine and the Czech Republic.

A comparative study

A final document of special interest is the doctoral thesis written by Daphne Green in the year 2000. It is entitled, 'A Comparative Study of Krishna

Consciousness in ISKCON, and the Practice of the Presence of God in CSMV (the Community of St Mary the Virgin, with Headquarters in Wantage, Oxfordshire)'. She spent a considerable amount of time with members of both communities. She wanted to study how Brother Lawrence's concept of the practice of the presence of God could aid in learning to encounter God in all things and all situations. She found many similarities but also differences. The place of the guru was much higher in ISKCON, and the role of chanting. The place of silence was much stronger in CSMV, and also their lifelong commitment to celibacy. The ISKCON devotees saw Krishna as eternally youthful, joyful and playful, expressing this in the fullness of Creation. The task is to go beyond the illusions of this world, in order to serve Krishna through seeing him in all living beings. The sisters were focused on the Trinity, and on a suffering Christ, and sharing in his sufferings for the sake of the world. One of her surprising conclusions is as follows, summarizing from her challenging concluding chapter:

> Members of ISKCON perceived Krishna consciousness as expressing their awareness and encounter with Krishna in the world, whereas CSMV members increasingly perceived the practice of the presence of God as the religious life faithfully lived out in the convent with an accompanying withdrawal from social and community involvement.[10]

As a member of the clergy, what did Daphne herself learn from ISKCON? She is now Chaplain to the Archbishop of York. She learned of the need for clear structure and discipline in the search to encounter God, and that she has a responsibility for this search herself. She learned of the importance of the senses in that quest, including the richness of the devotees' worship of the deity, and 'the ecstatic, exuberant forms of devotion', shown, for example, in *kirtan* and *sankirtan*, the former personal, and the latter congregational chanting to glorify God. This helps them to have confidence in their evangelism, and assured engagement with the world. They practise Krishna consciousness, whether in an ashram or outside in the world. She appreciates their devotion focused on the deity, in a way that could also be offered in her tradition around ikons, candles, the cross, statues. She is impressed with the concept of *lila*,[11] not found much in Christianity, the transcendental playfulness of Krishna and the sheer delight found in worship. Clearly Pentecostal, charismatic Christian traditions come closest here.

4

Three *bhakti* movements in the UK, and Christianity: 2. South Indian *bhakti* movements through temples

I worked for a long time as a theological teacher in Madurai, Tamil Nadu. Being in this most Hindu of Indian cities introduced me to Hinduism in all its complexity, in a way that books and lectures never could. I went for a six-month training programme in Selly Oak, Birmingham, and Lesslie Newbigin, who had been Bishop in Madurai, gave us teaching. But he wisely said that we would learn more in a week in India than in six months with him, not least from learning from Hindus themselves. This city of more than one million people was nearly 90 per cent Hindu, and a great centre for pilgrimage to its enormous city-centre Meenaakshi Temple, as well as to major temples in the region around, and to the thousand shrines and mini-temples on all street corners and village lanes. Apart from this, and most importantly, there was the religion of the home, where devotion was expressed at all kinds of levels, to all kinds of gods, on all kinds of occasions, routinely and daily, with prayer on the 'good and bad occasions' of life. And within all this, the focus on festival, of which there seemed to be a major one every week. An anthropologist friend researched the Meenaakshi Temple; he reckoned that on average, in a 12-month period, there were 10,000 people a day entering the temple, and probably three times as many for festivals. And the deities were not confined, but were taken out onto the streets of this amazingly busy and noisy city, for such occasions.

Whatever the philosophy or theology behind the classical dimensions of Hinduism – the Advaita Hinduism I had learned of in Selly Oak – what I encountered here was *bhakti*, or a kind of charismatic devotional practice, that had to be taken very seriously. Alongside it there was village Hinduism, as I encountered it on village visits, a kind of animism as I might term it, but which sustained people, in its marking of the stages of life and in giving an annual framework to their tough lives. I learned too of the faith and practice of Dalit Hindus, known then as 'untouchables', 'scheduled castes' or 'Harijans'. Was this Hinduism at all? How did it relate to so-called

Sanskrit traditions, or Brahminic traditions, which they felt very oppressed by? What of their oral traditions, and longing for liberation, to be free to be what God, not human society, made them? This was, and remains, an intense topic of debate and much more so in the seminary, and within the whole Christian community, 70 per cent of which was from Dalit background in the south, and 90 per cent in the north.

This chapter is about South Indian *bhakti* in the UK, and will focus upon two major temples, the Balaji Temple in the West Midlands, and the Murugan Temple in Manor Park, east London. I will also mention a new Tamil temple in Leicester, which is nearer in its development to how these major temples were in their origin. They are largely Tamil or Telegu in their administration, and in terms of devotees. But they are increasingly eclectic also, as other Hindus attend, particularly at festival times. I will also be reflecting on how they have related to the wider communities in which they are set, and to Christians in particular. What is evident throughout the British Hindu community is how few of them have a Dalit origin, particularly those coming from Gujarat, Tamil Nadu or Sri Lanka. Most Dalits are Punjabis, a proportion of whom have become neo-Buddhists in Wolverhampton, Birmingham or elsewhere.[1] Some attend Guru Ravidas temples. This guru/god is on the border between Sikh and Hindu. There is a Ravidas temple in north Leicester.

There have been some studies of the South Asians as they have moved to the UK. One such study is *Diaspora of the Gods*,[2] by Joanne Waghorne. She sees a movement to globalize what have been localized temple traditions. This applies particularly to the god Murugan, normally associated with Tamil Nadu, and with six hills there which house Murugan temples. These are Palani (the most important, in Madurai District, and second only to Tirupati, where the Balaji temple is on another hill, in Andhra Pradesh), Tiruchendur (by the sea in Tirunelveli District), Tiruparakundram (just five miles south of Madurai), Tiruttani (north of Chennai), Swamimalai (near Tanjore), and a sixth which is undefined, because Murugan is everywhere, and so this temple is found wherever there is a hill with a shrine to Murugan on its top. There are numerous candidates for this. They were not original national pilgrimage sites, but regional and local. These locations throughout the state help us to see how Murugan has become a symbol for Tamil religiosity, and also for the Dravidian consciousness that permeates culture and politics, where, since the 1960s, government has always been in the hands of the Dravida Munnetra Kazhagam (DMK – the Dravidian Progress Federation) or a split from this main party. Murugan is linked with the Sanskrit tradition, through his being the second son of

Siva. There is a definitive study of Murugan by Frank Clothey, entitled *The Many Faces of Murugan.*[3] The author's conclusion is that many Tamilians see the god and the region as virtually inseparable. Murugan's life has been mythically lived out in Tamil Nadu. Generic elements from both the Sanskrit and Tamil traditions have been fused with local and folk imageries in such a way as to make the god's holy stead attractive to people from all walks of Tamil life. His exploits speak to all dimensions of the Tamil imagination – whether he is seen as teacher and philosopher par excellence, or the one who dispels misfortune; whether he is the giver of joy in life or release from it; be he the mischievous lover or ideal ascetic the full range of human needs and emotions are expressed in the contemporary mythology of Murugan.[4]

Clothey writes this before the development of the Murugan cult in the Tamil diaspora. Now this god is found globally, and Joanne Waghorne coins the phrase 'transnational religion'. She quotes another sociologist, Susanne Rudolf, that 'local devout groups through informal networks, keep alive these examples of religiosity in a new context, just as happens with the religion of Imams and Bishops.' Another example: she looks at how worship of independent village goddesses is not found until the 1990s, being seen as low class and low caste. But now it has spread through London, including in the East Ham temple. This is a kind of neo-Hinduism and can be linked with Hindutva ideology. This British Hinduism has been described, by Burghart,[5] as the perpetuation of religion in an alien cultural milieu. Recently, there has been another example, the wider development of the cult of Ayappan, a god normally associated with a major shrine on the top of a hill in Kerala called Subaramalai. This is a centre for an annual pilgrimage which involves much asceticism in preparation, and where pilgrims can be identified by their black clothes. I was surprised to hear of a doctor from the UK who was going on such a pilgrimage with his wife in 2014, normally engrossed as he is with the religion of the Tamil diaspora. This may be the next transnational import.

A major player in the development of Tamil religion in London was a Sri Lankan called Sabapathipillai, who felt a calling in the 1970s to unite all worshippers of Siva in the UK who were of Dravidian origin. This began in Archway, north London, and he encouraged Tamils from Fiji, Malaysia, Singapore, India, Sri Lanka, Mauritius and South Africa to come together with their families to follow the Saiva Siddhanta philosophy found in Tamil Nadu. But Archway was not an Indian area, and the worship was very restrained and confined within the building. East Ham was the next temple, and a Tamil professor said, 'This is a place where I would not want to walk around at night.' But by 2004 there were seven main Dravidian temples in London. These are in Highgate/Archway (Murugan-centred), Wimbledon (Ganapathi), East Ham (Murugan), Tooting (Maryamman), Stoneleigh (Rajeswari Amman) and Ealing (Kanaga Thurkkai Amman). There are also temples to Lakshmi, and other Vaishnavite deities, and this shows the balance between Tamil and Telegu communities. The influence of the female goddess cults can be seen here. Sampathkumar was asked: what makes a good temple? He replied, 'A general feeling, a good atmosphere, a powerful deity, and good priests.'[6] Going onto the streets is also important, an act of grace from the gods to reveal themselves to the general public. This is normal in India, and growing in the UK, with the growing acceptance of Hindus as part of British life.

Balaji Temple, West Midlands

Let us look first at the South Asian diaspora in the UK, as seen through the history of the Balaji Temple, in Sandwell, between Birmingham and Wolverhampton. The early South Indians and Sri Lankans who came to the UK were normally professionals, the majority doctors or business people. The Tamil community included both those from India and Sri Lanka. The latter were not refugees in the late 1960s and early 1970s. They initially used to meet in private homes, and they had before them a picture of Balaji (Vishnu as in Tirupati), in southern Andhra Pradesh. (The temple there is on the top of a significant hill, and is the most popular and richest temple in India and a great centre of pilgrimage. I visited once, and it is a phenomenon of religiosity and also a centre of business and education.) But after some time, it was difficult to host gatherings of this professional community in the house.

My friend and informant, and one of the two key trustees of the temple throughout its history as a project, **Dr Rajah**, from Jaffna, Sri Lanka, tells me how he asked the leaders of the first temple in Birmingham, Gita Bhavan, to allow this temple to be used on the first Sunday of the month, for a gathering on Sunday afternoon. I was present at the opening of Gita Bhavan, one of the earliest temples in the UK, whose congregation was from the beginning largely Punjabi. Ninety per cent of the South Indian worshippers were professional, very different from the Punjabis, and they wanted to keep up their practices and rituals. Many were Brahmins – but they had no priest, and so they relied on lay leadership, even in worship. And once a month was not really enough.

There began a long process towards a temple of their own. As early as 1978 they became a registered charity, and began all kinds of fundraising efforts. From 1985 they began to look for land, and searched all over the country, from London, to Derby, to Peterborough and even to Wales. Criteria included being near an airport, and having good road and rail transport links. It took them nine years to find a suitable plot, after several rejections, and to get planning permission. I remember being approached about whether they could buy a redundant church. I pointed out this could not be an Anglican church, because of Anglican rules about selling redundant churches for the worship of another faith, and we were about to approach the Methodist Church. But they then decided that Christians had destroyed temples in Sri Lanka to build churches, and they did not want to do a similar thing in the UK. Therefore, they would focus on a new build, rare at that time.

They ended up with an unprepossessing brown-field site, ex-industrial land, in Oldbury, which is part of Sandwell, between Birmingham and Walsall. Its strength was that it was near the M5, M6 and M42 motorways,[7] and the Birmingham Airport and rail connections. They anticipated a national and even international clientele, which has indeed happened. They got planning permission, but then opposition developed, and I was told that the Bishop of Wolverhampton, who gave solid support, was nearly lynched when he arranged an open meeting in the nearby Tividale church. I faced a hostile crowd when I went for the laying of the foundation stone, with placards saying 'Leave us our green fields', and worse. I told the people gathered there that in India Hindus had given land and support for building churches throughout the country, but they replied that this was the UK and not India! I think there was a mixture of fear of the unknown, racism, religious bigotry and commercial apprehension. Spokespeople for the nearby Merry Hill mega shopping centre joined the battle, saying, in a slanderous way, that there would be half-burnt corpses in the nearby canal. There was also a genuine concern about parking.

The trustees acted with care and patience, and key was communication, and also such gestures as a very good Indian meal given to all the neighbours when the project was explained. They also gave a priority to a large car park in the big area they bought. In fact, visitors to the temple in large numbers have helped the economic regeneration of a declining area. It is reckoned that 2,500 come each weekend to visit the temple, and 5,000 are fed when there is a festival. What began as a temple for South Indians and Sri Lankans has broadened its appeal, with perhaps one third of visitors being from North India. Regular attenders are Gurkhas from a garrison in Stoke, not far away, and many IT workers from all over India, for whom temple-going is part of their way of life.

The temple itself has five shrines – to Siva, Balaji (Vishnu), Murugan, Ganesh and the planets (*navagraha*). There are nine to ten priests, five Telegu, four Tamil and one Malayali, and they all have quarters in the compound. Normal language used in the temple is English, with Tamil or Telegu interpretation, though of course the language of ritual is Sanskrit, understood by few except the priests. There is a *gopuram* (tower) in South Indian style, and there are plans for an auditorium for 1,500 people. They gained £3.4 million from a Millennium lottery grant, and the trustees, all doctors at the beginning, each gave £100,000 personally towards the matching funding required.

The age profile of British visitors (like in most churches!) is elderly or middle-aged. There are often more grandchildren than children. In Sri Lanka or South India, children and young people attend the temple. New arrivals tend to come with all the family, and regularly. The Rajahs say that the reasons people come to the temple are: to pray individually, as families, and to pray with the community; to make vows; to commission special *pujas*; to observe rituals for *nanmai* and *thimai*, 'good and bad times'; for social reasons and to meet friends, and to eat well. Above all, temples are about handing on the faith and culture, and indeed language. There is a Vedic – scriptural – school for young people, and this is attended by 80–120 children during a summer camp. There is also football, classical dance teaching and other cultural activities. This is to try to counterbalance the way religion in the home is also dying in the UK, where weekly worship is no longer normal.

A second key trustee is **Dr Narayana Rao**, who has been a leader in interfaith work in Birmingham since at least the 1980s. He came from Chennai – Madras as it was – in 1966. In Tamil Nadu, he had been involved with the Student Christian Movement (SCM) at Madras Christian College, when the great Chandran Devanesan was principal. This took him into voluntary work in a leper colony near the airport, and this changed his life. He met the dedicated Swiss missionary Dr Fritchi who had given his life to this work. His studies became affected as he spent every weekend in social work in villages. He also became influenced by Gandhian principles, as he went to camps in Gandhigram, the Gandhian college near Madurai. After his training, and early experience in Tamil Nadu, he went to England to study paediatrics in London. There he met an elderly colleague who had a model of the temple in Tanjore, and had a dream to build one like this in London. They formed the Hindu Association of Great Britain, and from this initiative was built the first Hindu temple, in Archway, north London. Several nationalities attended, and there were eventually trustees from India, Sri Lanka, Burma, South Africa, Singapore and Malaysia. Gradually it was taken over by Sri Lankans, and Dr Rao is now the only Indian left. As senior trustee, he took the Queen round in 2002, a great moment for the Hindus of London. Dr Rao comments that the purpose of these visits is to indicate respect for the diversity of faiths, to support interfaith dialogue, and to show that non-Christian, as well as Christian communities, are central to contemporary Britain. The temple's main deity remains Murugan, but Sri Lankan issues have dominated its recent history.

Dr Rao next moved to Smethwick in the West Midlands and became a GP, until he retired in 2001. He began there with a temple in his garage, dedicated to Vishnu, and to Sai Baba, who was an inspiration for him. Here there was a Gujarati majority. He longed for a South Indian temple to worship in. In Handsworth the temple was Punjabi majority. So he joined with Dr Rajah, and the project moved forward.

Today, it is not easy, because a strong working group is missing, and the original visionaries are growing older. Dr Rao believes that the temple should next have a priest from North India, and a Radha-Krishna stone image, to respond to the breadth of Indians now coming. But he acknowledges that new government regulations make it difficult to bring any new priests.

He speaks of his theological understanding. He feels that the human being is truly the living God in Hinduism, and would prefer the great sage Vivekananda to all the mythical gods found in the temple. He is very keen on the different hills, and is eager for them to be complete, and for each faith to provide guides to its hill. He is chair of the Hindu Council UK, which has its problems, he says. He has also become frustrated with the Hindu–Christian Forum UK. Perhaps he has been in the business of interfaith too long? In the temple, they have occasional lectures, though no regular dialogue. There is an annual Inter Faith pilgrimage around Sandwell which they join in.

More conventional are the beliefs of the Rajahs. They say that in Sri Lanka people normally worship the deity associated with their village. There is no Vishnu–Siva divide. They go to different deities for different needs, which are felt to be manifestations of the one God. Scriptures are not read much, and the way of expression of faith is especially through *bhajans*. What drives Dr Rajah to be a trustee and to work so hard, along with his busy medical practice, is that there should be a proper temple to hold the Tamil community together.

I interviewed **John Barnett**. He is the vicar of Oldbury, and Inter Faith Adviser to the Bishop of Wolverhampton. The current bishop has been there for a few years, and has made a couple of visits to the temple and had a very warm welcome. But he says the temple suffers, from his perspective, from being on the border with Birmingham Diocese. He makes no claim to have much experience or knowledge of Hinduism. His Adviser came from Birmingham Diocese, from the Sandwell area, and therefore has had a more continuous interest. He was on the Advisory Board to the Temple in the early days, and remembers strongly the local opposition, and also how the local councillors were split. The primary purpose of this board was to bring together long-time supporters, both councillors and civic leaders such as himself as representative of the established Church, the architects and others involved with the temple, including a Hindu group. His view is that the board did a good job in airing issues and preventing overreaction. After the opening of the temple, with opposition receding, the role of the advisory board also receded.

He owes much to the visit of Archbishop Rowan Williams to the temple, because after that John was given a half-time appointment in interfaith relations, along with half time in a parish in Walsall. Since then he received all the regular invitations to the temple, as well as representing the diocese on such occasions as health walks each year, armed forces Diwali day, the celebrations for the openings of new buildings in the temple, and the festival of Holi. There are engagements through the Sandwell Council of Faiths, and more than one Hindu has completed the Faith Guides Course in Birmingham, and they participate on the Sandwell Faiths Trail. There are good relations with the local councils, but almost no relationship with Muslims. But there is no ongoing dialogue, interfaith or otherwise, with Christians. One ongoing issue raised by the Archbishop was the question of access of the lower-caste Dalit devotees to the deities. The relationship with the white community is now all right, but there is little involvement with the churches, mainly through lack of priority from both sides. The evangelicals do not particularly target Hindus, maybe because they do not live locally. Overall he enjoys going to the temple, to a place of unfailing courtesy.

Murugan Temple, Manor Park, London

We move next to another major Tamil temple, in a rather different area. Manor Park, East Ham, is in a very crowded area of Newham, east London, and on emerging from the Tube one is immediately struck by the Indian and, indeed, Tamil context of the streets around. This is seen conspicuously in the South Indian restaurants, cafés and sweet shops, and the vegetable sellers on the streets. The population is largely South Asian, and by appearance South Indian and Sri Lankan. Enquiry reveals that first impressions are correct. There are many Muslims from a wide variety of backgrounds, and Africans, as everywhere in London. But there is a large minority of Hindus, Tamil and from other southern backgrounds. They were originally mainly from South India, but to them have been added large numbers of Sri Lankan refugees who have come in the last 20 years, many of them much more recently. We will focus here on the prominent Murugan Temple, just off the main Romford Road, and on the Christian responses to this. In both the nature of the context, and the response of the churches, there are considerable contrasts with the Oldbury temple and its environment.

I was privileged to meet **Rajagopalan**, one of the founding trustees of the Murugan Temple. He came to London from Chennai in 1973 as an accountant, and he began life in London by holding a house *puja*. He is a Brahmin, and in 1975 a group of Tamils instituted a formal Association. They bought a warehouse in Manor Park, because that was where many Tamils were living. They consecrated a temple there in 1984, and a purpose-built major temple in 2005. From the beginning, Murugan, who was the family deity of many, was the central deity. There were five trustees and a management. As with all these major temples, there is a practised businesslike approach to structures. Originally, Rajagopalan acted as a priest once a month. Now there are nine priests, and there are several thousand Tamils in the immediate area. These are mixed, and the temple has never had links with Sri Lankan politics and the Tamil Tigers (Liberation Tigers of Tami Ealam, or LTTE), nor has fundraising been allowed.

His experience is that there is no problem about being a Hindu in the UK, in London in his case. He has not faced any problems from evangelical Christians. Interfaith marriage is frequent, both with other Indian communities, and with other faiths. Also there is frequent inter-caste marriage, because of the kind of mingling that happens here. Normally the family then prays as Hindus. There is little interaction with Muslims, either from the temple, or in the area he now lives in in west London, where there is a local interfaith group. He feels some frustration to be so far from the temple in his old age, and he can feel isolated from his religious roots.

His son, **Kumar**, whom I know well, became a Christian at university, and I refer to him in the next chapter.

There are now about 20 temples in London, but young people are not easy to keep, and it is Sri Lankans who are more committed to temple ritual. The family still keeps up their temple in a village in the Vilipuram district, south of Chennai. *Kollam*[8] competitions in London are a way of keeping the women interested.

I visited the temple with Kumar for a second time, for research, and was impressed that there was a wide turn-out of trustees, including the only woman among them. They are mainly South Indian, with one or two Sri Lankans, though the area is increasingly Sri Lankan. Most of the South Indians are doctors, IT consultants and business people. The important deities are those from South India, particularly Murugan as the centrepiece. Many come in from Ilford and further afield, having moved out from this area, which is traditionally the first port of call for Tamils. The main languages of the temple are English and Tamil, with the priests now being required to speak English by visa requirements, and the need to do their job. I was garlanded and given *prasadam*, with no pressure to make any offering. They proudly invited me to their annual street procession with a chariot, when Murugan is taken round the streets of East Ham. Twenty thousand people turn out, not just Tamils but other Indians, and indeed indigenous people. Other processions are held within their building or compound, as they do not want to presume upon the locals. There is little involvement with Christians or other faiths. The trustee assigned to Inter Faith Newham has little time to go, and does not see it as a priority. 'We leave each other alone, and there is no trouble.' The exception is for the large number of interfaith marriages, mainly with Christians.

A third visit was on a Friday, when the temple was full of devotees, as happens every Friday, Saturday and Sunday, and also Tuesday. I was struck by this being a mini Meenaakshi Temple, the great iconic temple in Madurai. There people come for all kinds of reasons, and all kinds of activities are going on at the same time. Here, in microcosm, the same thing is happening. Individuals and families queued up patiently in front of the main 'holy of holies' where Murugan is housed, and the priest conducts *puja* and blesses them. Groups around are centred on the family, and not just Tamils. I met a couple who had brought their new car into the compound for a *puja* ceremony. The priest conducted this on a £26,000 new hybrid Toyota, and this reminded me of how a carpenter in Madurai conducted prayers over the wood out of which he constructed a new bed for us. The car owner was Punjabi, and his wife from Uttar Pradesh. The wife is an Indian dance teacher, and she says she has a *puja* corner in her house. There she has pictures of all the gods – Krishna, Durga, Jesus and so on – and even of their deceased and venerated parents. They laughed with me as they told me this – the gap between being human and being divine is very fluid in popular Hinduism. They were being given a free ornament from the temple, and they accepted this 'provided we do not have to do *puja* every day', with a twinkle in their eye.

Another couple were there to celebrate their fiftieth wedding anniversary, which they do very reverently. Relatives have come from the USA and Canada, and show the way that giving thanks to God is so central in their lives. Another family had come to dedicate a golden chain. One of the founding trustees had recently suffered the death of his wife, and the daughter-in-law was bringing up the grandchildren in Tamil Nadu, because they prefer to nurture them in that culture directly. The trustee tells me he is from Karikudi, near Madurai, and is one of the well-known Chettinad Chettiahs,[9] very successful business people. His son, true to form, deals in property, houses and land, in Sussex. He has 28 houses there, and used to have 80 in London. Father joked as I left, 'You won't make me into a Christian!' I replied, 'And you will not make me into a Hindu!' I feel a real sense of South India when I enter this temple. One woman said, when the temple was opened, 'Now my India has come here!'

Christians around the Murugan Temple

Manor Park Christian Fellowship This meets in All Nations Church, Church Road. Two hundred and fifty Tamils attend the church on a Sunday afternoon, and 500 when there is a festival. Sixty per cent are now Sri Lankan, and 40 per cent South Indian (including three or four Malayalis, from Kerala). About 30 per cent are converts. There are some outreach workers: Sister Rani, whom I met about 15 years ago there, and two converted women. These would be seen, in India, as 'Bible women'. There is no real relationship with the temple. Occasional conversions cause no stir, though mass baptisms would probably do this. Pastor Ebenezer (Ebby)[10] has been there for 29 years. By and large, conversions have been of individuals, and there is always movement, as they gain education and status and move out. Worship is 90 per cent in Tamil still, with English singing alongside it. There are occasional bilingual services, particularly when Jonathan Eden (see below) is preaching. English is also used in the Sunday school, youth meeting, and what they call 'energy church'. Expansion means they now have five branches in east and north London, some of them more Pentecostal, some less. Ebenezer described their ethos as 'gently evangelical'.

They do not engage in social work, but that is partly because of the movement out, and so many are not part of the local community. Caste comes in at marriage, and he would score them at 5/6 out of 10 in facing caste issues. There is little real mixing between Sri Lankan and Indian Tamils. The majority from Tamil Nadu are IT workers and students. They participate in the Evangelical Church Leaders meeting in Newham. Most of the evangelism is 'friendship evangelism', and through tracts given out carefully, making use of the electoral register. 'We tell people not to be critical of Hindus, or to attack idol worship, and to focus on a ministry of prayer, in which they believe.' He has always been well received when he has gone to the temple himself.

Jonathan Eden is a dedicated colleague, who first came to Manor Park in 1982. He still does not speak any Tamil, but was welcomed by the Tamils warmly, and by Ebby, and as an administrator joined with him in establishing a church then. He was seen by the Tamils as a kind of itinerant holy man, then aged 25! He came first as a missioner to immigrants, on a one-year commission. It was clear that 'hit and run' methods did not work out. He has seen many changes over the years in Manor Park and the church. An example is that *kallar kallachebbam*, a kind of storytelling in music, and very Tamil in ethos, has dropped away. One of the reasons is the God Channel, and also a 24-hour daily Tamil TV channel. Present immigrants are typically Vellore doctors, Tamil labourers from Singapore, Tamil Sri Lankan refugees, software engineers from Bangalore. Many do not stay, but pass through, and it is the elderly who are left. Jonathan's view is that this church is a community project, helping generations of Tamils adjust to their new life. It is a social project. In London, the idea of 'our community' has little meaning, beyond the circle of social workers and clergy. Some attend because they can only cope with the Tamil language; others just want to feel at home when they live in an English environment the rest of the week.

There has been a steady trickle of converts, normally because of what is seen as answers to prayer for practical needs. Particularly in need are mature students from Tamil Nadu who find they have no right legally to work, and are very poor and consequently depressed. They are literally hungry, without any benefits, and they go to the Murugan Temple, to a local gurdwara and to the church for meals. They also come on the once-a-year weekend away with the church. Normally this is attended by about 60 persons, but this year it rose to 120, many of them Hindus. Here they get food for the body, but also for the soul, since Indians love to hear good oratory, and that is what they hear.

Pastor Bakhtaur Basra He is pastor of the All Nations Church in the same road as the temple, and is a Punjabi of Sikh background. He came to faith through Steve Chalke, the well-known London evangelist, and when he first went to church felt he had come home, as did his wife. He is evangelical, but has very little contact with the temple or with Tamils. They do have Hindus coming along, and if they move towards baptism the church leaders do not tell them they must not go to Hindu weddings or to the temple. But they should not be involved in religious rituals. The church is actively involved with an evangelical movement called 'Hands across Manor Park'.

Canon John Williams He has been vicar of Forest Gate, a nearby parish, for 46 years! When he came, there was a white majority in the area, and a settled Caribbean community. Now, apart from the Asians, there are many Africans – 39,000 in Newham. His congregation is more than 85 per cent from ethnic minorities, with Nigerians the largest group. White people have mainly moved out to Romford and Ilford. The latest group to come are East Europeans. None of these Christian groups has much contact with Hindus, and he has had one half-Hindu convert in all these years. More conversions have been of Muslims. Still the indigenous community lumps all Asians together, and there is no formal Council of Faiths in their area.

Conclusion

Clearly we see both continuity and discontinuity represented in these stories. There is both a thoroughgoing indigenization of Tamil and Telegu families in the UK, leading to their growing confidence financially, educationally, and in their progress in their professions. This is even more marked in the second and third generations. Geographically, they become more and more widespread as they grow more affluent. At the same time, there is a longing for continuity with their past, which is also their present, and they wish it to be their future. This is about their origins, whether in Tamil Nadu or Andhra, and of their native village and the context that makes them who they are. This includes the deities who have watched over them as they have travelled to Chennai or Hyderabad, or Bangalore, and then to the West. The temple in the UK becomes a place where they can continue this rooting, and they are prepared to travel large distances to it on a regular basis. I have seen the same in Queens, New York, where Tamils travel from about four states, for *puja*, and for food and fellowship. These temples are also a symbol of the cultural identity of a group of Indians who are not Gujaratis, or Punjabis, or Bengalis. Hence the importance of Murugan, and the Ammam female goddesses, and of Balaji, the image of Vishnu so associated with Tirupati in southern Andhra. The temples are also a place of training for those of future generations, whom it is difficult to hold in the UK.

Key to the temples is the supply of Brahmin priests from southern India. This will become increasingly difficult to provide, as visa restrictions grow with the 'religious functionary' category removed, and the level of English required is raised. It would seem to be a challenge to begin to train priests in the UK, as does ISKCON. But these families are unlikely to be attracted to such a profession, bearing in mind the very specialized role of a priest as a *pujari*. They have their eye on higher things. It should be borne in mind that the priest is not a teacher or pastor, except incidentally. Moreover, the restriction to Brahmins lessens the potential pool enormously.

Another is the need for teachers of the faith. It needs to be taught, not just caught, in the UK. The role of the guru has been crucial in the south of India. But young people are not so willing to listen and be obedient to such a leader. Visiting teachers come from India, and that needs to continue. But the same needs to happen with South Indians within the UK.

The arrival of so many Sri Lankan refugees has greatly increased the number of Tamil Hindus in the country, both in London and now also in other cities such as Birmingham and Leicester. There is now a temple in Leicester, and several *dosai* restaurants. The temple is dedicated to Murugan and to Ayappan (as above). A Sri Lankan Tamil refugee is the priest, and he lost his family in the civil war. The temple is used by both South Indian Tamils and Sri Lankan refugees, and the relationship seems somewhat strained. So we see that the Tamil diaspora in the UK is getting wider, as is the spread of these gods. What is found among the Tamil refugees is that their religious practice is greater, and their community needs more intense. As time goes by, this may recede, but the temples and associations have provided an important support for the traumatized. This also used to be more associated with the support for the Tamil/LTTE militant cause. Now that that is in abeyance, it remains to be seen what follows.

Finally, the relationship with Christians has far to go. Christians generally, especially the established Churches, have given significant advocacy support for the building of temples, and have mobilized communities in favour. There have been significant friendships between individuals that have helped in this. And the temples have unfailingly been places of hospitality to Christians, mainly individuals, but also groups. But there has not been a high level of dialogue, either at a religious or issue-based level. There are few examples of anything regular. And both sides are responsible for this, as each gets on with its own life. There has been little proven need. The number of conversions has been steady, but too small in total to cause much of a backlash from the Hindu side. There has been a dearth of facilitators. And the imperative of dialogue and working along with Muslims has been central in churches and communities, particularly since September 11, 2001. This has met with a ready response from Muslims.

Moreover, their faith is easy to understand for Christians. Hinduism remains as something exotic. South Indian *bhakti* may be a tradition easier for Christians to relate to than Advaita Hinduism. But there has been little impulse to do this, from either side. There is involvement in councils of faiths and forums, in festivals and occasional events, but nothing yet of a tradition of theological, scriptural or philosophical dialogue. That is the challenge posed by the Hindu–Christian Forum UK, and by this book. It is important that the South Indians, and their Siva traditions, are not left out of such a journey.

5

Three *bhakti* movements in the UK, and Christianity: 3. Hindu conversions to Christianity in the UK; *Jesu Bhakters*

My doctoral research was on conversion in Tamil Nadu, to and from Christianity. This impelled me to consider conversion in the British Indian diaspora context. There were significant differences as well as similarities, and I outline these here. What was most moving for me, however, in both cases, was to witness the courage and determination of those I met, and their grasp of faith that often made me reflect on the challenge this can be to those of us who have been born into the faith in our own local culture, and have never been sorely tested, except by apathy or indifference.

I draw here on my own experience, and that gained through meeting South Asian converts to Christianity. I have also talked at length with those closely involved with the kind of converts I have been writing about and the churches they attend. This is a chapter based on contextual investigation.

A survey of Asian Christian converts was undertaken in 1992, and it was discovered that a considerable proportion of Hindus who walk into churches and can be counted as 'converts' in any one year have gone by the next year. The Alliance of Asian Christians was established to try to do something about this reality, and help individuals and groups to be firm and grow in their faith as Christians, and also to affirm themselves as Asian Christians. Things have improved in the years since. There is also no reason to think that the situation as regards Sikhs or Muslims is any different. I look here at some of the factors within the British context which will help explain these pressures, and also consider why it is that many do stay, and what are the issues they continue to face.

It should be noted that the proportion of new Christians within South Asian communities is much higher than in South Asia itself. Eighty per cent of those on the Alliance list then – in total 5,400 – were converts, at this earlier date. Muslims make up 12 per cent of new believers, and this number is rising, and is clearly much higher than is found in India or Pakistan. The Alliance of Asian Christians now focuses on mentoring of individuals, on networking, and on enabling conferences, for example on Women's Leadership among Asian Christians.[1] Patterns of conversion are very different from those in India. There the majority have been group, extended family or part family conversion. Here it almost always begins at least as an individual deciding to convert, or at most a husband and wife, whoever later then follows. When a woman becomes a Christian, men do not necessarily follow, though children may. When men convert first, the women will almost certainly follow. The possibility of independent living in the UK encourages conversion, as does the smaller independent nuclear family. This is the influence of the host culture. Conversion is usually of women first. Education, mobility and financial independence help. Whole families do come, but usually bit by bit; mother, father, children, grandchildren in turn. The occasion when all join together, from little children to grandparents, is very rare in the UK.

Women often feel oppressed and trapped by the cultural expectations of their extended families, which cut across the goal of independence encouraged by their British education and seen in the lives of their white contemporaries. Such women may feel accepted by Christ, who they feel is calling them to freedom. They then enter the inner struggle to face up to the situations in which they are set. In some Asian cultures, to beat a wife is a husband's right, where necessary; unemployment, drinking and economic poverty encourage such, and there has been much of these in some poorer Asian communities.

Such converted women are no longer willing just to 'take it'. Many of the husbands discourage their women from becoming Christians because being a Christian gives the women some status in the society, as well as this resistant streak. Where both convert together, it is a much more stable situation. Punishment from the community is more often ostracism than violence. Beating can occasionally be used to stop them going to church. The women may become calmer and more loving, and more full of hope, which enables them to bear suffering in the hope that one day the husband will change.

The Asian churches may be isolated from other churches, and the main contact is through friendships. Members may think they are the only Asian Christians around. They also tend to be isolated from the mainline churches, in theology, in style of worship, in structures of leadership and in language. Independence gives a certain vigour and life, but also great vulnerability to personal or doctrinal clash. It also leaves a possible vacuum between Asian Christians within the mainline churches, who may be fewer in number but also may be more mature in their Christian experience and theology, and their independent church counterparts.

Fortunately there are overlapping persons, such as those who are members of a mainline church but who attend fellowship meetings or evening services in independent Asian groups, or who share in the same weddings or funerals or other functions.

Statistically a large proportion of converts come through evangelical churches of various kinds, while those in the mainline churches tend to be second or third generation or more, having come from India already as Christians. Asian Christian churches have been necessary in this generation, not least for linguistic reasons. In the future they may remain for cultural reasons, but the linguistic reasons for their existence will fade.

An example is the city of Wolverhampton where, when I researched ten years ago, there were the following Asian churches:

1 an Anglican-style church led by a Sikh convert couple, with about 35 members;
2 a strongly conservative evangelical fellowship, led by an American who has worked in the subcontinent, and feels that working in Wolverhampton is an extension of that missionary work; this is the strongest group, with 250 members;
3 an Asian congregation meeting at St John's Anglican Church, as a separate community, with 110 members;
4 an Asian Christian Fellowship at an Apostolic church, with 70 members;
5 Bilston Evangelical Church with 30 members;
6 a Baptist church with 25 members;
7 a Pentecostal church, Assemblies of God, with 40 members.

These numbers may not seem high, in a city of more than 200,000 people, with many Asians. But they come out of what was only a handful of Christians 30 years ago. Seventeen per cent are Punjabi, a large percentage having converted here. Throughout the country only one in four South Asian Christians were Christians before coming to the UK, and this quarter is only reached because of South Indians or Sri Lankans.

My information has now been updated, and there is little change in the overall pattern, though some variation in churches and fellowships, and an overall modest increase in numbers. Mainline churches have a few members or families at most, Asian Fellowships have increased, and the general fragmentation has not been much reduced. The American above has died, but his work has continued based at a Methodist church, and still with around 150 members and 100 attending on a Sunday. There is a new All Nations church, with an Asian Fellowship within it, with 30–35 worshipping in Punjabi, some for linguistic, some for cultural reasons.

About 100 worship at the two English services. There is also a Calvary church, with 70 members, led by a Pentecostal Punjabi, and a few Asians worshipping in a Nigerian-led Pentecostal church called Oasis. St Luke's Anglican Church prefers to have an integrated congregation, and numbers are increasing a little. It also engages with Asian mothers at their school with a midweek coffee morning.[2]

In addition, as in South India, there is the category of secret Christians. Numbers are bound to be hard to estimate, by the very nature of the secrecy. It is likely that the majority are of Muslim background, where the consequences of openness are nearly always particularly harsh. There are certainly also secret Christians among the Tamil Hindu women in East Ham, London. They can be visited at home, and prayers can be held there. Some husbands allow them to come to church but not confess their faith.

The result of comparative isolation is that the Christian maturity of these converts may be low. The majority are new Christians, and leadership tends to be in the hands of those who converted first, whatever their leadership capacity. The sermons tend to be repetitive, with variations on the theme, 'Come to Christ and you will be saved'. Ethical teaching is dogmatic, with a clarity about what is right and wrong that takes little account of the complexity of the British context in which they are settled, or of any recent biblical scholarship that would suggest that things may be less cut and dried than was once thought.

Identity questions are central for South Asian Christians. Where do they belong? At one level they are not part of their past; they have obeyed the text, 'Come out from among them' (2 Corinthians 6.17 AV). In the present, they often do not feel accepted by the Church in England, where they are settled and where could potentially be their greatest support. Culturally they remain essentially in continuity with their past, and this tends to pull them back, their association with their compatriots of other faiths being closer than their bonding within the body of Christ, which theologically includes themselves and European Christians of every variety. They come closer to the independent or Pentecostal white or mixed churches, but even here there can be cultural divisions which eventually break through.

An exception can be when the advocate, the influential figure in conversion, is a European. Such may be returned missionaries who have spent time in Asia or East Africa, and share a common language with their Asian counterparts, and understanding of their culture. They may be quite authoritarian or paternalistic in their leadership, but clearly attract by their loving concern. They may also impose a theological and conservative orthodoxy, which prevents development, in particular, of a more Asian Christianity, or one that is in any form of dialogue with Hindus, Sikhs or Muslims.

In the mainline churches, such white leaders may be much more open, but not have the same influence over Asian Christians since they are only in limited contact with them. They will tend to have a liberal approach to other religions and to questions of dialogue. They may be more interested in Asians who are Sikhs or Hindus than they are in Asian Christians, whose existence they may often forget, either subconsciously or even consciously, since their conservatism is an embarrassment to their own 'enlightened' views. They forget how different it is to view Hinduism when one has never been a Hindu, as compared with a situation where one has suffered at the hands of Hindus, and is afraid of being dragged back, either oneself or one's children. Caste and other bonds, including that of common origin in a particular part of India, are also very significant, and not necessarily understood.

The future of these Christians is uncertain also. In which direction will their children go? Will they even know or be interested in the language and culture of their Indian background? It is often young Westerners who find themselves fascinated on a visit to India, while many young people of Indian origin are not enamoured at all, and are only too glad to get back to the UK. Moreover, living in the West means that they find themselves expected to think in an individualistic way – 'I' and not 'we'. This is not easy for the older generation, but educationally comes naturally to the younger people, leading to a potential generation clash, not least about religion and churchgoing.

They feel the lack of community in church life within the mainline churches, where there is a strong church–home divide. This is felt particularly by Asian groups within mainline churches who find themselves part of two cultures; the main church group may be warm and accepting to a point, but does not share the closeness of cultural bond which permeates every aspect of life at home and beyond for the Asian members of the congregation.

Thus far we have seen difficulties in relationship to the church for converts. But there are also the problems related to their wider families and communities who are not Christian. Acrimony often arises related to life-cycle events. These events are seen as inclusive by other faith communities, but difficult for converts. Often they are pressurized by other Christians – including those responsible for their conversion, who do not understand the significance of participation in such events – to absent themselves completely. They may impose such a mandate on themselves and then feel considerable guilt or ambiguity of feeling. On the other hand some liberal Christians may encourage them to participate beyond the point where they remotely feel comfortable. Each may feel differently. Converts from Hinduism seem to find a variety of ways of attending significant funerals, and it is the exception that someone stays away completely. I know of a Sikh who converted who was more ready to take part in family functions than his wife, who felt not strong enough to do so. Another retains his Sikh silver bangle, one of the five Ks (key Sikh symbols). He feels it is a mark of cultural and not religious identity. Other Sikh converts would be horrified at this.

Normally the convert will not bow down before a Hindu image, nor eat blessed food. Some will not go to weddings to avoid offending Asian Christians. Some may be forced by their families to do what they would rather not do, for example to go through a ritual under a Hindu priest. Some of their Asian Christian leaders understand this, and would not add to their own feelings of guilt.

Generally at the beginning, the attitude to the convert's former religion is all negative. In time, he or she gets a more balanced view of past and present. The Old Testament is seen to have clear links with Asian culture. Many can accept that knowledge of God had been there in their former religion, but corruption has distorted this. Christianity is true, and where salvation is found, and concentration is on the positive, rather than deriding what has been found in the former faith. A minority of converts feel strongly that to do this would be to deride the faith of their mother and father. Rather they wish to affirm that it is from there that they gained their knowledge of God, to which has been added the particular revelation in Jesus Christ. An even smaller minority may wish to be known as Hindu Christians.

The absence of a liturgy for 'engagement' occasions was mentioned to me as a difficulty for converts, since in Asian culture this is considered as significant as marriage. These things become all the more important for converts, who wish to emphasize that such events are also important for them as Christians, and wish there to be a religious element in what happens. Pradip Sudra wrote an engagement liturgy in which engagement is seen as a foretaste of marriage, as the Holy Spirit is the foretaste of heaven.

Marriage itself leads many converts back to Hinduism, since Christian marriage partners are often not available from within their caste communities. There is a need for marriage brokers in this context, something strange for European ministers.

The issue of caste remains important here. Biblical arguments cannot remove the issue. Caste consciousness is there even at the lower end of the spectrum, though there is a gradual erosion taking place. I heard of one case where a marriage could not be arranged because a convert would not speak of his caste background on principle. A larger proportion of Asian Christian converts are from the Dalit castes than the Dalit proportion in the whole British Asian community, since Dalits in general did not emigrate in large numbers. They did not have the means, and were too downtrodden to have the initiative required. Many also were in bonded labour. The Ravidas Sikh/Hindus are an important group among these.[3] But in general far fewer converts, in proportion, are Dalits than in the Dalit-dominated Christian Church in India.

Theological problems are not normally relevant when there is relapse. Ex-converts continue to hold Jesus in affection, but their problems have usually been with the church, or with overwhelming cultural issues. Eurocentricity has an inhibiting effect on Asian Christians and on potential converts. Asians in the UK as well as those in Asia need freedom to enable them to contribute theologically from their own background. They can also reflect on Acts 15, and as the Gentile Christians were able to find a way of living with the Jewish Church, so they can find what is essential in coming out from Hinduism or Sikhism or Islam, and what can be maintained in continuity.

Relapse may take place to find marriage partners, and because of pressures to conform to an alien church community culture. Also, there may often be a lack of acceptance in a mixed or mainly white church, so that the converts can feel lonely even when a church, as a whole, is loving. The converts look different and are different. Their own families do not understand spiritual factors, only changes of behaviour. It may take 10–15 years for a convert to gain a stable understanding, depending on the personality, estimated one convert leader. The person often needs support for years, particularly if he or she is an individual. White people can give such support to Asians, though often can be very insensitive. But Asian leadership is vital, whether in the mainline churches or in Asian Fellowships.

An example of Asian leadership is that in Manor Park, East Ham in London, among the large local Tamil community, the majority refugees from Sri Lanka (see also in Chapter 4, about this congregation). Between 150 and 250 attend the Tamil church each Sunday afternoon, often combining this with a mainline church membership elsewhere. The church is led by Pastor Ebenezer, from Tirunelveli District. Worship is evangelical, but not Pentecostal, and the hope is to be inclusive of the varied background of the wide variety of members. About 10 per cent of those coming at any one time are enquirers, and a number have been baptized over the years.

Ebenezer's leadership is enormously strengthened by the involvement of his wife and the use of his home, where there is an open house most of the time. The family is totally identified with the church and its variety of ministry to the Tamil community, as featured in a number of my case studies. There is a European administrator of the church (Jonathan Eden, see previous chapter), a situation which allows Ebenezer to concentrate on the pastoral ministry, so important and heavy with a displaced community such as this. He has a sure instinct in this area, and it is not surprising that the congregation grows and conversions happen. At certain times when I have been there, I have seen Ebenezer doing patient work as a marriage broker, a crucial area if members of the congregation are to be retained at this vital moment in their lives.

Theologically the assumptions are conservative, both in terms of doctrine and ethics. Worship is of a chorus-dominated variety. Speakers often come from India and Sri Lanka, this being one of the well-known Tamil congregations for visiting preachers to visit. Among them are those who offer the healing ministry, for physical but also psychological healing, much sought after by members of this type of community where there are many tensions around. It will be interesting to see if this kind of expression of Christian faith can survive a further generation and continuing engagement with the UK's secular society. Observation shows that young people are still very much part of the Sunday congregation and other groups.

Another example of a minister here is Sister Rani. She was born in a Christian family in Bangalore and came to work in East Ham in 1982 by personal invitation. She does personal evangelism, counselling, Bible study, women's meetings, hospital visiting and translation work. She feels the main reasons for conversions are that people's needs are met spiritually, and they have healing – physical, mental and spiritual. Hindrances are the state of the Christian world, and the sense some have that their Hindu gods are great. She encourages them to look only to Jesus and not to the evangelist, and her only tool is the reading of the Bible. Theologically she likens Hinduism to the book of Leviticus, while Christians have moved on, and above all, are blessed with hope. In discussion with Hindus, she avoids arguments – she does not claim to know much – and concentrates on the positive points about Christianity. In general, she feels it is easier to come to the Lord in the UK than in India or Sri Lanka, and easier still for the younger generation. There is quite a lot of loneliness here, and a need for comfort and peace, and that is why so many come to Christian faith.

I end with two examples of converts, very different from each other.[4] The first we call **Selvi**, in her early twenties when she converted. She was the third girl in the family, and felt unaffirmed, with little self-worth, within a large Hindu Punjabi family. She was permitted to go out only to work. She felt down, and only identified loosely with her own religion. Each day she passed a church on her way to work. One day, she entered and sat quietly for some time, enjoying the peace and quiet – her work with young children and her own crowded household lacked both these things. She began to call in each day to this church, which was open daily. She saw an advertisement for a 'Holy Eucharist' at lunchtime, and took time off to see what this was. One of the women in the congregation took the trouble to sit with her and explain. She was introduced to the woman priest, who then met her regularly. She learned about the Christian faith, and began to read the Bible daily in secret. Eventually, she felt called to tell her parents that she wished to submit herself to Jesus as Lord, and felt loved as never before.

The parents' response was, as she expected, very negative, particularly because of how they would be seen in the community if she came out publicly. But she remained firm, with a confidence that surprised her. Gradually the situation at home softened, and her father agreed to look for a Christian husband 'from the same caste'. 'I will do what I can to make her happy,' says Father.

When I met Selvi, I found myself amazed at her courage and at her maturity. Her knowledge of the Scriptures sustained her in a very lonely journey, being loyal to her Lord and obedient to her parents, as the Scriptures tell her to be. Eventually, she was baptized into an Asian Fellowship. Plans had been made for her to be baptized in a very public fashion in the large Anglican church mentioned above. But she decided that was too public an occasion for her parents to endure. So she went forward locally. Her parents did not attend, but permitted her sister to represent the family on this key occasion in her spiritual journey.

A second example is that of **Kumar**. He is from a Tamil Brahmin family, brought up in London, where his father was a trustee of the Manor Park Temple (see Chapter 4). His father found his conversion to Christianity difficult; he said, 'We are not very happy, but go and fulfil your dream; this seems to be your *karma*.' He gradually realized that 'we have to adjust in a foreign land.' His son prepared for ministry in the Baptist Church in London, and at that point he became proud of him, as he went to hear him preach and also saw his caring nature. At Kumar's graduation, which he attended, his father felt, 'He is an Indian, but he is getting a good name as a Christian!' This adjustment took a long time, longer for him as a public figure than for his wife, Kumar's mother. He was also sad that Kumar gave up a career as an accountant, and potentially a large salary, and still does not have his own house. When Kumar was a student pastor, his father still introduced him to family visitors as an accountant; nevertheless, his parents were glad he was appointed to an important role within the church. But positively, Kumar enabled church people to come and pray with his father when in hospital, and this gave him moral support. He was very happy because God is one.

Crucial too in the adjustment was Kumar's marriage to a Northern Irish Christian. At first he had kept quiet about his conversion whenever he went to Tamil Nadu. This changed when he went with his wife and they visited the churches in Chennai. His mother says she has no regrets. Kumar has two siblings in the USA, but at least he is here, and so supportive. He put on the sacred thread as a Brahmin, but came into contact positively with Christianity through attending a Roman Catholic school, and acting as one of the Magi in nativity plays. He became a Christian at university, through the witness of a fellow student whom he admired. When he told the family, he was told above all to keep things quiet publicly. His brother said, he remembers, 'You have become a *Shudra* now.'

When Kumar married a European Christian, he encouraged the priest at their wedding, which was attended quietly by his family, to preach on the text 'Perfect Love casts out all fear' (see 1 John 4.18). 'God is Love' is the heart of Christianity, and he wanted his family to hear that they need have no anxieties.

He has struggled since to free himself from the over-Westernized Christianity that he was baptized into, while remaining part of a mainline church where he is now a minister. An old faithful Hindu friend of his died, and Kumar wrote to me at the time:

> I cannot believe that my friend will not be accepted by the love of God. The fruit of the Spirit was so evident in him. Often it appears that people are not led by missionaries to understand Christ as the fulfilment of their quest, but that their very quest is demolished.

He told me recently, 'I learned of grace from my father, and devotion to God from my family and community. My brother's questions and observation of Christian practice and rhetoric have enabled me to review my own walk with God.' 'If the established British churches and the Indian Church in Britain exercised humility and were willing to learn from Hindus, not only would they grow in faith, but their witness would be enhanced.'

I feel Kumar has been freed from the rigid exclusivism that would confine his family to hell. At the same time an easy universalism would seem to deny the costly journey that he has made, which he feels has been a journey towards personal freedom and hope. His reflections have led him gradually to a position where he would like to call himself a *Jesu Bhakter*, and he is in a small network of such persons on both sides of the Atlantic.

Such converts as these two, and many others I have met, remind me of a quotation from Dag Hammarskjöld, the Swedish former UN General Secretary killed in an air crash over Congo in 2011. He wrote *Markings*, a spiritual testimony from a very private man, in diary form. One of the last entries is a testimony to freedom:

> I don't know. Who – or what – put the question, I don't know where it was put, I don't even remember answering.
>
> But at some moment I did answer *Yes* to Someone – or Something – and from that hour I was certain that existence is meaningful and that therefore my life, in self surrender, had a goal. From that moment I have known what it means 'not to look back', and 'to take no thought for the morrow' . . . As I continued on the Way, I learned, step by step, word by word, that behind every saying in the Gospels, stands *one man* and *one* man's experience. Also behind the prayer that the cup might pass from him and his promise to drink it. And behind each of the words from the cross.[5]

It is increasingly hard to be a Christian in either India or the UK. There are different challenges that make this so. In the UK it is the challenge of secularism and the postmodern way of life. Secularism makes all religions out of fashion. There is an aggressive new atheism which goes further than this. Postmodernism means that if we are religious, we should confine that side of life to the private, and compartmentalize it so that it will not invade the rest of our life. A gift of South Asians of all faiths to the UK has been their open religious commitment and practice – Sikhism, Hinduism, Jainism and Islam are all clearly ways of life if they are anything. They have brought the dialogue about faith into the forefront of public life, and encouraged a Christian confidence in public as well as private life. Within this context, converts to Christian faith, if they have weathered the kind of difficulties mentioned in this chapter, can be a strength and support to British Christians, whether European or South Asian in origin. Their examples of a faith lived out in often difficult circumstances, involving giving up much, to gain what they feel is the 'pearl of great price' (see

Matthew 13.45–46, AV), can inspire the apathetic, or the Sunday Christian so often found in our churches.

For the Indian Christian, we can reflect how conversion is one of the ways God works in the life of an individual or group. Because the question has become so political in India, this does not mean we should not stand by in solidarity with those who take this step here in the UK. The convert needs to be fully accepted as being a gift and not just a problem, as we acknowledge the work of the Spirit in those who come to us. We should also reflect on what Kumar said above, that the churches need to see the convert as the bridge to his or her families and friends who have not converted. He challenges us to consider what we can learn from Hindu traditions at their best, and not to write them off as merely Brahminic or oppressive in their power. All religions are a mixture of good and bad, and we need to pray for the discernment of the Spirit in considering what we must refuse to compromise with, what is indifferent and what we can welcome. As the convert gains in confidence, he or she may help us in this, if we do not force a great gulf to be formed between the person's present and former faith. Interfaith dialogue is a way to help this process. Converts can have a place in this as time goes by, since they can see both sides of a complex picture.

6

The Swaminarayan Sampradaya movement

The Swaminarayan denomination within Hinduism is a growing and increasingly important Hindu tradition both in India and in Western countries such as the UK and the USA. It is especially recognizable to many Hindus and non-Hindus by the very beautiful temples built by its devotees. These temples are open to all Hindus and non-Hindus. I have visited their large centres in Ahmedabad and Gandhinagar in Gujarat, and in central Mumbai, also their vast new temple in New Delhi, and also their traditional stone *mandirs* on the outskirts of Chicago (see Chapter 8, on the USA) and in Toronto. They have major centres too in parts of Africa, and other US cities (including New York, which I have seen).

In the UK, I have visited their amazing temple in Neasden, north-west London, just off the North Circular Road. This is like a piece of North India transported to this unlikely area of the capital, behind the suburban housing estates of north London. Thousands of British Hindus go here regularly, and not just from London itself, and not just Gujaratis. Here too is a professional and permanent exhibition about Hinduism in general, and about this movement. Many school children, students and enquiring groups of non-Hindus often get their first feel for Hinduism here. Opposite the temple is a Hindu school, the first in Europe, which has a very successful academic record – and across the road is an excellent vegetarian Indian restaurant. This *mandir* (temple) was opened in 1995, after earlier *mandirs* had preceded it from around the time of the East African exodus to England. The estimated cost was £12 million, but a vast amount of voluntary labour was given (the temple brochure mentions an estimate of 3,000 such persons), both local and devotees coming from India for up to three years. It was opened by His Holiness Pramukh Swami Maharaj, the current head of the movement, whom I met personally in Ahmedabad when I visited.

There are also a number of smaller temples and community centres around the UK, in Ashton under Lyne, Loughborough, Wellingborough, Coventry, Birmingham, Nottingham, Preston and so on, making 13 mandirs in total. My knowledge is of the one in Leicester, which I give as an example, and which opened after many years of planning and fundraising, in October

2011, in a two-day festival involving not only other Hindus, but also the city mayor, the Council of Faiths members and other well-wishers.

Who was Swaminarayan? History of the movement

Bhagwan Swaminarayan, also known as Sahajanand Swami, lived from 1781 until 1830, and from 1799 was based in Gujarat. He was a Vaishnavite of Brahmin background, and was venerated in his lifetime as an incarnation of God. There are differences between different branches of the movement, but the view of BAPS (see just below) is clear, that he was a manifestation of Parabrahman (the highest reality); all other deities including Krishna are ultimately *avataras*, but he himself is not an *avatar* of any other deity. His home is in his divine abode, Akshardham. This divine abode manifests on earth in the form of the guru, and Swaminarayan is believed to be present in and work through him. As such, he is seen as the human manifestation of God.

The various successors to Swaminarayan are designated in order from one to the other (cf. successors to the Dalai Lama), and they are all considered manifestations of the divine abode and ideal devotee, Akshar. The present successor is Pramukh Swami Maharaj, the fifth in the line of succession. Elderly now, he will designate his own successor. He is enormously respected by the more than 900 *sadhus* and millions of lay persons of the fellowship. He has been immensely energetic in travelling around the world, including the UK, encouraging the development of the movement and giving it direction.

Key to the movement was the development of an order of monks, known as Paramhansas, which Swaminarayan trained and initiated. There were 500 at that time. They took five main vows, including non-attachment and non-greed. Best known was the renunciation of family contacts and direct contact with women. Parents are to become as other parents from previous lives. The only exception is that, when one of the parents dies, the *sadhu* should go through a ritual bath of purification.

Swaminarayan was a campaigner for women's rights and the abolition of *sati* (widow burning). He taught that education was the right of all people, men and women. People of all castes and creeds joined his movement.

Over the ensuing two centuries, splits have occurred. The main group found in the diaspora is known as Bochasanwasi Akshar Purushottam Swaminarayan Sanstha, or BAPS for short, and their main temple in the UK is the Neasden temple above. Another group of the movement have their main headquarters in Queen's Park, also in north London. There are several other smaller groups in the UK. Overall, there are said to be 20 million members of the movement worldwide, and they are said to be the fastest-growing part of Hinduism globally. BAPS does a wide range of social work, and educational and youth work, and claims to have 55,000 volunteers around the world. Its members also produce many audio CDs, DVDs and books, and we can view these in their bookshop in Neasden. This is outside the introductory exhibition on Hinduism and the Swaminarayan tradition. They give free there an attractive and colourful guide, *Understanding Hinduism*, which looks at the complexity of Hinduism in general, and seeks to explain the Swaminarayan tradition, and Bhagwan Swaminarayan its founder. His Holiness Pramukh Swami Maharaj is introduced at the end as inspirer of the temple, a people's guru, 'reaching out to all, regardless of age, class, colour or creed', as one of Hinduism's great spiritual teachers. It is noteworthy that one of Pramukh Swami Maharaj's predecessors was a low-caste tailor, who was not a monk when he was spiritual leader of the movement.

I have visited a similar magnificent temple complex with exhibition in Gandhinagar, Gujarat, called Swaminarayan Akshardham. There was a terrorist attack on this a few years ago, said to have been by Pakistani terrorists.

I have met two of the *sadhus* at Neasden. One, **Yogivekdas Swami**, is the senior monk at the time I met him, in 2012. He qualified as a doctor in Leicester and then felt a calling to become a monk. He heads up the temple and enables the monks to go out on teaching missions elsewhere. He exhibits a deep spiritual presence as he welcomes a visitor like myself.

The other is **Paramtattvadas Swami**, also with origins in Leicester. I acknowledge here my debt to him, as he has looked through and corrected a longer version of this chapter. He is an academic and is just completing his doctorate from the University of Baroda in conjunction with the Oxford Centre for Hindu Studies, where his guide was Professor Gavin Flood of Oxford University. His aim has been to go beyond Indology or Sanskrit studies, and to apply Western theological tools and methodology, while remaining faithful to Hindu tradition, a kind of comparative theology. Swaminarayan is his case study, where the centring on God as personal clearly provides an entry point.

At a personal level, he commented on the requirement to leave behind his family totally. He referred to the belief in reincarnation. His parents and family were part of his previous life, and he is enormously grateful for them. But in the next physical life, he would have to leave them behind, as do all persons. So he did this within the same life by taking monastic vows. His new family are the *sadhus* with whom he trained and with whom he now lives in Neasden.

Challenges, possibilities and difficulties for Christians in relating to this movement

Swaminarayan had a famous meeting near Baroda in 1825 with the Anglican Bishop Heber of Calcutta. This is seen as an early example of dialogue. Heber had heard that Swaminarayan preached one God and a moral order. Heber hoped the meeting would lead to Swaminarayan hearing the Christian gospel. Swaminarayan hoped to get British help to build a temple, a residence hall and a hospital. Heber said he could not do this, because of the links of the movement with idolatry. He also disapproved of how followers saw Swaminarayan as a manifestation of God, with rays coming from his face. The dialogue went no further, though the meeting is noted in Swaminarayan history.

Today, and positively, those in this movement are very friendly and open to the wider community. We find this in the UK and also in the temples I visited in India and North America. They are very committed to the interfaith movement, and want to play a full part. I have long known this in the Leicester Council of Faiths, where they have long had their own two faithful representatives. I have known this also through Nitin Palan, responsible for such outreach from the Neasden temple. He has played a major role from the beginning in the Hindu–Christian Forum UK (see Chapter 10). Many events have happened over the years at Neasden in Inter Faith Weeks and at other times. At the temple, there are photographs of distinguished visitors such as Prince Charles, Sir Richard Branson, Tony Blair as prime minister, Archbishop Rowan Williams, Diana, Princess of Wales, and others. Prime Minister David Cameron and his wife Samantha Cameron visited at the time of Diwali in 2013.

Their temples are easy to visit. Hospitality is generous, and the food the best of vegetarian food. They have trained educators to be able to offer an understandable framework and to answer questions.

Theologically, Christians will be led to consider whether they can be empathetic to the idea that Swaminarayan can be likened in any way to Jesus Christ, having both an incarnational time on earth ('he that hath seen me hath seen the Father', John 14.9 AV) and an eternal form in heaven. It is a similar challenge to that relating to Krishna in ISKCON. Christians will naturally vary greatly in their response, as superficial similarities soon fall away and serious theology is discussed.

Another much-discussed question is the position of women within the movement, and the reality that the *sadhus* are not permitted to meet one to one with women in their own movement or with outsiders. Academic work has been done, particularly in the USA, which has affirmed the respected place women have in the movement as a whole. Swami Paramtattvadas told me of the work of Angela Rudert (submitted to Cornell University in 2004) on Swaminarayan women in the USA. She considers how women can and do assert power through their own initiatives and spaces. (There are many other examples of such studies.) This is clearly so. But there is still a complex reality involved in dialogue with *sadhus*, such that within my own Anglican tradition nearly half of those becoming priests, women who are theologically trained, cannot meet with monks. They can of course meet with theologically trained Swaminarayan women. But my experience is that this is a stumbling block for those female priests who would like to engage at all levels, as I, as a male priest, can do. This is not to condemn the movement for their gender arrangements and rules, but to suggest that opportunities of dialogue thereby require greater effort.

7

Three geographical studies: 1. Leicester, England

Introduction to the case studies

The following three chapters are case studies of three places. The primary focus is in Chapters 7 and 8, which are representative of two major centres for Hindus in the West: the UK and the USA. The third is much shorter – on Sweden – and is here as an example of small Hindu communities in Europe. They are the ones I happen to know, and can provide a snapshot, beyond the major countries involved – because of course there are Hindus in nearly all countries in the West, and small communities, and the spread of Hindus is likely to increase in the future.

The two long chapters related to the UK and the USA are not like to like. In the USA I have included only cities I have visited, and, except for Chicago, all are in the east of the country. There are major omissions, not least California, but this provides, I hope, a feel for the whole. My British example is much smaller in geographical area – just the city of Leicester – though not in terms of intensity and importance of Hindu presence. It will be explained why I feel that this is representative enough – and it is where I have lived for the last 14 years. I was thinking of writing a separate chapter where I make direct comparison between the two contexts. But, on consideration, it is clear that such material is included in the main content of the two chapters, and that would seem to be enough. A major difference to point out at the beginning is that Leicester is a single city, with a great concentration of different faiths, including its large Hindu minority, and this community has been vital to the development of the city over the last 40 years, since the major immigration began. In contrast the American cities I visited are much bigger, and have a far smaller proportion or concentration of Hindus. So also nationally, there is no concentration of Hindus anywhere like in Leicester. As a proportion of the total population of the UK, Hindus are much higher, and they are concentrated in certain areas, besides Leicester, especially in east and west London.

In Leicester we can see the powerful influence of Hindus who came via a double migration, usually from East Africa and further south in Africa.

Here Uganda, Tanzania and Kenya are particularly important, though smaller numbers have come from Zimbabwe and South Africa. These Hindus came with a much broader experience of life than those coming direct from India. They had risen in society economically, socially, professionally and culturally, and this is why they were moved on with independence coming to those countries. They became a threat to the new rulers, and they moved, where possible and if they had the necessary documents, to the UK, seen by many as the mother country. They brought with them long experience of living as a minority alongside other faiths, and above all with Christians. Many had been educated in Christian schools. From early on, they played a significant part in the interfaith activities in the cities to which they came, as well as making a significant contribution to city life at all levels. Though we should not exaggerate the ease with which they fitted into life in a city like Leicester, they found certainly the earlier steps in integration fairly straightforward.

Those who came direct from India, very often through arranged marriages, or for job opportunities, found things more difficult, especially for language reasons since often they spoke little English, and because they were not so used to a pluralistic society as those from East Africa. Leicester has benefited from having a high proportion of those whose origins were in Africa.

Only a small proportion, in comparison, of Indians coming to the USA came via East Africa. They did not have the required papers, and the choice was usually between the UK and India. There are a significant number of Guyanese and Trinidadian Hindus in New York, more noticeable than in the UK.

But generally, migration to the USA has usually happened through the 'green card' system, and this ensured a very high level of professional and educational entry, and also that people came already with a good economic status. They tended to come as individuals rather than as groups, and made their way forward wherever there were skilled employment possibilities, or professional or business openings. The majority of Indians came to where British Indians already were, though the National Health Service (NHS) employed large numbers of Indian doctors and nurses throughout the country.

There is also a significant difference in the regions from where migrants came, and therefore in the Hinduism they brought with them. In the UK there is a Gujarati dominance, not least in a city like Leicester. This is partly because of history, in that many Gujaratis were part of the diaspora that went to Africa and hence came on to the UK. But they are also a group ready to migrate with the ambition of building up their businesses and other openings. Of course there are plenty of Gujaratis in the USA, but not such a dominance.

In the USA there are large numbers of South Indians, professionals, and they come both from Tamil Nadu and also in considerable numbers from Andhra Pradesh. The Venkateswara Temple in Andhra is said to be the richest temple in India. It is much reproduced, with grand buildings, in the parts of the USA I visited, and other South Indian gods surround the main images of Vishnu and Parvathi. Where Tamils are significant, there will probably also be an image of Murugan, the brother of Ganesh, as found in Tamil Nadu (see Chapter 4 on South Indian *bhakti*).

Leicester

I choose Leicester for my case study in the UK for several reasons. The first is that I have lived here for the last 14 years, in the main city, which means that my neighbours have been Hindus, Sikhs and Muslims, and a minority of Christians. So I write from within what has become a city that is seen, with good reason, as the most Indian city in the UK, and indeed in Europe. The second is that Leicester is viewed as the Hindu capital of the UK, for historical reasons, as will be seen below. The third is the mixture of Hindus here. It is a good place to consider varieties within British Hinduism, as experienced in one medium-sized city. A fourth reason is that interfaith work has been long established here, and Hindus have been major players in what has happened over the last 30 years. Christians and Hindus have been much engaged together in this story, alongside Muslims, Sikhs and others.

A recent article in *The Independent* newspaper has the headline, 'We are all in this together: how Leicester became a model for multiculturalism (even if that was never the plan)'.[1] The article reflects on how the UK obtained its dazzling array of new citizens with little conscious planning. Nobody planned for Leicester to become the most multicultural city on the planet. 'It just happened that way.' The original idea for many of the earlier immigrants was that they would work for some years, get enough money, and, if they were farmers, 'buy a tractor' and then go back. But in fact, most did the opposite. They got into the rhythm of life here, and began to bring their families, from the 1960s. New arrivals sensed this could be a land of opportunity – though early beginnings were tough. One Sikh, interviewed by *The Independent*, said his father had shared a house with 48 people when he first arrived! Attempts to stop people coming failed badly, as the news that this was a good place to come to penetrated the Indian subcontinent, and East Africa.

East Africa became a major source of immigration to Leicester, whether voluntarily, or through the kind of expulsions seen most prominently in Uganda, with Idi Amin's famous action in 1973, but also by more phased movements out of other East African countries. The city council of the time tried to stop the wave of immigrants coming to Leicester, taking out adverts in the *Uganda Argus* stating that conditions were no longer favourable; there were waiting lists for housing and for schooling, with social and medical services stretched to the limit: 'Leicester is full. Do not come.' But they came all the more, finding opportunities opening up through family associations and professional possibilities, and by developing businesses to replace the declining old industries. Hindus were in the forefront of this movement to Leicester, as they made it what they considered 'their city'. They began to develop their temples from the late 1960s, indicating that they were here to stay. To date, there are now at least 18 temples around the city, particularly in the high settlement areas to north and east.

As time went by, Hindus became major players in Leicester, both in the professions, especially the health service, and in the development of the city economically, politically and educationally.

Demographics tell a major story, as the numbers of non-Westerners in the city rose inexorably. In the 2011 census, white indigenous people were just 45 per cent of the 329,000 population. The non-white population was 49 per cent, with East Europeans and others accounting for the remaining percentage. Another part of the story, the significance of which is not yet clear, is that the Hindu figure of over 50,000 had been overtaken by a Muslim total of 61,000. In the previous census of 2001, Hindus had been the larger community. These figures are explained partly by fresh immigration of Somalis (perhaps 14,000) from mainland Europe, all Muslims; and many other Muslims came from traumatized countries. A significant number of Tamils came from Sri Lanka, by far the majority Hindus, propelled to the UK by the civil war. Around 200,000 came to London, and from there several thousand moved on to the cheaper city of Leicester, seen also as more welcoming.

What has also happened is that the increasingly successful Hindus have begun to move out, first to the leafy suburbs on the edge of the city, and then from there to towns and villages around, in the county of Leicestershire. They can drive from there easily to their temples in the city. Muslims now have around 50 mosques of various sizes, but they attend them very frequently for prayers, and above all, for the evening *madrassas* for the education of their children. So the outward move has been much slower, with the first mosque in the Leicestershire town of Oadby, bordering on the city, only opening in 2011. There is as yet no Hindu temple in Oadby, and the nearest outside Leicester are two or three in Loughborough, 15 miles away, an important university town.

All these groups own the city of Leicester as their home, and things normally go on well between communities. There can be tensions from time to time, but local interfaith structures and the generally positive contribution of both the city council and the police have helped to keep things generally peaceful. The city has become a magnet for those coming from Europe and wider afield to see how Leicester does manage things. A key response, when I am asked about this, is the mixture of faiths here, and the positive effect of the balance between so-called Indic faiths – Hinduism, Sikhism, Jainism – and the so-called Abrahamic faiths – Judaism, Christianity and Islam. Another factor has been the long and positive involvement of the churches, and especially the Church of England, in being proactive in enabling diversity to be managed, and tensions held in balance – whether originating in the city itself, nationally or internationally. This has resulted in the last two Bishops of Leicester, both very committed to interfaith engagement, being known as 'our Bishop' by the faith community leaders.

Three main structures have been developed for interfaith work. The first is the Leicester Council of Faiths, first formed in 1986, and one of the earliest in the UK, in response to the growing threat of the National Front, and initiated by the Archdeacon of Leicester and the Mayor of Leicester. This has had its ups and downs, but has continued to be a central factor in enabling all faiths to feel part of the structures of the city, with the city council consistently providing modest funding for part-time staff and premises, though this has been much reduced under the cuts imposed by the coalition government from 2010 onwards. This means the council owns the faiths of the city, as a positive factor, and this is a key element behind its slogan, 'One Leicester', prominently displayed throughout the city – on many lamp posts, for example. On the Leicester Council of Faiths, Hindus have four places by right of nomination, and in addition, the Swaminarayan movement has two places of their own. This is an anomaly, with Roman Catholics, for example, having no place in their own right, only as part of a Christian group of four. Major faiths have four places each, and smaller faiths two each. The present chair of the Council is a Hindu woman; the previous one was a Bahai woman, and before that a Sikh man.

The second structure is the Faith Leaders Forum, established by the Bishop in 2001 in the aftermath of September 11, 2001, the attack on the Twin Towers in New York. This meets regularly and is able to discuss major crises quickly, and face difference more directly than the Council of Faiths, where the emphasis is on representation and harmony. Hindus have always been prominent here, though Muslim issues tend to predominate, for obvious reasons.

The third structure is the St Philip's Centre for Study and Engagement in a Multi Faith Society, developed from 2004, and becoming a Trust in 2006. This was initiated by the Diocese of Leicester. It became fully ecumenical, but apart from grants the main funder remains the Church of England. It is one of four centres nationally recognized as Presence and Engagement Centres.[2] Training takes place of Christians at all levels, from village lay people to clergy and bishops, with the intention of their owning where the UK and Leicester/shire now are, taking this positively as an opportunity for engagement and theological reflection, and for taking seriously the understanding that everyone living in a Church of England parish is the responsibility of the parish priest.

What does this mean in a parish like St Philip's, where Christians are less than 10 per cent of the population (census of 2011), with Muslims by far the majority, or St Theodore's, Rusheymead, where there are similar figures, but by far the majority of the rest are Hindus (see interview on page 108)? What is the role of a church like this in Rusheymead? The Centre also does a wide range of training for officials from the council, for recruits to the police, for medical students, for school children and teachers and so on. In all these, the emphasis is to show that the multi-religious world is diverse, and that Hindus are a very important part of this globally, within the UK and in Leicester. There has also been a Hindu–Christian Dialogue group (see Chapter 10), though this is not functioning at present. In all such ventures, the challenge is to show that there are other religions in the world than Islam and Christianity, which, of course, is one of the purposes for writing this book.

For our purposes, another important initiative has been the developing work done by the Oxford Centre for Hindu Studies. Their initiatives among Hindus will be mentioned in the interviews below. But they have also initiated a monthly series of open lectures, leading to dialogue, on topics central for Hindus but also potentially engaging for Christians. Hopefully these can lead to a revival of dialogue between the two faiths on a regular basis.

I will now introduce the reader to a range of Hindus whom I have long worked with, and whom I have interviewed in depth. This will give a feel for where British Hindus have come from, and where they are now. I will then also provide details of encounters with some Christians who have worked with Hindus at a parish level.

By way of introduction to Leicester, and indeed to the UK, I end this section by comparing the seven areas mentioned in the introduction to the US case study which follows (see pages 114–15 for these seven areas).

1 *Vivekananda* is of course a great international figure, venerated on both sides of the Atlantic, as the founder of the interfaith movement. But his immediate impact was where he delivered his first addresses, in Chicago, and where he conducted an extension mission afterwards in the USA. His impact in the UK was much less, at this peak time of empire and the Raj, where Hinduism was what was seen in the subcontinent.
2 *Vedanta* has permeated the culture much less in the UK, and Vedanta Societies are without great influence. There are now important missions such as the Chinmaya Mission, which incarnate similar principles. They are Indian in feel, based on their guru in Delhi, though teaching Vedantic principles – see the interview with Preet. Mention should be made here of the dominance of the Gita in nearly all British Hindu study groups and movements. It has become like the Gospels in its centrality, much of it through *bhakti* movements.
3 *Yoga* is found all over the UK, and in Leicester also. But it is more limited in its spread than, say, in California or Boston. It is probably more linked with Buddhism, or secular groups, though someone like Hemang Bhatt (see his interview below) conducts very full classes in temples or halls, and nearly all are Indian participants. Many Christians are very suspicious of *yoga* (see the later section on spirituality). On the other hand, there are strong attempts to develop Christian yoga groups. Associations of this movement with 'New Age' is seen as attractive by some of the young, or those disillusioned with conventional Christianity; for others this is a reason to avoid it.
4 *The guru movement* has always been most linked with the USA, with followers in their tens of thousands. Such gurus have found a more fertile ground there, particularly in the east and west of the USA. The impact in the UK has been less, and less permanent in its effect. Young British people, including from Leicester, have of course made their way to India to seek out spiritual nourishment and transformation.

5 *ISKCON*. A study of its importance in the UK can be found in Chapter 3. ISKCON's importance has probably increased in recent years, as it has engaged deliberately with Christians, through the Oxford Centre for Hindu Studies, and through the beginning now of its involvement in primary school education.
6 *Transcendental meditation*, again, is much less dominant in the UK than in the USA, though there are practitioners of it. I rarely hear it mentioned in Leicester, and it is seen, if at all, as linked with Zen Buddhism.
7 *Alternative medicine* again is found, but not linked too much in the public eye with Hinduism, as opposed to India generally.

The public face of Hinduism in the UK is seen around temples and festivals, and in a city like Leicester we are thinking of many different temples. Hinduism is part of the experience of children in schools, who may visit a temple as a part of their religious education. Festivals such as Diwali are celebrated in schools as a matter of routine these days. Then names of gods will be learned, and their stories related, just as and sometimes more than New Testament stories.

In public life, Hindus and Hinduism have now claimed a large public profile, both in city and national contexts. There is a Diwali gathering in the House of Commons, as well as celebrations in Leicester. The city sponsors the Diwali festival lights and fireworks, and is willing to block busy roads to enable vast crowds to attend. Individual Hindus' involvement in city life and politics is clear from my interviews, and this is seen nationally also, in both the House of Commons and the House of Lords.

Hindus in Leicester

TV Mojaria

This senior citizen of Leicester is known as TV! He has been here for 40 years, and came as part of the compelled exodus from Uganda. This fortieth-year anniversary was celebrated in the city's cathedral in June 2013, with representatives of all concerned faiths, in the presence of a central government minister, the elected Mayor of Leicester, and many others significant leaders, local and national. The sermon was preached by the Bishop, Tim Stevens, and he highlighted the way the government of the time, that of the conservative prime minister, Ted Heath, honoured British overseas passport holders, and received a total of 28,000 in a matter of weeks. The country had benefited greatly from this open-door policy. Ugandan Asians were dispersed, but many found their way to Leicester, and the city gained much over the years, and not just through diversification of food.

One of these was TV. He had been active in Uganda as an accountant, and he got a job within three weeks of coming to Leicester. He had been president of his caste association, the Lohana Community, now actively organized in Leicester with its own temple. His prominence is shown by the fact that he was an Asian delegate to a conference called by Idi Amin. The participants wrote a 200-page report which was ignored – and another prominent Leicester man, a Muslim, was part of the leadership of this.

Amin wanted integration through intermarriage. TV's comment is that Hindus do not encourage even inter-caste marriage, yet alone other liaisons. The reality was that Amin could not abide the Asian dominance in business and the professions, and in landowning. The Ugandan Asians were given 90 days to wind up their affairs and leave. Some panicked and went to India. Eventually, because the exodus was not taken up urgently, an order was given for all to leave within three days. TV left urgently, and arrived in a camp in Suffolk with his wife and children. At 4 a.m. the next day, relatives arrived from Leicester, to give them a place to stay.[3] TV was amazed at how welcome they seemed, and the amount of voluntary work offered in support.

TV found his way socially through his membership of the Lions Club. There were 20 members from East Africa. TV wanted the organization to be integrated, locals and East Africans. But TV was a baby within the organization, and failed to enable integration. However, he encouraged the giving of food parcels to needy families. He also joined the Patients' Advisory Service at the General Hospital. Here he encouraged the introduction of a prayer room, and vegetarian food, a subject where there were disputes to engage in, such as whether this food could include egg or fish!

In Uganda, TV had not been much involved with religious and temple life, as opposed to cultural and charitable engagement. This was where he began also in Leicester. He attended the annual meeting of a new temple called the Jalaram Temple, and though not a member himself, he found himself elected secretary in 1983. There was no Jalaram temple in East Africa. It is a cult based on the guru Jalaram. He was a saint from Gujarat, who lived in the nineteenth century and is well known for his healing miracles. TV became a devotee, and an expert on the stories of this saint, which he narrates to all who come to the temple. The miracles included the raising of a Muslim boy from the dead. The movement has spread further afield, though the Leicester temple is the only one in Europe. Its members are now found in Gujarat itself, in Tamil Nadu, Calcutta, Toronto, Houston and Australia.

TV became president of this temple, and they raised £1 million in three years, the new temple being opened in 1995 in Narborough Road, near the Church of the Martyrs. TV believed above all in the openness and inclusiveness of a temple. So he enabled the placing of a rather special medallion of six religious leaders on the ceiling of the main temple, right in the middle. This means that Jesus, Gandhi, Mahavira, Guru Nanak and two others are blessing the worshippers. This comes out of his strong commitment now to the Council of Faiths, of which he became a long-serving Hindu member, and then a life president. 'All faiths are welcome' was at the core of his belief. He was influenced by a painting in the Swaminarayan Temple in Nairobi. For him also social and community work was central, and much of this took place from this temple. Education was also important, and he wrote a guide to the temple for the countless visitors, whom he normally received, rather than the priests who knew little English. He invited the Oxford Centre to give lectures in the temple premises, and to teach A-level Gujarati, for which grants were available. He obtained a five-year grant for the development of a learning centre. He spends about an hour a day in the Jalaram Temple, and this is where his heart is. This is why he refused to be involved in politics locally, and he is not interested in the politics of India, where he has only been twice.

He finds no issues in religions relating, and he gets on especially well with Christians, and even with Muslims, whom he meets at functions and through the Council of Faiths and Faith Leaders Forum. He had no issues when his younger son married a Westerner, and he was happy he married a Christian. Now there is a temple in their house. His wife goes to temple, and at Christmas they celebrate a Christian festival.

Summary TV is an example of a typically upright and responsible Hindu. He offers the same qualities in Leicester as he had been nurtured in in Uganda. He provided the kind of leadership that the new community needed, largely out of a commitment to civic responsibility. Successful in his career, he found time later to develop his religious life, focusing on a saint who nurtured his life. He is a man in whom there is no guile, and who is valued by those of other faiths, as well as his fellow Hindus. He provided strong rather than charismatic leadership, at an important time in the development of his community.

Important addendum TV died in November 2013, after this interview was taken. I add here my own personal tribute to a 'good man', who was appreciated and loved by those of all faiths who were privileged to know him in Leicester, as is apparent from the above interview account.

Rashmi Joshi

Rashmi came from Tanzania, as did a number of the leading Hindus in Leicester. The stereotypical view that all came from Uganda through expulsions is not true. He is from a Brahmin background, and his father worked in the secular field, but also as a voluntary priest. His mother also knew the ceremonies, and carried them out in houses in Tanzania. Rashmi learned much from her when he came to Leicester at the age of 16. When he was old enough, he used to drive her to lead functions, and also went with her to the temple each evening. In Tanzania, he was brought up experiencing an easy relationship between faiths and communities.

But when he came to Leicester, he found that each group of Asians did their own thing, as they recovered from the upheaval brought by the enormous changes in their lives. Local people here had little idea of the religious and cultural needs of these new communities, and so the newcomers had to look after themselves. A small group of Hindu leaders got together, and established two temples. One was the now famous Sanatan Mandir, in Belgrave, in 1972, one of the earliest in the UK. (This was in the old William Carey Memorial Baptist Church, ironical since William Carey had been the first Baptist missionary to North India in 1799. He had been a minister in Leicester, as well as a cobbler, the profession of the lowest of castes.)

The second temple was started in 1969 and became the Hindu Mandir, in St Barnabas Road. The project was encouraged by visitors from India such as Shyma Devi, from an ashram in Vrindavan, who made a major contribution financially and worked with a group of women, focusing on the goddess Mattaji. They raised large sums of money as their prosperity grew, and built the present Mandir, and now its extension.

Rashmi became assistant secretary of this temple, and a major player within the community leadership in Leicester. He has been a prominent radio presenter on the Leicester Hindu radio station for 17 years, his programme being aired early in the morning four times a week. This is an important component in the nurture of Hindus, and the enabling of their education and devotion. He also took up the mantle of interfaith work, enabled by his good English, and conviction that this was vital for the cohesion of Leicester. He has been a key player in both the Leicester

Council of Faiths and the Faith Leaders Forum. He was the obvious person for me to approach when we established the Hindu–Christian Forum, and it met often in the Hindu Mandir. He enabled the temple to make donations to Christian Aid each year, in Christian Aid Week, and developed a close relationship with nearby St Barnabas Church. He is nicknamed 'Haribol' ('I invoke the name of God in you'), because that is the greeting he always uses when meeting others, whatever their faith.

A further development is that he accepted a nomination to be a candidate for the Labour Party in city elections, and has now been a local councillor for a number of years, seeing this as part of a calling to serve the wider community.

He is no longer associated with Hindu Mandir. There were problems related to control of the temple, and a new guard wanting to take over. He and other elders were voted out. The leaders did not like his interfaith priorities, among other things. They asked him back, but he said no; he feels that politics is now his priority. He has now joined another temple. This story illustrates the complexity of power relationships in such institutions. He feels the Hindu community remains fragmented, particularly its leadership, and has far to go in its journey to maturity. That applies to national bodies as well. He has been involved with the National Council of Hindu Temples (NCHT) and is a trustee of Brahmo Samaj.[4] He has considerable admiration for ISKCON, which seems to have done away with Brahminic domination, and through Prabhupada spread the teaching of the Gita through the West. His sister is an official of ISKCON in Germany.

Rashmi is now in his mid-fifties, and has taken up his priestly role more. He carries out some rituals in private homes, and occasional marriage ceremonies. These include officiating in a private Brahmin temple in Leicester. Recently, he conducted a wedding between an American Christian and a Gujarati bride – 90 per cent in English. Another last year included a Swedish family. An Orthodox priest from Sweden joined in. The Hindu side wanted to show him what Rashmi would do, and what images would be involved. They had a meeting before the wedding, when everything was explained stage by stage – including the inclusion of Ganesh, and who Ganesh is! The priest had no problems. Rashmi had swotted much before his first wedding, and prepared a special service order. He followed the Christian way of doing things – preparing carefully and timing correctly. He used a website, and his wife helped. He has also assisted at funerals and at the coming of deities to a new temple in Wellingborough, 40 miles away, when he was one of four officiating Brahmin priests, for three days.

Rashmi comments on the contemporary situation in Leicester There are underlying tensions in Leicester, which may erupt like a volcano. Hindus are not aggressive by nature, but show dismay at outside groups coming in – such as the English Defence League (a right-wing, militantly anti-Islamic organization). This can be classified as a faith tension. Hindus tend to murmur at temples, or in libraries, but are unlikely to go on the rampage.

An underlying issue is not that their numbers are now less than the Muslims, but questions of conversion. The young, and those with weak personalities, are influenced by other faiths to move to Islam or Christianity. Often this is through marriage. A growing number of Muslims are involved. They put on political pressure, as over the Iraq war. Rashmi fears that Leicester, within 10–15 years, may become as Muslim-dominated as Bradford. Muslims are well organized and can mobilize people very quickly, unlike the fragmented Hindu communities. Issues in Gujarat have often been significant between the two communities, particularly at the time of civil disturbances and deaths of 1,000–2,000 Gujaratis, mainly Muslims, in 2002, which led to much tension in the city. (My updated comment: will the result of the Indian election of 2014 lead to renewed tension in the future, particularly if Narendra Modi visits Leicester?)

Populations do change. With the influx from Uganda, for example, whites began to move out from the inner-city areas of Belgrave and Highfields. Muslims took over Highfields and now are doing so in the outer area of Evington. In north Leicester, it is felt that Somalis have preference for social housing, in what has become a major Hindu area. There are also potential flashpoints, with the coming of Sri Lankan Tamils and East Europeans.

Summary Rashmi Joshi is clear that so much of his commitment to Hindu leadership in the city, and to the consequent political involvement, comes out of his early years in Tanzania, and what he learned from his parents. This he has tried to hand on to his four children, all of whom are maintaining his heritage and teaching. He works immensely hard in community work, temple and media work, and in interfaith engagement, especially with Christians, and has contributed greatly to the harmony of the city, sometimes at personal cost to himself: he has suffered from the internal factionalism often found in any of the temple-based faiths, where influence in a temple is seen as so important, with Hindu priests being only employees, and the boards and executives holding the power as elected officials.

Manjula Sood MBE

Manjula came to Leicester in 1970, in the midst of the snow, straight after getting married in India. Her husband Vijay Paul was from Amritsar District, in the Punjab, and as he set off for England his father exacted two promises from him: that he would remain a vegetarian and that he would marry an Indian woman. Paul and Manjula got married ten days after they met, and she left for England after two months spent waiting for her visa. Their first home was in a small, dark and cold flat in Highfields. She had been brought up in a house with 25 rooms, and the contrast was enormous.

Manjula came from a religious family, of a Chattriya caste. Her family were members of the Arya Samaj, and followed Swami Devananda Maharishi. From this source, she was taught the Gayathri Mantra as a basis for life. Arya Samaj does not emphasize rituals. God has no form, and you can worship God in any form. No need for fasting – do not torture yourself. Women do not veil themselves, and have equal rights. Her grandfather founded Arya Samaj in Kenya. Followers will not eat meat or consume alcohol.

In Leicester, this group hires a hall once a month. Its members learn the Gayathri Mantra as children. The scriptures of Manu are important. Arya Samaj is about discipline and way of life. Central are the Veda Slokas, the basis of the four Hindu stages of life. *Yagna* (fire sacrifices) are conducted for purification; special herbs are put into the fire. Their weddings are very simple. Hindu Punjabis from East Africa are particularly involved in this movement, and it is more active in Birmingham and London.

The Gita Bhavan is Manjula's temple; this is Punjabi ethnically, and uses Hindi as an inclusive language. This is an important temple, she feels, because all can feel comfortable. She gets concerned about caste temples; Sanatan Mandir is much more inclusive.

Manjula has also followed Sai Baba since 1980. This, she feels, has made her more open. She has dedicated herself and her achievements to Sai Baba, from where she gets the mantras 'Service to humanity is service to God' and 'Hands that help are holier than lips that pray'. It is not a matter of bathing before prayer, but of purifying one's soul. She learned that we should spend money on the poor and needy, rather than on religious organizations. Baba has taught her to respect all faiths – never think badly of any faith. In each religion, spirituality is vital; for example, she appreciates Friday prayer and Ramadan. For her, Baba has not died (though physically this happened a couple of years ago); she can have a conversation with him when driving. Devotees expect his reincarnation to happen in Mysore, in the form of Christ, in a few years' time.

She made a point of visiting prisoners when she was Lord Mayor, as the outflow of her Hinduism. Her Hinduism has a practical outcome. She does not fear about anything, but only fears God. Her approach to life she summarizes by the title of the Abba song, 'I Have a Dream', and by this sentence: 'Care for today, not worrying about the future, or being sad about the past which we cannot change.' We should not impose our values on others, and dialogue is central. Being negative will not get us anywhere. Even ecological disturbance is partly caused by people's selfishness. Hence the deep significance of fire, leaves and flowers in Hindu prayer rituals. She loves the meaning of cow as mother.

Even political meetings should be a beacon for God and humanity. She respects every religious building. God is everywhere. In no scriptures are women second class. Durga gives her strength as a woman, as does divine Mother Mary. She loves the devotion of Mary to Jesus. Equality, values and respect need to be taught, as well as how to pray. She was very proud to be born in a Hindu family where her grandfather was a great campaigner for women's rights.

There were few Muslim families in her city. Leicester educated her in diversity. In Leicester, she has learned much more than if she had remained in India.

The great challenge of her life was when Paul died of a heart attack. She felt the 25 years of her marriage had been a real gift. He was a model for her political career. He had encouraged her to become a primary school teacher, one of the first Asian women to be so, from 1973. Early on she had a bad experience with her headmistress, who asserted that she 'must do as the Romans do in Rome' – and should not wear a sari. She replied that when the British were in India, they did not wear saris! She had to extend her teaching probation by one year. Manjula felt that it was her country of India that was insulted, and not just herself. Moreover, she had no money to buy new clothes. She appealed and won the battle and was relieved from her extra probationary year, and confirmed, 'I am acceptable for my teaching, not my clothes.' She empathized too with an Indian pupil who was told not to wear trousers, though she wanted to cover her legs.

Her second head teacher went to India on a bursary, and learned nothing. He just bought jewels for his wife, and nothing for the school. He appeared to have no interest in India; he claimed that there was too much multiculturalism, and would not allow Eid or Diwali to be celebrated.

The third head teacher was very different, and through her Manjula became known throughout the county. They made a link with a school in a very rural area. She took Asian mothers to the north of the county in exchanges. But she remembers, as late as the 1980s, she went to a county school for Diwali, and three teachers left the assembly. On the other hand, three teachers were trained on *tabla* and harmonium by a teacher from Delhi brought to the UK by her husband Paul. One indigenous father said, 'I don't want my child to be taught by a wog.' Her head teacher said, 'I am not moving your child to another class. Manjula is one of the best teachers.' The father then took his children away. Words like 'gollywogs' were in reading schemes at the time, and she got the books removed.

Manjula's next step was to campaign for Asian meals in schools. Also cutlery was a question, and the difficulty of using a knife and fork. She bought 24 teaspoons with her own money, when the head teacher refused to buy any. She also set up an advice centre about benefits, and English classes for mothers.

Things were sometimes thrown into the playground. When coaches came bringing people from Malawi, Manjula remembers they were afraid to get off the coaches. Members of the National Front were around, and were a challenge. Manjula was not angry; she just wanted to get on with her work. She said to her neighbour, 'We are here to stay. Let our children play together. Fear of the unknown is what stopped this.'

Integration This is a two-way process. Manjula believes we must go out to communities and talk to them. Institutions like the Council of Faiths or St Philip's only reach a few. To this end, she has done Morris dancing in the Haymarket theatre, and taught songs of all kinds. She has taught the Asian stick dance to indigenous people also. She introduced Commonwealth Day, and residential camps in Leicestershire and France to get Asians out of their urban environment. Multicultural exchange needs to be both ways round. She wanted grannies, together, to learn about English culture and Indian culture, as they shared tea. She started culturally mixed swimming groups. Her general view is that *buildings do not give you happiness, but rather people, teachers, and communities* (old school buildings do not matter so much).

Politics and faith Manjula said to husband Paul: 'If the Asians had gone into politics in Uganda, it would have been difficult to expel them!' He stood as a councillor in Belgrave, and he was elected as one of the first

Asian councillors. Peter Soulsby, council leader and now elected city mayor, tried to save Paul with resuscitation when he had a major heart attack during a political meeting. Manjula was devastated, but accepting: 'Death is in God's hands.' 'Thy will be done' was her Hindu attitude. She stood for election in her late husband's place, very reluctantly. At one point she thought of resigning, but Peter did not accept her resignation, saying she was a good councillor.

She met some sexism; for example, in a temple, she once had the microphone taken from her by a man. She commented, 'You took it from me because I spoke better!' She was prevented from performing the *arati* at Navaratri. Some woman said, 'Widows should not so this.' Manjula did not return to that temple for two years.

She loves going to churches, and feels peace there. She went to Holy Cross Roman Catholic Church to pray, at a time when she felt she was at a crossroads as to whether to resign. She prayed to Mother Mary, and heard a voice, saying, 'Why are you defeating the woman in you?' She had a vision in February 1997, and she has never looked back. She lit candles in the cathedral and put flowers in churches, on Paul's death. She continues this practice. Charity giving is central to all faiths. She believes in never hating anyone, something she has learned from Christianity, as also the centrality of forgiveness. No one should throw stones at others – and she thinks of the woman taken in adultery (John 8.3–11). She is glad to have five cousins married to Christians, and each carries on his or her own faith.

She feels she has learned from Muslims about unity and solidarity, and charity. When she first came to Leicester, a Muslim mother made her a meal, and bought a new pan to cook a vegetarian meal. This was a wonderful gesture. Manjula sold a shop, and the Muslim buyer found £500 in a drawer. He brought it to her, and said, 'I am a Muslim and I cannot take a widow's money!' She was touched by his honesty.

My comment Manjula's contribution to Leicester has been enormous. She was the first Asian woman Lord Mayor in the country, and also chair of the Council of Faiths for several years. She is a symbol of the more cohesive side of Leicester, and all this came out of major struggles – personal, within the communities, in politics and in the educational sector. She has come to represent the best of Hinduism, expressed in the three 'Ds' that she says are at the core of her life: devotion, duty and discipline. She has rightly been honoured with two honorary doctorates from the two universities in Leicester, and an MBE from the Queen. She is clear that her political work should never come before her family.

The Majithia family

Ramesh and Kirthi Ramesh is another product of Tanzania, where he did his O-level school qualifications, before being sent to the UK for A-levels, on a British overseas passport. He went first to London, and stayed with a relative above a restaurant where it said outside, 'No dogs, no coloureds'. A Muslim helped to get them a flat. Later, he graduated in mechanical engineering and went into teaching. In 1970 he moved to Leicester and married Kirthi. The marriage was arranged; she was from Gujarat. Her family were very pietistic and loved ritualism, and Kirthi had learned Sanskrit and also Indian dancing.

Ramesh had always had a hunger for spiritual things. In Tanzania, as a boy, he had seen a yogi buried in the earth for seven days, with a complete fast, and the man had come out alive. This made a big impression. He then purchased the Gita and the poems of Tulsi Das.

In London, he joined a church in Cheddington, which was the nearest 'House of God' to where they lived. He had heard of missions in Tanzania, but had had no direct contact with Christianity. But he did learn the English game of cricket, and he had taken part in a match with English counterparts. He was a spin bowler, and his team won. This interest continued when he came to England. In London, he visited Westminster Abbey, where he heard a 'terrific' sermon and beautiful carols, and songs like 'Go Tell It on the Mountain'. He did not really know at the time the difference between Hindu and Christian. He learned the phrases 'You are saved' and 'You have accepted Jesus Christ'. But he reflected: what of my family – are they not saved? The answer came: No! They will not go to heaven. He parted company with Christians as a result. He began to go to the Ramakrishna Mission on Sundays, and listened to Indian speakers.

Ramesh was a free spirit, always independent. When he came to Leicester he used to go to Ram Mandir, which was struggling, to help the temple of his caste – a Chattriya community. He also went to the Sanatan Mandir, which was a mixed community temple, according to its constitution.

But his burning interest has always been in *education*, in the pursuit of truth; this led him to be part of many spiritual organizations. He feels spiritual power is there, rather than in the temples. It also led him to take early retirement from school teaching to become the main voluntary teacher in Sanatan Mandir, which became the most popular venue for outside groups to come and experience Hinduism: university students, future clergy, school children and any number of other groups.

He was ten years in the Vishva Hindu Parishad (VHP), as local secretary and president; this was for his own development, not for political interest. He says to Christians, 'Broaden yourselves.' He calls them to move to a more inclusive approach.

He began to take a children's class in Ram Mandir as early as the 1970s. He was president for the social activities, as they tried to help those from Uganda settle down. He started the children's class at Sanatan Mandir in order to help Preet, their son. He set up a Young Hindu Heritage Centre, where he explained all, and answered all the questions around the 'Why, Why, Why' of symbols. He tried to root the children in the tools of their faith, and explain: if you do not respect yourself, how can you respect others? If you do not respect your own mother, how will you respect other mothers?

He found reading the Gita at first very hard, when there was no guidance. Five families then came round to study, and they have long had a weekly study group. He tried to help youngsters also to study it. His view is that chapter 12 is central, and he loves comparing the place of Krishna here with that of Jesus. He loves texts such as 'I am the way and the truth and the life' (John 14.6), and other texts from the Fourth Gospel such as 'I and the Father are one' (John 10.30). He has learned so much over the years from visiting groups and their questions, particularly from Christians.

Ramesh became a member of both the Statutory Advisory Committee on Religious Education (SACRE) and Leicester Council of Faiths, and as a trustee, wrote the magazine of the temple for many years, though he is sad he had no feedback from the community.

Overall, he feels that Leicester is so fertile for Hindus, and there is a growing interest in true spirituality from well-to-do Hindus. He has been very happy with the growth of such organizations as the Chinmaya Mission, with its educational focus on the Gita, yoga and spiritual awakening, and also its charitable focus. He mentions three outstanding young people who are central to this movement in Leicester, one of whom is his son Preet. But overall, he is wary of movements which become exclusive and consider themselves superior to others, and you become negative towards others. There are some, but rare, true gurus. He has one himself. And he believes that Prabhupada was an example, but there are not so many.

Preet The son of Kirthi and Ramesh, Preet is now in his mid-twenties. He learned his faith at home, where he was enveloped by the devotional environment. He was taught chanting and all the basics, with Hinduism always around him. This included Hindu epics on TV, and in children's comic books. He went to the Saturday morning club at the temple from the age of six, and he attended events and festivals there. As he grew older, there were more English-speaking teachers there also.

Preet was taught English by his father, and Gujarati by his mother. Early on, he knew some prayers in Sanskrit, and he learned Hindi through watching Hindu epics on the BBC. He attended Loughborough Grammar School, where Hinduism was taught in general studies. The Christian chaplain was very open and offered talks on different faiths, and from the junior school upwards the children celebrated festivals. He never revolted against his upbringing, and from the age of seven he attended the Gita class which met at home (see above). It was a place where open discussion took place, and comparisons were made with John's Gospel and other Christian Scriptures.

He took part in the Leicester Hindu–Christian Forum from 2000 to 2004. He was very struck by the contributions of Shaunaka, of the Oxford Centre, and Israel Selvanayagam, the one a white Hindu and the other an Indian Christian. He then went to the World Parliament in Barcelona. He found this fascinating, learning among other things about indigenous religions, and also practical issues such as Water Aid, AIDS and so on. The pre-meeting in Montserrat was a powerful experience as he took part in a prayer circle which involved prayers from every different faith.

He then went to Cambridge University, and he tried to follow up his dialogue interests there. In Freshers' Week the concentration was on night clubs, but the Christian Union had a Cheese Tasting Café, an alternative to the clubs. There he made some friends, including a born-again Christian. He went to his baptism, and there appreciated jazz-style hymns. He went to one Bible discussion, but found it very literalist. He was not used to such an approach, nor could it be found in Hinduism. He knew wider views existed from the Hindu–Christian group in Leicester, as well as from school. His questions were not taken seriously by the Christians he spoke to in Cambridge.

He joined the committee of the Hindu Society, and was its education officer, and also responsible for interfaith events. Sharing of music was important. He enabled meetings with Jewish and Islamic Societies, also with Jains and with Buddhists. The Catholic and Methodist Societies were open, but the conservative Christian Union was not interested. He then became president of the Society, and was able to initiate a Hindu chaplaincy, with an official status. He and his fellow members worked for a prayer room, and an Eastern Religions Centre. This involved all groups, including ISKCON. They also carried out cultural programmes and charity work.

He obtained a government grant of £2,500 to set up an Inter Faith Forum. It held Diwali dinners each year in Wesley College, Cambridge, and garden parties and so on. People from eight different faiths participated in the Forum, meeting every two weeks. Jewish participation raised questions of race as well as faith. This helped to keep communication going, with leaders changing each year. The Forum has sadly now declined.

From Cambridge, Preet moved to Harlow, and then London. A year later, he joined the Chinmaya Mission; Ramesh Pattni became a guide to him, and he felt fed spiritually. He was now working in a large accounting firm with many Hindu colleagues. He was given a budget to finance a network and a Diwali event. The Chief Executive came, and stayed two hours, and Shaunaka from the Oxford Centre launched the society.

Chinmaya Mission is very study-focused, which suits Preet's personality. It is based on Vedanta philosophy, and appeals to young professionals. It has a structured approach to theology, with philosophy presented in a practical way. It easily relates to young people, because all is in English. Youth activities here are done outside the temple structure, including drama and sound-and-light shows. Preet goes on retreats to India, with like-minded young people, when there are three lectures a day and other activities. Over a hundred people journeyed from the Indian diaspora.

Open dialogue is what Preet likes most. He can relate to Muslims at a cultural level, including discussing Bollywood. Last year, he really enjoyed going to Amritsar with 60–70 people – a great visit. Despite being Hindu, not Sikh, he was allowed to take part in the daily ceremony of carrying the Guru Granth Sahib, the holy book, into the temple. This is of course one of the holiest objects in the Sikh faith. This was a great interfaith experience.

As regards Christians, he feels that sometimes they practise a quiet inquisition. But the moral and ethical values of Hindus and Christians are common. He is not against Christian mission. If you have a good thing, you want to share it – that is OK, but not to do it aggressively. It can become intrusive. Chinmaya Mission is about gentle evangelism also. This is OK, and happens naturally. We should recognize that dialogue with another faith is different from pulpit preaching.

Summary This family represents three aspects of British Hinduism. Ramesh is self-educated, and very committed to educating the non-Hindu community, much more important to him than having power in the temple. He is seriously interested in learning from Christians, particularly when he can see synergy; but like many such Hindus, he remains unhappy with what he sees as the exclusivism of Christianity, and prefers Christian Scriptures that can be interpreted inclusively. Impressively, as a senior, he continues to learn about his own faith and its scriptures. Kirthi is a very spiritual woman who loves her faith and singing songs, and writing poems about it. Preet is an intellectual young man, committed to enabling other young Hindus to take their religion seriously in this way, as well as to make sure that Hinduism is handed on well to his own generation. He is even sadder than his father at how difficult it has been to engage young Christians, the majority of whom are now of an evangelical background.

Hemang Bhatt

Hemang is an unusual priest in Leicester. He is part time, being also involved in an IT consultancy business. He is a dynamic young family man, and is very committed both to his family and work, and to his priesthood. He, of course, has the qualification of being a Brahmin. He does not focus completely on temple work, but conducts ceremonies freelance. He is very independent-minded, as will be seen, and he is devoted to a guru in Gujarat, where he trained for three years as a priest.

He feels his thinking is very close to what he thinks is a Christian position – he believes strongly in one God, shapeless and formless, who sends different messengers. Siva is an *avatar*, as is Vishnu. Buddha, Jesus, Krishna are on the same level, with different timelines (see the lovely depictions at Jalaram Temple, Leicester). Krishna and Jesus have close links since both are full of joy and love. *Murthis* are not God, but made of metal – just as the Son on the cross is not God, but made of wood, by human hands. Jesus is not an idol, but represents the divine Son of God. When we bow before the cross, this is the point of focus, not God.

Washing the *murthi* daily is about keeping it clean. Giving the *murthi* fashionable clothes is about respect. Cleaning is about good maintenance; this tells us that while we clean the *murthi*, we should clean ourselves from within. Images will wither away. The Holy Spirit is the nearest concept to Brahman. Throwing milk is about cleansing; reciting and chanting is also a good way of popular devotion.

The Swaminarayan movement is very rich, and predominantly Gujarati. Its members have built multimillion-pound temples in Gujarat and around the world. Now they could do more towards helping the needy. Their temple communities are great places for networking, and giving a sense of belonging. They are good also at teaching Hinduism to children.

We should be very open, and not fence faith with barriers. Truth can be 'both–and', not 'either–or'. 'Might be right' should be our adage, not

'I am right'. Our challenge is to help people to grow step by step – crawling is needed by a child before running. We do not teach a PhD to a junior child. The journey of faith is a serious one, and is not just play acting.

He conducts ceremonies as tradition requires, while advising worshippers to follow the deep philosophical meaning behind it and not make it a mere ritual.

Hemang supports the ideas of the Arya Samaj (see under 'Manjula Sood'). A Brahmin trying to find God follows a system passed down by the saints, and he or she lives, breathes and follows it, and shares it with those who could benefit from it. But he feels that this movement is now very fragile and is on life support, hardly keeping going. It is not concrete enough for British Indians, for whom idealism will not always work.

In general, he hates closed doors, and is against dogmatic conservatives in any faith. So he does not like missionaries either way. His view of evangelism, from whatever faith, is that so often it opens doors by preaching, but then there is no way out. If you go out of the door again, you will enter hell. Heaven is here in the sheepfold, with its images of honey and milk, health and virgins. You need to keep people in. Mother Teresa was a different kind of missionary. Anyone is welcome, including women. He gave me a contact with a woman Brahmin who has acted as a priest in Leicester, since her son was killed. We are all children of God. Mixed weddings are all right, whether all faith or non-faith, so long as the *Vasudhaiv Kutumbakam* ('Love thy neighbour') idea is followed.

Leicester is a good place for Hindus, since Christians here are very welcoming. Christians have shown great love and accommodation – hard to match, he believes. The Hindu community is going through a great transformation, some coming to faith, and some going away from faith. Politically they are divided. There are increasing tensions with Muslims, which are not spoken about. Hemang's guru says it is better to bring such problems into the open, and that it is dangerous to keep quiet. He finds the British Hindu Voice (see below) approach a bit emphatic, and linked with Hindutva ideas.

The 2002 situation is still not resolved in Gujarat, where it is said that 1,000–2,000 Muslims died in communal violence. But Hemang claims that some Hindus believe that in previous riots more Hindus have died for every Muslim over the years. Hindus used to feel that they had their head down, and they were right to fight back. We should see also the contrast between Pakistan and India. You should not look at your temperature, but why you have a temperature.

In general over here, Hindus are happy to lead quiet lives; they bring up their families well, run their businesses well, and work quietly within the

NHS. Vast businesses such as Mittal are Gujarati, led by a Hindu family. Vegetarianism is important, with a high proportion of Gujaratis following this way of life. Krishna endorses this – do not hurt animals, but coexist with them – as in the Vedas. We should not hurt any animals, but live non-violently with all, as Gandhi enjoined: Love thy neighbour, including the animals.

There is a large image of Siva in his main room. Siva has a prominent three-pronged trident, and Hemang interprets this with conviction, as being about three things: reconciliation, and destroying what hinders; spirituality within; and fighting enmity against others. He emphasizes that his idol is not an idol but an image, to emphasize contemplation and meditation, and being kind to animals. Union can come if you follow the three prongs of the trident. He displays also the Dancing Siva, which encourages enjoyment of the world God has made. Hemang likes to be seen as a singing priest. He also likes to conduct rituals in the house, since this emphasizes that God does not live in temples alone, which are often full of politics – God is just as much in houses and offices.

Summary Hemang represents a modern Hindu leader, who reflects about his community, its strengths and weaknesses, without being overmuch part of it. This is also true of his distinctive theology and spirituality, with its lack of dogmatism, inclusiveness and almost gnostic feel, where popular religion is acknowledged, but he and those like him have risen beyond it. Like many Hindus, he is pro-Christianity provided it is not exclusive.

Bharti Acharya (means 'teaching')

Aged 49, Bharti is one of five children, all devoted to their Hindu journey; she and her two sisters are unmarried. Their father was an enormous inspiration to them all. Bharti learned so much from her family upbringing, where she picked up the faith at home and in the temple. Father believed in discussion, learning and debate. He died in 2001, but by then had instilled so much in his children, and what he taught was a generous inclusivism. He learned all this in Tanzania, and brought it over in 1972. He was one of the founders of the Inter Faith Forum that came before the Council of Faiths. Members went to the houses of each other, and learned so much there. This was the atmosphere in which they were all brought up. She continued learning from every opportunity, of the Bible and Christianity as well as Hinduism. Her mother was also central for her; it was she who taught her how to be a good human being.

Central to family life was their evening meal, which was accompanied by prayers together – the BBC even came once to record this, and their family life. The BBC producers liked the fact that they had a statue of Mary and Jesus in their home temple, and a cross, brought from Tanzania. Each of the Hindu gods was given under different circumstances, and bring so many blessings; for example, a brass Ganesh from Rishikesh brought by her sister. When her father died, her mother cooked every day for the deities, to raise her morale. Morning prayers are varied, with each family member doing his or her own thing. Bharti prays silently, her sister fully verbally. They are a Brahmin family, but do not practise as priests.

The whole family has been part of the history of the major temple, Sanatan Mandir. Bharti remembers how, at the beginning, Krishna was represented by a cardboard figure! She believes that the gods, when properly installed, were living deities – and she relates two miracles that she connected with these *murthis*, including one that happened to her brother. These *murthis* are not just stones! The force of the one God can operate through them. God is infinite, while we humans are finite.

The forms of God found in each faith are acceptable. There are many roads to London, and so why not many ways to God? She includes Jesus easily and readily, and has a Bible and a Qur'an in her house. Prayer, core ethical principles and charity giving are common to all faiths. Most problems are about culture rather than religion. Her problem is with Christians who say Jesus is the only way for all, and not just for them. She believes in the famous simile of the elephant. She does not ask Christians to accept Krishna. If Jesus is the Son of God, why can there not be other sons and daughters? Her problem is with conversion, and her father, as a Gandhian, worried about the conversion of poor people in particular.

We talk about Swaminarayan, and she finds its attitude to women strange; it is women who sustain religion, not lead people astray, so why can they not be leaders? At Sanatan Mandir all are welcome, whether heterosexual or gay. ISKCON is good, though she does not want to limit herself to Krishna when she has the whole ocean as a focus for her devotion.

She loves Leicester, but recounts how it is not perfect: she had faced some really racist incidents when she was younger.

ISKCON in Leicester

A recent development in Leicester relates to ISKCON. It is mentioned in Chapter 3 as one of the *bhakti* movements in the UK, under the leadership of Pradip Gujjar. The ISKCON school has started successfully, and after two years has 180 children. Most, but not all, are Hindus, and the school is clearly open to all. Only a small minority of the Hindu pupils are from ISKCON families. There is no pressure to become followers. Pradip comments that some Hindu parents come back to a living faith through the school. The interfaith openness is shown too by their going to the local Anglican church for a Christmas function, as well as speakers coming in. The head teacher is English, from an International School background in Hong Kong.

The other development has been that ISKCON has acquired a city-centre site in an old bank. They are in the process of converting this into a temple, and in the same complex they plan a restaurant, a café, and a function space which will be rentable. So the profile of ISKCON is gradually being raised in these ways. In addition, the members have a small farm outside the city, where they are now rearing nine cows.

Swaminarayan in Leicester

For this movement see Chapter 6. The movement has a prominent new temple in Leicester, as mentioned there, and this is one of the 18 temples in the total above. It is the only purpose-built temple in the city.

British Hindu Voice (BHV)

This was formed a few years ago as a pressure group and think tank, unlinked to any temple or existing organization. It is not a mass movement, but a focused organization, led by a few prominent individuals concerned about the kind of issues mentioned below. It is Leicester based but speaks on national issues. I interviewed two of these individuals, **Mukesh Naker** and **Sachin Nandha.**

They feel that Christians do not take seriously the dialogue with Hindus, with no consistent follow-up. Hindus see themselves as pluralist, as compared with the exclusivism of the Church. They embrace all religions. There is diversity, it is true, among Christians; but underneath the apparent pluralism, they end in exclusivism. This makes dialogue difficult, between an exclusive and a pluralist faith. It does not seem to be a level playing-field, and church doctrine gets in the way of easy interaction. Trust is very limited, and there is a lack of parallel organizational structures. An example, says Mukesh, is that when the previous Archbishop came to St Philip's, he was asked a question about why a statue of Jesus can be in a Hindu temple, but there is no Krishna in St Philip's. The Archbishop said he would reflect and reply, but there has been no response since. Hindus are aware that it is impossible for the Church to accept another religion or idea of God, in parallel, due to its internal doctrines. Hence the Church encourages words like 'toleration', whereas Hindus find this word condescending, and prefer 'respect'. The word 'toleration' hints at the psychology of the Church, where Hindus are to be tolerated, as they may have some nice parts to their culture or religion; but ultimately, the church narrative is superior. So until the Church confronts its own internal contradictions and struggles, it will remain difficult to engage Hindus with authenticity.

Overall, Hinduism is being regenerated in the West, in the diaspora. We are at the beginning of a Hindu renaissance among youth. It is very important to engage young Christians in the dialogue. Mukesh and Sachin emphasize the growing geographic spread of the Hindu diaspora; for example, the Leicester Hindu radio station has listeners in Sweden, and South Indians work for Nokia in north Sweden. There are different challenges in dialogue: are we looking at things from a doctrinal perspective or from an experiential perspective? We need a new inclusive vocabulary.

Hinduism can be very confusing to the outsider. Government, politics and religion are separate in Hinduism, whereas they are together in the Abrahamic faiths. (My comment is that it is different now in India, where all three now come together, as in Hindutva thinking and action.) But in the UK, government and politics and *dharma* (religion) are separate. Equality questions are a major challenge in the UK. In India, key questions relate to questions of secularism.

Examples of issues they have raised are a Hindu demand for a separate crematorium in Leicester, and the lack of receptivity of the city council (when it accommodates Muslims in all kinds of ways). Another relates to the grooming of young Hindu girls, which the Hindu community is not ready to face up to. Hindus should stand up for themselves, when the authorities do not take action. There have been eight to ten cases around the country, and the authorities have not taken proper action. There have been 56 cases of groomers, mostly Muslims, and the Muslim community has not taken proper action. There is a great fear of upsetting Muslims. In Rochdale, no action was taken for ten years.

Further issues BHV has highlighted:

1 *Hindu representation at director level in the council.* There are 50 directors, not one from an ethnic minority. So also among the police: 7 per cent of the force are from ethnic groups, but 90 per cent of these are serving at the lower level.
2 *NHS doctors and nurses.* Many of these are Hindu, but not involved in policy-making. Another equality issue.

3 *Hindus in Afghanistan.* There were 100,000 before 2001, and now there are only 2,000. One Hindu woman was about to be deported from the UK, and BHV were able to stop this.
4 *Hindus in the Sind.* Here, 20 Hindu women each month are forced to marry Muslims and be converted. One Hindu woman was forced to marry a Pakistani politician, and BHV instigated a protest from a Sindi organization.
5 *The government-financed Near Neighbours Project.* This is based at St Philip's. Very few of the grants have gone to Hindus or Hindu-led organizations, as opposed to Muslim and Christian groups. BHV enabled a meeting with its organizer at the Sanatan Mandir. Forty Hindus attended, but there has been little progress in terms of grants.
6 *The Leicester Council of Faiths.* BHV consider this group to be largely dysfunctional over Hindu issues like that of the crematorium above. The criteria for appointment to the Council, and the process, are unclear. The Faith Leaders Forum is useful, but has no executive power.

Mukesh and Sachin have now initiated a federation of Hindu and Jain organizations, facilitated by BHV. Lack of organization was a problem when there were plans for a temple in Oadby, just south of Leicester, where many Hindus now live. Individuals did not get their act together when the door was open as far as the county council was concerned. This shows the need for that kind of organization. The Muslims have their very effective Federation of Muslim Organisations. (BHV failed to get the Sikhs to join with them, and instead the Sikhs formed their own body.)

Nationally, they list a number of further issues:

1 Former Mayor of London, Ken Livingstone, called for London to be a beacon for Islam, speaking in a mosque.
2 Political parties in Leicester are drifting into common stances and this is dangerous, because it means there is a dearth of debate.
3 Bradford has become a Muslim fiefdom, empowered by the Respect Party and George Galloway, with no place for the Hindu minority.

BHV needs to keep a regular dialogue going with the Hindu communities, and to keep records of this. At a national level, there is a need to go back to the communities and find what is difficult. The Church of England can do this much more easily. Hindus have very different theologies and diverse structures, which makes things very complex; moreover they often go to two or three temples. At least BHV responds quickly compared with other Hindu organizations. 'Our purpose is to add value to the community – this is our *seva*.' Gujaratis dominate BHV, but not exclusively. It does not have large numbers, and does not wish to – time and passion are both needed to support this organization.

The recent big question for BHV has been the inclusion of *caste* in the equalities legislation, along with race and gender and so on. It was never an issue in East Africa from where so many have come. It was included because of Christian lobbying. Moreover, marriage questions come to the fore, and the problems that happen when people marry out. Theologically, divinity is in each person; but the social issue is that people are protecting their own interests, through caste identities. Even Dalit Ravidas temples are about protecting their members' interests. Caste should be an internal dialogue within Hinduism, about how we learn to respect the other. There are plenty of Hindu reform organizations working on these matters. The biggest problems, claim the BHV, have been caused by Dalit Christian organizations, working from outside, as well as from within the UK.

Summary One of the key questions is: whom does the BHV represent? Its members are certainly articulate and assertive, but on behalf of whom? Themselves, certainly, and they do not mind being a minority, speaking things as they are and protecting the interests, as they see it, of a discriminated-against minority. But if they are to make much headway on their causes, they need to seek wide support from those they speak for. They have little base in the Hindu temple constituency, but it, too, as BHV feel, has no real mandate to speak for all Hindus. BHV can seem to take over from longstanding community leaders, when both are in one meeting, for example, with the Bishop or city leaders. Its members appear, to outside observers, to be strong on issues and weak on personal relationships. But their feeling that the Hindu Voice should be more heard is appropriate, and the Hindu national bodies are often weak and divided. (Comment of BHV: The weakness in traditional Hindu bodies stems from a lack of understanding and clear articulation of the legal and cultural framework they have to operate in, that is, the UK legal system and the knowhow to navigate through British methods of dialogue . . . the younger generation will soon bridge that gap.)

A mixed Hindu–Christian family

Nikita and Jay, aged 19 and 15, children of a Hindu–Christian marriage Both parents are practising in their two faiths. They have been brought up in the religion of their father, having a small temple at home, and visiting the Sanatan Mandir two or three times a year. Their mother

Jill was confirmed at St Philip's in recent years, and they attended the ceremony to support their mother, and have been occasionally to St Philip's.

Their general observation is that Hindus and Christians are very different, with different beliefs and customs. Hindu temples are a lot louder. And taking off shoes marks a big difference. They find Sanatan Mandir a very friendly environment. Grandparents used to have morning Hindu prayer in the house.

At school, they studied many religions. In Leicester, there are so many different faiths, and people seem to get on, and are open to different opinions. They have not and will not take baptism, nor will they have arranged marriages. Nikita thinks it is good to know both faiths, so they can grow up more open and happy. They are happy to be mixed race, which is not unusual in Leicester. Moreover, they have lot of friends who are Muslims.

Raj, father of Nikita and Jay, and husband of Jill Raj is chair of the Hindu Forum Public Affairs Committee. He believes that Hindus are very strong in Leicester, but they are not strong on leadership. The BHV is trying to change this, but he is not happy with their style. But the challenge is: how should Hindus move forward? It is vital for them to work in partnership with other communities and faiths. Hindus are nationally a good example of good neighbourliness. But they tend to be divided into groups meeting separately.

Raj is also chair of the governors of a local primary school, where he finds that the proportion of children from different communities is changing often and rapidly, with East Europeans a new factor. His business partner is a leading Muslim, which surprises people.

Some are very cautious about their mixed marriage. His parents said, 'We don't have divorces, and so it must work.' For them it was important that both were vegetarian and non-smoking. Moreover, Jill does what she is expected to do, attending temples sometimes, and having functions at home. Raj attends churches, though not Holy Communion. He was impressed with the confirmation service, and the use of holy water at dawn. Some communities say that a married couple should be of one faith, but this is not so in their case. His mother takes Nikita to the temple, and teaches her Gujarati. It is important the children are raised primarily in one culture – in their case in the Hindu culture. They therefore have Hindu names, chosen by priests, and have Hindu ceremonies. It is important that they know their roots.

Mixed children are a group on their own; a child's religion and his or her name are vital badges of identity. The parents see their son and daughter as mixed; the rest of society judges by how they look. Dual-heritage children from lower classes face more difficulties, or those of single parenthood.

Jill is sometimes sidelined within the Hindu community. She understands this, but Raj does not like it: 'Some people are just blinkered.' She wears a sari, but did not at her own wedding, which was at a registry office, since the couple did not want to have three weddings, which would have been a logistic nightmare.

The parents of Raj went with them to India, taking their spices so that they could feel at home. All the parents are supportive. Raj had left Uganda when he was 12; his mother is from Tanzania. Jill's parents are fine about the marriage. They were worried at first, but on the whole accepted the situation. Her father loves going to watch cricket and football with Raj. He introduced his son-in-law to a cricket club – the first Asian to join! Jill's mother loves making English desserts, and Raj appreciates them. He is very accepting by nature.

Summary This family can stand as an example of an educated middle-class mixed family. There is little angst, with an adjustment here and there, largely from the Christian side. It can also be the other way round, where the Christian part of the family is dominant. This kind of marriage and family is increasingly common, and seems to be the way that things are going in the UK. Vital is not just tolerance of difference, but respect both ways round. This is considerably more difficult to achieve when a couple marry across wide caste difference, or across the Hindu–Muslim divide, for obvious reasons.

Some Christian responses

Most Christians, even in Leicester, have had little sustained experience of meeting with Hindus, except incidentally in shops, hospitals, schools or business life. Usually these experiences have been very positive. There follows a fairly random selection of those who have tried to go rather further, as clergy and as lay people. They come from a range of theological positions, and answer honestly about what they have experienced. Overall, they can be seen as representing some of the typical thoughts of non-specialists.

Pete Hobson

Pete was vicar of the Martyrs church, in whose shadow the Jalaram Temple and social centre were opened. This church is of an open evangelical tradition.

What was the response of the congregation to the building of a prominent temple nearby?

1. Generally a sense of good neighbourliness with the Hindus. 'We got used to their presence and went shopping with them.'
2. The East West Community Centre was opened nearby. It was to be a place of meeting, especially in its lunch club; but it has become a Hindu centre, where *bhajans* are sung by the senior women and the men play cards each afternoon, and they have an excellent Gujarati lunch.
3. One convert from Hinduism, and a family of Asian Christians in the congregation, feel that the Jalaram Temple was imperialistic, symbolized by an arch put over the road outside. The church congregation did not accept that the new building, to house the community centre, would be really open to the community. Pete, as vicar, could go in any time and be recognized, with his clerical collar, and be very respected. He observed how much time and energy the Hindus give to bereavement when someone dies.
4. Joint concern was shown for the Gujarat earthquake in 2002 – with prayers and a collection. Pete went down to the temple to give the money.
5. Early on, an Unfamiliar Journey course was run, based at St Philip's and taught at the Martyrs. Attendants visited the temple and were very well received.
6. Members of the temple or the church were not particularly able to hold dialogue, or interested in it, except for TV Mojaria (see above). The Hindu priest was invited by Pete to the major annual police multicultural event, but sadly pulled out because TV would not allow him to go, clearly not seeing this as the job of a Hindu priest.
7. Pete found it much easier to engage with Muslims, at the local mosque and through St Philip's, and the Islamic Foundation, near Leicester.
8. There are four Hindus working within the diocesan office structures, where Pete now works. They join in the devotional life there – in this they are very different from Muslims. The Hindus seem to see no problem.
9. The lay people generally feel that Hindus are in error, and it would be good if they were converted. But they do not make evangelism with Hindus a priority – and probably they would not know how to begin. The majority of clergy in interfaith parishes move from a position of exclusivity to inclusivism. Pete has done this. Lived experience has strengthened his position: in the middle, neither conservative evangelical nor universalist. (My comment: this is the common experience of missionaries to India, such as myself.) This change is happening in the West. Of course, some find their position hardening, both in India and in the West.

David Clark

A senior priest, David felt a calling to leave his major parish of Oadby, just outside Leicester, which was rapidly becoming multi-faith, and to spend the last five years of his ministry engaging with people of other faiths in the main city. He wanted especially to make a journey of spiritual pilgrimage and discovery. His concern was that he did not have the capacity to go deeper; so he gave up, and spent over five years intensely involved with the Leicester Council of Faiths, which came to depend much on him.

On the Hindu side, David knew well three temples, and he found it all an overwhelming experience – very deep and difficult to get into. Ramesh and Kirthi (see above) became important to him in his journey; there he knew he had met a deep philosophy. Another Hindu leader, Ashok Jogia, was also significant for him, and the Yogeswari movement. It is millions-strong worldwide, with a thousand members in Leicester. But he could not give the time needed. As with many other Christians who wish to get involved with other faiths, Islam quickly takes over.

He was influenced by a book by Deepak Chopra, *Life after Death*, which pinpoints the great gulf between Eastern and Western world views. Much of the Eastern view has been taken over by the New Age movement in the West.

At David's church, Hindus began to come to the Christmas midnight service, about 100 in the end, and this made a huge difference to the service. They contributed greatly to the piety. They came several years running but it gradually stopped. In interfaith relations, tenacity is essential. 'Just playing around', or 'faith tourism', is not enough in this ministry. With Hindus on the Council of Faiths, the challenge of accommodating difference was difficult. None were effective at this; similarity and harmony were what they emphasized all the time. He was sad when he invited a leading international Jesuit to come and speak, but very few came to listen. He felt very frustrated that almost no Hindus appeared, even when he had rung them the night before.

In general, he feels the Church of England never really backs this ministry and those who persist with it. It does not see dialogue as being at the heart of its concept of mission. The problem is that Christians are a minority with a majority complex. They need to be realistic about what they can do. Living among other faiths is vital. The Church of England tends to put people in the wrong place. They need to show to all around what is their faith and practice, and so there is a challenge about where to live. Evangelical Indian Christians feel that people like David have sold out, but even they find that Hindus are largely impervious to the gospel. Two further challenges: how to create young people with a heart for dialogue; and how to find British Bede Griffiths-type figures!

Group at St Alban's, the church on the same road as Sanatan Mandir

This group was led by a 74-year-old woman, Maureen, deeply associated with church and community centre. When the first Hindu family came in 1970, her father said, 'This is the end. We will even lose our shops.' He died two weeks later. But Maureen has been happy here – she has much respect for Hindus. All her neighbours are of different faiths; she is nosey and learns from them. She even dances in a sari – she has five – in the community centre, and regularly takes part in the Navaratri festival and in weddings. She does not see the need to go to India; it is all here. Neighbours came to the funeral of her husband, and she goes to funerals of Hindus.

She gives chocolates to Hindus and others for Christmas. She welcomes Hindus into the church – it is open each weekday – and they come for shelter and peace, and light candles. They are surprised when they are not required to take off their shoes. She made a point of visiting the local temple when the son of a priest was murdered, a major incident in Leicester. Generally, Hindus are more helpful than locals. Private hire of the church hall is nearly all by Asians. Use of the community centre is 80 per cent Asian and 20 per cent white.

There was initial murmuring about Asians feeding pigeons, and also there is a problem of rats and mice. Feeding pigeons is seen by Hindus as feeding their ancestors! We need to educate them, and Maureen went to the temples to try to teach them. There are two views of whether the area is 'run down' or not. This little group finds the present-day Leicester exciting. Maureen even says it can be like heaven for her at times. She is happy too that the lack of drinking and smoking has led to the closure of some clubs in the area.

A colleague says there were initial stories of overcrowding in both the neighbourhood and Asian homes. This happens when any new group comes in. Many of the original inhabitants move out. Maureen was seen as 'slumming it'. If someone said that, Maureen said, 'There's the door!' Her daughter married an Antiguan; the Antiguan family did not support this as they did not want a white daughter-in-law. But there are gradually more mixed marriages. Hindus are having trouble with some of their young, and many are sad when marriages involve marrying out. There are now

Sikhs and Muslims moving in, with four small mosques in the area. But in general, Asians are more family-minded; they look after their elderly, and send their children for tuition, as they would in India.

The group view is that theologically there is one God and that we approach him in different ways. Central is that we respect each other. In both faiths, there are clear parallels in the concepts of the contrast between light and darkness, good and evil.

Terri Skinner, priest of St Theodore's, Rusheymead

Terri came to this parish three years ago, from Loughborough, 15 miles away, with very little background in multi-faith ministry. She felt a sense of calling to this parish, but not to the make-up of the area. She had been in Africa for two years, which gave her a feel for cross-cultural work, but she had not thought of interfaith contexts. According to the diocesan website, the parish is 86 per cent non-white. The local primary school is 92 per cent Asian, with statistics of 65 per cent Hindu, 13.5 per cent Sikh, 13 per cent Muslim and 4 per cent Christian. The school governors are applying to the education authorities to have Christianity taught as just one of the religions.

The church is open evangelical, and Terri found a congregation unsure of itself and afraid about its future. They were desperately in need of encouragement. They had had a popular full-time priest for 20 years, and now Terri was to be only part time. One of her roles has been to help the congregation feel positive about its future. In the congregation now there is only one person from Gujarat, two families from Pakistan, various Caribbeans, two Americans, an Estonian and a Hungarian! There is a challenge of intra-congregation integration. The church had been built in 1980 for a new and modest housing estate. Today, one third of the congregation live in the parish, one third nearby and one third further afield, but with roots here.

The Church of All Saints, with its focus on Asians, is not far away (see Sunny George interview and associated interviews below). Sunny came out of this church. There is also the Life Abundant Pentecostal Church within the parish, with a congregation from Kerala, and bigger than St Theodore's. And there are various other Asian congregations, including Tamil Roman Catholics, and all have become linked together in a prayer fellowship through South Asia Concern.

Terri feels she still has her 'learner plates' on after three years. There are several activities in the church and hall, and many Hindus come. They like Bible stories, when told to their children. But there is a huge jump from that to becoming Christians. Several have a kind of faith in Jesus, from within the Hindu culture. In three years, there have been no baptisms of any kind. What is the future? This is her question. Hindus come to midweek activities, but not to the Sunday service, and no one has even asked to discuss baptism. Dialogue is very friendly with mothers, but not at any deep level, even though the two Americans were with them as co-workers for some time.

The theological challenge is Jesus as the Way, the Truth and the Life – what does that mean here? Terri has more questions than answers. She feels she sees Jesus in others, though they do not know it.

Discussion with four parishioners

Of these four, three are seniors, and two are churchwardens. The seniors came as young mothers, 42 years ago. There was only a church centre, and they prayed for a church to come here. From 1973 onwards, Asians began to arrive, one on a street, and then more and more. Quickly, it happened that no white people moved in, and many moved up market. Now East Europeans are beginning to come here.

In the church, and community hall, Asian mothers and grandmothers began to turn up at various activities. At first they tended to sit separately, for linguistic reasons. But gradually, they came together with the white mothers. Some of the parents now attending used to be children here. In most groups, Hindus are the majority, though people from some of the other minorities come. They have no problem in hearing biblical stories, watching Christian DVDs, and taking part in nativity plays and other activities. There is a strong sense of learning from each other, and the atmosphere at St Theodore's is much welcomed. After a death, the Hindus bring food for others. In general, there is an acknowledgement of each other's cultures, often hybrid now, and when one of the Americans tried to speak Gujarati, one of the Hindu Gujaratis said, 'No, speak English, please. I am English!' There have been few negative experiences; these are rare if you reach out in love, for love is a universal language. If Hindus really want to be Christians, that is fine, but not essential, provided they have love. If a person has a sincere heart, God can see that and reach him or her. The inclusiveness of Hindus makes them easier to relate to than Muslims. Christmas lunch is a time of opening out to adults, though being aware of vegetarian needs. Older white people also need such support, as they can be very isolated.

Prayer is something that can cross barriers; an example is praying for a sick child in church and in temple. Or a Hindu placing a prayer request for someone who is depressed; the response to such a prayer does not depend on whether someone comes to church or not.

On the whole, the children know more than their parents. Christian children have usually been to temples through their school. The church itself has a range of charity projects, and Hindus readily participate in these. They raise money for Romanians before Christmas, in a shoebox project called Samaritan's Purse, and in this cause they have a Girlie Night, both Western and Asian in its content.

All Saints Asian Church (Anglican)

The minister in charge here, training to be ordained, is Sunny George. He has enabled this church to grow to around 70–80 persons on a Sunday afternoon. This church, previously known as St Gabriel's, had been closed as redundant. It was reopened two years ago, and is situated right across the road from the brand-new and imposing Swaminarayan temple (see Chapter 6). The mission of the church is both to nourish born Asian Christians, enabling them to worship in their own languages and in a charismatic way, and to engage in outreach to Hindus and Sikhs. There are a number of converts in the congregation from these two faiths: ten Hindus and the rest Sikhs. Sunny begins by giving enquirers John's Gospel to read, and prays that they may find Jesus as the Light of the world.

I met three such converts in Sunny's house, and I include a summary of their stories, to provide a full picture of engagement in Leicester.

The first is **Subodh** (known as Stephen). He came from a rich Kenyan Gujarati Hindu family, associated with the Arya Samaj and RSS. His brother was one of the leaders in East Africa, and then when they came to England, in Leicester. Subodh went then to Birmingham University. Here he only self-identified as a Hindu when approached by Christians, when he defended his faith. He was influenced in his hostel by a Christian who said the grace before a meal, and said this in a serene way. He had never experienced this before. Through this contact, he accepted an invitation to attend a house church, and a Bible study group in the hall of residence. He was 22 when he accepted Christ, and his converting verses were Isaiah 55.6–7:

> Seek the Lord while he may be found; call on him while he is near. Let the wicked forsake his way and the evil man his thoughts. Let him turn to the Lord, and he will have mercy on him . . .

He felt suddenly free of the law and burden of karma. He returned to Leicester and faced opposition from his family members, who all remained staunch Hindus. At home, they accepted he did not join their prayers, and did his own devotions. They even insulted Jesus, calling him a snake. But Subodh has for ten years been involved in an evangelistic ministry in Leicester and in India, attached to Pentecostal missions.

A second person, **Chandra Kant**, had as a young man become disillusioned by Hindu rituals that were carried out in his house. He was influenced first by Bhavan, wife of Sunny, and then by the warmth of welcome into their house. Sunny does not attack other gods, but just focuses on Jesus, without pressurizing. We do not need to go to different gods for different purposes. Jesus can offer all, and comes to us; we do not need to run after him. Chandra decided to give Jesus a go; there he finds healing and peace (even when, as now, his daughter is very ill). He had thought that Jesus was the God of white English people, but he now knows he loves us whatever our race.

The third convert is **Bhavan**, wife of Sunny. She comes from a Punjabi Brahmin background. Her key text is Isaiah 41.10: 'So do not fear, for I am with you . . . I will strengthen you and help you; I will uphold you with my righteous right hand.' Her testimony includes both dreams and healing stories, as she was released from the power of Siva, and from a sect who followed Radhaswamy. In her half-sleep, she was led to say that she respects the other deities, but that Jesus Christ is the living God. If she is frightened, she picks up her Bible, and these disturbing visions go away. Her prayers are acceptable to the family, especially her very ill mother. Sunny was allowed to lay hands on her. But Bhavan's father has never accepted Sunny in 21 years. Bhavan prays that he may be saved through her prayers and through being the father of a believer, remembering St Paul's words in 1 Corinthians 7.14 (RSV): 'For the unbelieving husband is consecrated through his wife, and the unbelieving wife is consecrated through her husband.'

Summary These summaries represent common strands in conversion stories. Positively, these persons exude a peace and surety that shines out from them, particularly from Bhavan. In general, they are a lesson that Christian mission is at its strongest when it stems from the positive affirmation of Christ, and not when it denigrates the other. This is what enables the converts to become missionaries themselves. And this kind of mission is part of the reality of Hindu–Christian encounter in the West.

8

Three geographical studies: 2. The United States

Any study of the Indian diaspora, and its relationship to its Christian context, is bound to include the USA. The proportion of Indians to the population may be considerably less than in the UK, but its economic and social status is very high, probably on a par with Chinese and Koreans. And its religious and cultural influence goes far beyond the Indian community, influencing the whole of society in certain important ways.

Developments have been much wider than in the UK, and less specifically India-related. Though India will always remain important, in some ways it feels much further away. This is partly explained by the fact that Britain and India were irrevocably linked from the time at least of the seventeenth century and the formation step by step of the Raj, the Empire, and later the British Commonwealth, which became the Commonwealth. Hinduism was the majority religion of the Raj, and this led to a commercial interest in maintaining its strength, notably from the East India Company, in order to ensure synergy in a trading partnership, and due respect to traditional Hindu rulers in the so-called princely states.

At the same time, Christian missionaries were sent to convert Hindus from a religion that was seen as dark, if not demonic. Hinduism was known not by how it was experienced in Britain, which was a rare possibility until recent years, but by reports sent back by missionaries, which tended to see it as idol worship and little more. The chapter on India (Chapter 2) shows that attitudes gradually changed. But Hinduism was not really experienced in Britain itself until the 1960s, and the coming of the diaspora to its shores in large numbers.

There were missionaries from the USA to India, also, and I met some recent ones in India when working there. But there were far fewer, and the churches they formed much smaller. And these were not in the same way linked with the colonial movement. Nor was their influence on their home churches so considerable. They were much more a side show. Moreover, they came from a country born out of colonialism into freedom.

The US constitution was egalitarian through and through, and its history was unrelated to the complexity of India and its Hindu-dominated and caste-ridden society. Caste and class can easily and superficially be linked. India had been a caste-based society since time immemorial, and the UK was notorious for its class divisions. If caste was attacked in the name of Christian egalitarianism, the Hindu could easily cite class as a parallel division. In the USA, it was money that divided people, a very different and obvious barrier to ways forward. But opportunities, it could be claimed, were open to all who made an effort, and who had the gift of enterprise. Of course, what is written here ignores race, and that became the equivalent of caste or class, and in some ways more powerful, because it was impenetrable. To be black, until recent times, was an even bigger barrier to progress than to be Dalit or low caste, or to be working class or low in educational status. The point made above also ignores questions of gender in all these places.

The key event in the story of US engagement with Hinduism, most would agree, took place in 1893, at the World Parliament of Religions in Chicago. This was largely an American Protestant affair, though Europeans also featured. But it is remembered above all for the arrival in Chicago of a short, saffron-robed holy man from India, one Swami Vivekananda. Such was his impact that when he began to speak as an unofficial delegate, it was as if all the world was fixed on him – a bit like when Jesus came to the synagogue in Nazareth (see Luke chapter 4), and the audience were stunned. The interfaith movement which has been one of the significant religious developments of the twentieth century, now well into the new millennium, dates its beginning back to then. The great Eastern faiths, with their inclusivism and pluralism, became part of the agenda of the West from this date on. The apparent exclusivism of Christianity and Islam confronted now an alternative world view.

The first place to feel this impact was the USA. And more narrowly, but not much less so, the great edifice of Hinduism in all its manifestations became part of the history of religion in the USA. Indians in any large numbers only came to the USA with the opening up of immigration policies in the time of Lyndon Johnson in the 1960s. The points system, in terms of skills and education and financial resources, led to so many professional Indians coming from then onwards. They brought much wider dimensions of Hinduism than those found in India, and all the geographical contexts that came with the immigrants. But this took time to become rooted, and meanwhile, we can see several main ways how Americans, and American Christians, met Hinduism.

(I owe some of what follows to the comprehensive study *American Veda*,[1] by Philip Goldberg. He is described as 'ordained Inter Faith Minister', a title now found on both sides of the Atlantic. The book is described as an account of India's remarkable impact on Western culture, and there follows nearly 400 pages of detail. The author makes a large claim in his first sentence: 'In February 1968, the Beatles went to India for an extended stay with their new guru, Maharishi Mahesh Yogi. It may have been the most momentous spiritual retreat since Jesus spent those 40 days in the wilderness.' A big claim, and the ensuing pages seek to justify it, with conviction.)

The first encounter of Americans with Hinduism was through the direct legacy of Swami Vivekananda, and the second through the Vedanta Societies that were formed in the years following throughout the USA. They appealed to Americans in significant numbers, and through their influence the world view of the USA often took on a Vedantic feel.

Goldberg outlines what he considers seven core Vedantic principles that have been adapted in the West,[2] and I think they are a very helpful list:

- Ultimate reality is both transcendent and immanent, both one and many. God can be conceived in both personal and non-personal terms, that is as formless Absolute, and in numerous forms and manifestations.
- The infinite divine, while ineffable, has been given any number of names: Brahman, Allah, Lord and so on. 'Truth is one; the wise call it by many names' (Rig Veda 1.64.46).
- The Ground of Being is also the essential nature of Self. 'This self is Brahman'; 'thou art that' (Upanishads).
- Our innate unity with divinity is obscured by ignorance.
- Individuals can awaken to their divine nature through any number of pathways and practices; no single one is right for everyone.
- Spirituality is a developmental process, moving through a progressive series of stages.
- The aim is to realize one's true nature, be liberated from suffering, and reach liberation, enlightenment, *moksha*.

We will see links between this and so much in my interview records, far beyond what is detailed in my two visits to Vedanta Societies in Boston and in Chicago, outlined below.

The third encounter occurred through the passion that developed for yoga, in its Hindu form, and even more through Buddhist influence, which was even more widespread – and many did not distinguish between these two related faiths in terms of their spiritual influence. Yoga centres are everywhere. They can be associated with *bhakti* also, as found in the Centre in New York, or increasingly in the ISKCON centres. Much yoga is now fully secularized, and part of calming the mind for those involved intensely in the competitive American way of life. Yoga has become a multibillion-dollar industry, and its promoters often say it has nothing to do with Hinduism. But there is a Hindu American Foundation in Washington, for the promotion of yoga from a pluralistic Hindu point of view.

The fourth influence came through the guru movement. There was a constant traffic of Indian gurus, many genuine, many bogus, who came and went from the USA, but often stayed and formed associations of disciples, both local and national. Some were ascetics, others the opposite with their alleged involvement in tantric sexual practices. Some were unambiguous in their wish to be the centre of a movement, almost divine in their charisma. They built up major centres, especially in California. The majority were male, but some were female.[3] Some had branches in India, particularly in the Himalaya region, and devotees spent long periods in India; others cut their links, and became American through and through. Some were American from the beginning. Conservative Christian denominations would have no association with such groups. But fringe Christians, and very liberal groups, found themselves often associating with a guru, as well as with their churches, something easily labelled as 'New Age'.

A fifth way was through particular movements, most notably ISKCON, the Hare Krishna movement (see Chapter 3), whose influence waxed and waned but, as we shall see in our case studies, has settled down to a denominational place in American society. It has come of age. It has always also had an interest in having dialogue with mainstream Christianity. I mention this movement specifically because of its membership, moving from mostly American, to a mixture of American and Indian American. Other movements such as Swaminarayan (see Chapter 6) are almost entirely Indian, and in practice Gujarati.

A sixth way is through the transcendental meditation movement (TM) and the movement towards self-improvement that fitted so well with the American culture. This again has often lost its religious roots and has become big business, opened up through the internet and web learning.

A seventh way is through that of alternative medicine with an Indian origin (Ayurvedic medicine). This may be combined with one of the other areas. In the 1970s and 1980s, psychedelic drugs were also seen as ways of realizing the transcendent, with the Beatles and their song 'Yellow Submarine' part of a popularizing of such. That route has now gone out of fashion.

It is to be noted that none of these ways, with the exception of ISKCON, focused on the deities normally associated with Hinduism in India, and with temple worship. Goldberg comments, 'India's mythology and the outward forms of its religion have attracted only a small number of Americans.'[4]

My journal

Before taking the reader through my American journey, I should mention two persons whose guidance and writing are key to this story. The first is Diana Eck, mentioned in my visit to Boston, whom I found an inspiration, with her single-minded devotion to her Pluralism Project. But so also her key book, *A New Religious America*, with its subtitle, *How a 'Christian Country' Has Become the World's Most Religiously Diverse Nation*.[5] Chapter three, entitled 'American Hindus: the Ganges and the Mississippi',[6] is an evocative historical and geographical survey covering areas from California to Boston, written in a very personal style. The second is Anant Rambachan. He is a Hindu academic from Trinidad, who has been a professor for many years in a Christian college in Minneapolis. He is prepared to be critical of his own Hindu traditions, as well as being thoroughly Hindu. This is an unusual combination, as well as his empathy with Christianity, but also his awareness of its problems. It is not surprising that he has long been a consultant to the World Council of Churches, where I first met him, and he has been a great encouragement to me as I have undertaken this book, and this journey in the USA.

I had spent a sabbatical of two months in the eastern part of the USA, five years ago, visiting similar places to this current journey, though then I also went to Buffalo and Vancouver. Buffalo, in Upper New York State, I felt, has some distinctive likenesses to Leicester, in size and economic and religious diversity. Vancouver is the major settlement for Sri Lankan Tamils, the majority by far Hindus, 200,000 in total, mostly in the area known as Scarborough. This time I went much more intentionally, to prepare for this book, and all that I write of here occurred during a month's visit.

Clearly I cannot and will not claim to be anything of an expert on Hindus in the USA, or in these cities, and of their interaction with Christians. The reader is referred to other books and reports as he or she goes through the text. But I hope there is enough material here to play its part in this book as a whole, as one of its 12 chapters. I hope also it can provide comparative material for the chapter on Leicester, and for comparison with the UK and India, both of which I know so well.

I chose these cities because of the contacts I already had there, and because of their representative and significant nature within the USA, and for Hindus there. The big gap is California, for which I had no time, and maybe is more significant for Buddhists. What I provide here are really snapshots within each city. I believe I met significant people, both religious leaders and academics, both Hindus and Christians, both members of the Hindu diaspora and indigenous Americans. It goes without saying that I thank enormously those who gave their time and received me so graciously.

My visits were to Boston, Dartmouth (New Hampshire), Chicago, Washington DC, New York City, and nearby Princeton and Drew. I will group the interview material around various themes, and reflect on them together.

Vedanta

I had two main direct encounters with Vedanta, as I visited their societies in Boston and Chicago. But Vedantic thinking was of course underlying much of what I met elsewhere. The Swami in Boston is North Indian, but has been there many years. In Chicago there were two swamis, an American who felt the call in 1973, and a North Indian who had just arrived a few weeks before I visited. In Boston I had a long discussion; in Chicago I attended a Sunday morning service.

Swami of the Vedanta Society, Boston

I met Swami Tyagananda in the Centre of the Vedanta Society (known as the Ramakrishna Vedanta Society). This seems to be modelled on a US Protestant church, with a meeting room like a church, and Sunday services. The Swami is called a 'minister'. The worshippers celebrate Christmas and Easter here, and they have carol singing. They use a common songbook which I saw, and reminded me of the hymnbook used in the multi-faith school my children attended in South India. They love the Sermon on the Mount. They have texts from different faiths around the walls. There is Hindu worship of Jesus, using songs appropriate to this. There is a large picture of Ramakrishna,[7] and his vision of Jesus. *Prasad* (blessed food) is given from here, and lights are lit around this picture.

The Swami was educated in Bombay, and studied at St Saviour's Jesuit College. He had many Christian friends and there was never any attempt to convert him or to force worship on him. He told me a story about a new principal coming there. He said early on that a local Hindu temple was like a fish market. The Swami, 15 years old, responded, 'Well, the church is like a graveyard!' There was a major row. But the next day, another priest apologized, on behalf of the principal. He understood that the principal could not do this directly. They then became good friends – an example of direct and honest encounter, which the Swami carried through to his coming to Boston.

The Society, he says, is not a *Hindu* society but a Vedanta society. Vivekananda was for all people, as was Ramakrishna. Westerners, Muslims, Buddhists and Christians come to the Centre. Like Ramakrishna, he never condemns anyone, and no one should feel, in dialogue, that they are denigrated. The Society members are not conscious of differences of faith. Vedanta is part of Hinduism, of course, but it is a philosophical tradition offered to all who seek a deeper life. In this congregation there are no priests, and no life-cycle sacraments. Weddings are done by priests in local temples. Many Christians have come to the society, and believe they have become better Christians as a result. What are his views on conversion? He understands that this does happen. He addressed a Hindu–Christian discussion group in the Massachusetts Institute of Technology, and the group was co-led by two Hindus, one of whom had converted to Christianity. They led it together, and this impressed Swami. He told a story of an Episcopalian priest who, 35 years ago, came to ask the Swami here then if he might become his follower. The Swami said to him, 'No, but go back to the Bible and read it anew.' And that is what the Christian priest did. It is not surprising that the Swami admires greatly the Catholic priest Abhishiktananda, whose heritage in the West is best known through Father Bede Griffiths. Abhishiktananda is most obviously a Christian Vedantist.[8]

The Swami has been invited to speak to Christian congregations as a Hindu speaker, and once he gave a talk to Mormons. He is also a Hindu chaplain in Harvard. In some places he is very consciously a Hindu representative; in others he is a philosophical teacher.

The less theologically loaded terms we use, the more open people are, he believes. When he spoke to the Mormons, he did not use one word from Vedantic Hindu texts, or of Sanskrit. This is not a problem, because he believes that at root there is a commonality between faiths. He tries to present his philosophy in a way that enables the particular listeners to respond. He is aware that there may be an immediate barrier if we say, 'Krishna says in the Gita . . .' Hindus cannot just give neat answers; it is not that kind of religion.

Swami Tyagananda gave me a small book, to be recommended to readers of this book: *Vedanta: A Simple Introduction.*[9]

Vedanta Society Sunday meeting, Chicago

This centre is in a beautiful and peaceful setting, a long way out from the city. We were welcomed by a senior American Swami, Varadananda, of Catholic background, who joined in 1973. He learned of Vedanta, and the technique of meditation, from books. While serving in the army in Germany he read a book of Vivekananda which he had found in the army library. He went to India three times. He was told he could keep everything in his Catholic Church. It was an all-American centre until 1965. The swamis go wherever they are invited, and people take what they want from the visits. They have regular classes, but not dialogue groups as such. He has no problem about Christians who evangelize, but Indian Hindus do. He has no problem about someone converting voluntarily. He loved Shantivanam, in Tamil Nadu, when he visited.

His Indian colleague, recently arrived from North India, **Swami Ishatmananda**, led the service, attended by about 50 people, mainly Indian. The theme was 'Why should we meditate?', and was one of a series of such talks. He began by talking of Vivekananda, and his love of the USA, which is a country that gives confidence to the downcast, not like shy, fearful Europeans. Vivekananda coming to the USA was like India coming to the USA. He spoke three words at the 1893 Parliament – 'Brothers and sisters . . .', and there was then five minutes of applause. It was about power from within this magnetic saffron-robed monk, coming from another world.

Different religious shrines are present in their Ganges retreat centre near Chicago. In one of the three in Michigan, there is a shrine with a cross. Jesus is giving his life for love, love, love. The Buddha shrine points to all that is within you. Islam has a crescent and star, representing wonderful brotherhood and sisterhood at its best – Allah Akbar. Vedanta is inclusive of all humanity. In California there is another centre, called Taboko, with different shrines, and clergy can come and teach in their own shrines. The rituals are different, but love is at the centre of all of them. The *ishta devata* (the preferred way of approaching God) varies, but the heart is the same. Jesus had the higher mind, and Christian ways of meditation are to be much commended, and also the focus on pain and suffering – Jesus led the way in our facing up to these.

The Vedanta Society in USA focuses only on teaching. In India, its members play a lead in initiating social work among tribal people, which the Swami did until recently before he came to the USA.

Academics and universities

I met several significant academics or university-connected persons in this field, and I consider here the main themes that arose.

Parimal

I met Parimal, a Hindu academic, in his Harvard office. His department is the Department of South Asian Studies, and this brings together different disciplines such as Sanskrit, Urdu and Hindi. It is a geographical rather than a religious focus. There is no training of Hindu religious leaders as such in the USA, and they do not predominate here in his department.

He reflected on Hinduism in the USA. It is marginalized by Buddhism, which is everywhere – so many Americans are attracted to it as a philosophy of self-improvement. In Cambridge (Boston), for example, there are a whole range of such possibilities, focusing on meditation and yoga. It fits the American culture. Hinduism has a great weakness: its leaders are not intellectuals and are theologically weak. Business people are struggling to fill the shoes of intellectuals, which is very different from Buddhists again. This makes participation in interfaith discussions difficult for Hindus; no one knows enough, and there is no equality of leadership across faiths. Intellectual leadership being weak, Hindus are reluctant to accept there are differences in their traditions. Priests are not intellectuals and understandably know little except the required rituals. Sunday classes have now been started, but what are they to teach? It is a real challenge. The story usually begins with Indian families coming together in an area, to look at such education, often encouraged by grandparents. They will tell epics and cultural stories. They have also started linguistic schools. Much of going to temples is about cultural identification and the induction of children. Traditionally, in India, the main education is through being brought up in a Hindu household.

The Swaminarayan movement has camps and systematic classes, and also campus groups. The Swaminarayan system depends on one man in Ahmedebad, and from there are passed down commentaries on the Gita, the Upanishads and so on. Parimal's view is that they have an impossible position about women, and why should we respect impossible things? It is also very Gujarati (see again Chapter 6).

Parimal's question is that, in general, should Hindus find their primary identity as being Hindus – is this meaningful in any city or country? Is educational and economic success not central? Is there not bound to be asymmetry compared with Abrahamic faiths, where religious faith is the primary identity?

Hindus are forced back on the Gita as their sole scripture, though that is against their tradition of multiple scriptures. Hindus end up accepting a mono-scriptural tradition that is impoverished, and follow Christian and Islamic models of exegesis and hermeneutics. Moreover, they are very split, which means they lack communal resources. They can often be very communal. Parimal speaks very highly of the Oxford Centre for Hindu Studies and its community role. Who will provide such teaching here? He also commends liberal arts classes which can be used by Hindus, for example to discuss whether Rama was the perfect man. People can be led to think through exegeses of texts in such classes.

A fundamental question for Parimal is whether Hinduism should be seen as a religion among others. In India there are no real seminaries, and programmes generally are sectarian, or regional. His view is that Hindus only want to become a shared religion when they are feeling excluded. A generation ago, they were more relaxed, in India and in the USA. But in general, issues for Hindus are less intense in the USA than in the UK or India.

Conversion is no great issue in the USA; if you want to convert, go ahead, good luck, and why worry? Main issues relate to Dalits in India, and what is seen as Christian exploitation of weakness. But the demographics mean that the Dalit issue is not a big one here. Parimal never really meets the conversion issue, nor does it occur to him. So also with interfaith marriage; this is less of a problem all the time, and he married a non-Indian. He is aware that context matters, and in the suburbs of New Jersey, for example, it may be a bigger question (cf. Rajiv Malhotra and the Infinity Foundation (see below), with its anti-academic bias).

These comments are very valuable, with Parimal's emphasis on the asymmetrical situation between Christian and Hindu partners in theological dialogue. His colleague at Harvard, Frank Clooney (see below), is very appreciative of the way Parimal expounds this in his response to Clooney's book *Hindu God, Christian God.*[10] There has been little Hindu theological work for several centuries of the kind found in Christian tradition. We are not dealing with like for like. But Parimal wishes someone would take up the challenge, and this is where the work of the young Swaminarayan monk in Oxford, Swami Paramtattvadas, is an example (see under Swaminarayan, Neasden).

Diana Eck

Mention has been made of Diana's Pluralism Project above. I thank her for an excellent DVD about a small city in California, Frelimo, which can be compared with a smaller Leicester, and claims to be the most religiously diverse community in the USA, as does Leicester within Europe. I have suggested that Leicester could produce a similar but different DVD about the city and its diversity.

Diana's work is generally accepted as a comprehensive mapping of religious presence in many cities in the USA. Many Westerners are interested in a spirituality that they have left behind. Her project is one of engaged research, based at Harvard (see <www.pluralismproject.org>). She heads up a research team of mainly young people, both in Harvard and throughout the USA. They focus on field research in different cities, and, as the website says, they 'explore the religious diversity of the USA and its meaning for the American pluralist experiment'. This work is highly rooted in her own discovery of India, and of the Hindu family of faiths, as seen in her several books. I cannot highlight enough the importance of this unique project.

Diana recommends Danam, a network that has an annual conference at the same time as the American Religious Academy. It is a Hindu organization (see its website, <www.danam-web.org/>).

Subramaniam Swamy

An Indian academic, and member of the Janata Party, Subramaniam Swamy is a significant voice on the right who engages in Hindutva-style rhetoric. He has written an article, 'How to Wipe Out Islamic Terror',[11] saying that India has to solve the Muslim and the Christian problem forever. Muslims and Christians should be required to say they are really Hindus, or they should lose the vote! The mosque in Ayodya is to be destroyed. No conversions should be allowed. All Hindus are encouraged to vote en bloc. He has also taught that Bangladesh should hand over land, to compensate for India taking Hindu refugees from that country. Mujahideen should be banned – Hindus are targets of such radicalizing Muslims. Subramaniam taught his academic discipline of economics at summer school, at Harvard, for several years. Students wanted him out, because he foments hatred against Muslims. Forty faculty members protested also. Diana Eck tried to get him off the syllabus, and succeeded eventually. She was attacked for being pro-Muslim, some even saying she had a Muslim girlfriend! See the publication *Indian Abroad*, which actually complimented Harvard.

Rajiv Maholtra and his Infinity Foundation

I met Rajiv Maholtra in Princeton. He writes major books, of which he kindly presented one to me.[12] He is very controversial, because of his intention to strengthen the Hindu identity in the USA, and because of his perceived negativity towards Christianity, which he views as irrevocably exclusivist and inevitably polarized from Hinduism with its inherent pluralist and inclusive nature. There is an inevitable clash, particularly with mainstream evangelical Christianity. A key question is: where is God to be found? For Maholtra, God is everywhere, including in the *murthis* in temples and homes. If the Holy Spirit is everywhere, why not in such *murthis*? In general he sees dharmic traditions and Abrahamic faiths as incompatible with each other. This is shown politely but vividly in a long dialogue he had with Mark Tulley, which he asked me to watch.[13]

Frank Clooney has also engaged in dialogue directly with Maholtra. Other scholars I met felt that the attitudes of Maholtra make such dialogue pointless, since they are written off as Western academics. I met him on the advice of Frank Clooney, and we had a polite engagement, where I felt we were not able to touch on fundamental questions. One of these relates to India and how Dalits have been exploited in the cause of missionaries seeking to make Christian converts. Another is his anti-academic bias. He is particularly negative to those Christian scholars who claim to write on behalf of Hinduism, or Hindu–Christian theology. He sees them as imposing the model of Abrahamic faith study onto the very different study of Hinduism. He also feels the image of India is undermined by focusing on its divisions and problems. Diana Eck gave examples to me. A book by Paul Courtright on Ganesh[14] is very disliked by Malhotra and his followers. They do not like the celebrity status of Karma Sutra. In the same category is work by S. Kripal, who wrote a book on the diaries of Ramakrishna, seeing homoerotic sides in him.[15]

Comments from Richard Young, professor in Princeton Rajiv Maholtra is involved in a curious struggle in the USA as to who controls the image of India. Is it to be liberal progressives, or people like Rajiv, who want to make clear India is Indian Hindu? He claims to have Christianity defined, as he sees it. *Breaking India* is his most provocative book. He emphasizes a division that excludes Dalits and Dravidians. There is an atmosphere of paranoia, fear, anger, and Dalits have become pawns of the West. He develops a conspiracy theory that the US government, evangelicals and academics are conspiring to destroy the Indian–Hindu ethos.

He is not really welcomed by Hindutva groups here. Though not an academic, he wants to be part of Princeton and use that position. His books are launched in the university. Verbally, he mercilessly destroyed a Dalit pastor. Vineet, the Hindu university chaplain (see below), took away the microphone at Princeton, as he tried to keep the peace when the pastor tried to tell the Ambedkar story. What does 'Dalit' mean here and in India? Rajiv is not happy with either Anant Rambachan or Rachel McDermott, both significant scholars who have guided me.

Vineet, Hindu chaplain in Princeton

Vineet has been here for five years and is very reflective about his work. Amendment One of the constitution affirms clearly that there is to be freedom from religious persecution, and he says that this means there is no need for the kind of discussion there has been recently in the UK about caste, and including it in equalities legislation.

There have been national questions about animal sacrifice, health and hygiene, and voodoo. There is a great deal of difference between Indian American Hindus, and the American Caribbean Hindus on these and other matters. There seem to be two different worlds. In Princeton, there are just two Caribbean Hindus that he knows, but there is no procedural way to know what is the faith of a student or of a faculty member. There is an estimate of 1.6 per cent of students (of 5,000 undergraduates) who are Hindus. In a liberal arts college like this, there is no engagement with Hinduism in any classes, and religion is not academically a priority. Religions of India, or South Asian Literature may be there, but not the teaching of Hinduism as such.

But religious life is vibrant. Princeton has a Hindu life programme, which comes under the Vice President for Campus Life. Vineet is coordinator, and brings in such scholars as Jack Hawley (of Columbia University) and Frank Clooney, and Americans who are self-identified as Hindus. He says he is happy to use the word 'chaplain', even though it has a Christian history. He is broad in his approach to Hinduism, while the chaplain at Columbia is ISKCON and much narrower. Vaneet is in touch with about 100 students and two faculty members. Two students are Gaudiya Vaishna followers of Krishna; others follow different gods. Telegus are many, and there are Tamil Brahmins. More Gujaratis are in the state universities. There are Tamil Brahmin students. There are weekly gatherings in what is called the Inter Faith Prayer space, though no dedicated images are allowed. They discuss many things, including holding balanced discussion about Indian politics.

Another university experience in Dartmouth, New Hampshire

I went to see the University Chapel at Dartmouth, and was surprised to find a temple to the goddess of learning, Saraswati, in a side chapel. I attended a meeting of the Hindu Association. I was told there are 200 active Hindu students, and 100 families of Indians in the university circles. Those present at the meeting talked with me in a very friendly way when I assured them that I was not trying to convert them. The Telegus from Andhra Pradesh were quite strident about this in particular, and they explained their negative view of Christian missionaries, whether in South India or here. Such missionaries do not come on the campus here, though they go to Hindus' homes, and are soon sent packing.

ISKCON

Visit to Kenneth Cracknell in Vermont

Kenneth Cracknell, an English Methodist minister and pioneer in the interfaith field in the UK, was one of those who inspired me after my return from India. He spent his later years in ministry as an academic and teacher in Texas, and is retired in Vermont, near the Ivy League university in Dartmouth, New Hampshire. I look here at his long time in Texas, where he met ISKCON in depth, and this has been his major Hindu engagement in the USA.

Texas cities are enormous, like small countries. The Sikhs initiated dialogue in Fort Worth/Dallas; individual Hindus were there, but they did not at first flock together. There were few temples at first, when there were already vast numbers of Buddhist centres, many wealthy, and run like churches. At the Texas Christian University, all students had to do a course on interfaith dialogue. Kenneth taught elements of Hinduism to them all, but there was no real Hindu–Christian dialogue. The exception was the Hare Krishna students, who engaged in informal dialogue and home visiting.

Baptists were the dominant Christian denomination, followed by Methodists and Lutherans. None were keen on interfaith dialogue. One exception Kenneth experienced was when he took a Baptist minister to a Sikh temple, and he commented, 'God is surely here'.

Kenneth met Goswami, who was a secular Jewish convert to ISKCON in New York and assistant to Prabhupada. He became president of the ISKCON General Body, and was always welcoming to his Centre in a former Baptist church. ISKCON transformed the neighbourhood by inspiring social uplift in a poor vicinity. Goswami gave a lead in saying,

'We should no longer sell flowers in the airport, but work for the community.' They did this by moving into a very poor area and uplifting it. Goswami reminded Kenneth of an early Methodist. But the problem comes, with any movement, with the death of a charismatic founder (cf. John Wesley). Goswami – Tamal Krishna – died in a car accident in India, which was devastating to the members of this community. Kenneth helped them in the mourning process – he happened to be in the right place at the right time.

The ISKCON temple in Dallas is now very grand, and there is also a specialist restaurant. Much professional money is involved. A woman devotee, a paediatric consultant, used to dress the *murthis* at 2 a.m. each morning! The complex is equal in size to the vast temple in Bangalore.

Tamal Krishna wanted a Gaudiya Vaishnava university in the USA. In Dallas he signed up as a student, without qualifications. He went to master's classes, and brought out his essays as a book. He then went to Cambridge to do his doctorate under Julius Lipner.[16]

Americans are often confused and do not know that Sikhs are not Hindus and not Muslims. They have a steep learning curve to go through, and lack of Hindu organization does not help. But there is little tension between Muslims and Hindus in Texas, partly because there are few Gujaratis. Texas is full of highly paid Indians – mathematicians, IT specialists and so on. South Indians predominate.

Caste was never brought up, unless someone had just been to India, or they had read a relevant book. It is like the sound of cicadas in West Africa (where Kenneth worked) – no noise, but they are chirping all the time in the background. 'All are equal' is constantly drummed into the American psyche, and so there cannot be anyone in favour of caste. Caste has de facto been replaced by money, big cars and real estate. There is, however, a difference between old and new money. This is the equivalent of the caste system in a place like Boston, near where they now live. There you need to be one of the old families, known as Boston mandarins or Brahmins. For example, it is said that the Cabots talk only to God. Here in New England, there are many syncretistic Christians, influenced by yoga and Buddhism. In Texas, all ask as a first question: 'Which church do you go to?', but never in Vermont.

In general, Kenneth struggled with the Chicago view, that you cannot be a believer and an academic. Religions departments are like this to a high degree. People in these departments look at the goldfish bowl and stare, but have no idea what it is like to be a goldfish (though culturally they may be very Christian).

Anuttama Dasa

This major figure in ISKCON in the USA, and also internationally, was introduced to me by Kenneth Cracknell. So also his wife Rukmini, who received me very graciously in their house on the edge of Washington. Anuttama is a key player in the Vaishna–Christian dialogue which has been going on since 1996, on an annual basis, in the USA, and began before this in Wales. Another recent initiative is that he has started a Vaishna–Muslim dialogue; four annual day meetings have been held. Key and most challenging topics have been: 1) The name of God, 2) What do I love when I say I love my God? 3) What do I do when I say I love my God? 4) Sacred aesthetics: 'no graven images' – what does that mean, when it appears that Hindus make as many graven images as possible? Turkish Muslims, black Americans, Indian Muslims, Sufis, join in what has been a very deep encounter.

For the annual Vaishna–Christian dialogue, about 20 people come and it includes a night stay. He would love there to be such a dialogue in India, and he asked me to pursue this possibility. There is also a Hindu–Jewish dialogue in nearby Maryland.

Anuttama said he had been a brilliant but arrogant scholar, who claimed he was Vaishnavite and not ISKCON. But he remembers writing a card after the death of a Catholic friend: 'Because of him I was able to rediscover my faith.' He was an ISKCON monk from 1975 to 1985. Before that he was searching as he studied philosophy, which he found had no meaning, no focus on truth, and was only about contingent matters. Greek and Western philosophy failed him. Then he tried economics, which was no better. Then he began to study scriptures: the Gospels, the Gita, Buddhist scriptures. For a period, he went to a Methodist church, and to many temples. From the Bible he took the text 'seek and you will find' (Matthew 7.7), and absorbed the parable of the sower (Matthew 13.1–9). He decided to search for the good soil. He found it in Denver, with ISKCON. He joined for a week, and was then told to shave his hair if he was staying. He stayed week by week and eventually remained for seven years, and now 37 years (from the age of 20 to 57). Having met Rukmini, he decided not to be a monk any more, and established a business to help the order financially.

Traditionally, ISKCON had been the first place for younger American converts. And then came all the stories of child abuse and so on. It has become now, since around 1988, a congregational movement, the first such Hindu movement. It has become a denomination, and the time has now come to pass the torch to a new generation. The Governing Body Commission was established, under Prabhupada, with a number of gurus who were to work under this commission, to minimize the possibility of splintering. There are now 35 persons on the Commission. Anuttama is the Minister for Communication. The average age is now 55–60. Eight to ten are from the USA, one or two from the UK, and six from India. There are only two women. The devotees meet twice a year for five to ten days. It is increasingly effective, focusing on strategic planning. It is decentralized, not like the Vatican. There are no international resources. The Child Protection Office is an exception in being centralized. Some are now questioning whether the movement should be more temple-based.

There is now a resurgence of outreach in a more mature and gracious way. It is more a case of elderly people knocking on doors, rather than younger street-movement evangelists. Mission and evangelism are central, as in all *bhakti* movements and Christianity. Older, married people are much keener and nicer as missionaries than the overbearing young. There are now fewer long-term monks. Members are monks for a period. From the 1960s to 1980s, there were many who had ashram experiences in the East. But now, people carry on working at their jobs while becoming initiates. The Holi festival has become an important unifying festival. There is much interest in *kirtan* (chanting together) in the large cities, and in yoga groups (not mainline Buddhist groups). There are *bhakti* festivals and *kirtan* festivals throughout the USA, including on university campuses. These may involve Sanskrit mantras, dancing, lighting sticks, sitting on the floor, swamis coming to lead. Over five hundred students took part in New Jersey. The festival was begun by Indians, and others follow. There are bands from different traditions, including Gregorian chanting, Rumi, and ISKCON chanting.

ISKCON thrives on festivals. Anuttama's view is that the Ramakrishna Mission/Vedanta Societies will decline if they depend only on the didactic. ISKCON has two hours of *kirtan* before a main service, which is much liked by young people. The New York Bhakti Center has a six-hour *kirtan* every week, going round different temples and yogic centres. There have been *kirtans* lasting 24 hours, and in Bengal, five days. In Benares there is a 24-hour *kirtan* every day!

The younger generation are focusing on core chanting, and relating to yoga groups, and even secular groups. They are not so inclined to scriptures. It is a question of revolution through sacred sound. These practices produce a humble heart as the holy names of God are sung.

Rukmini

Rukmini spent 25 years in ashrams in different parts of the USA and India. This was until she married 20 years ago. She was initiated by Prabhupada, having followed a guru in Montreal when she was 16. She met the Beatles, and being artistic, made paintings in Boston for Prabhupada's books. She is of Jewish background from Chicago, on her father's side. During the Second World War he had flown from the USA, and taken out living skeletons from the concentration camps in Germany, where he saw terrible things. He was very kind and generous. But she found the rabbis could not answer her why, why, why questions. She came from a counter-cultural generation. She was searching, searching for an authentic life, and could not connect with the life others were living in Boston. Her parents were from the Dr Spock generation, and they let her go to search. Prabhu came to live in the New York counter-cultural area of the Lower East Side. Other gurus went to the more upper-class 'tea and sari' areas. Rukmini went to ashrams in Boston, New York City, California and India. She runs a jewellery business which helps to fund the movement, and also helps abused children go to college.

Dhanurdhar Swami

I heard this Hare Krishna monk speaking at the New York Bhakti Center, to perhaps 50 people, the majority American and some Indian, and one Iranian woman whom I met, who has to lie low as a member of ISKCON when in Iran. Some were clearly enquirers, many devotees, and Christians were clearly welcomed there in both categories.

He had returned from spending 25 years in India. His mantra is: 'You learn more from seeing than listening.' He was given notice to leave Vrindavan, and this nearly broke his heart: he prayed, 'What you want, God, I will do.' He looked for guidance to the letters of Prabhupada, and one letter said, 'New York is the place; it is special. I began my mission there – on 22nd Avenue.' His reflection: 'Today we are walking in love, to see the tree which Prabhu saw beginning. If you have love in your heart, then you will have compassion for others.'

What is *bhakti*? It is the deepest form of meditation, because you have a connection with the object of your meditation. You are always trying to get closer and closer. You chant the *ishta devata* meditation – meditation on the holy name – as you try to get closer. There is no difference between the name and what is being named. The *bhakti* process is about giving and receiving: you give yourself to the other, and receive back in relationship. *Bhakti* is the path of grace and love – which gives you spiritual love in your heart. Doing *kirtan*, chanting the holy name of God, is the best response. Yoga is made easy by music; he commends the six-hour *kirtans*. The best mantra for meditation is the one a guru gives you.

Preachers reach the point when the listeners realize that all are experiencing the same thing – you can reach this point occasionally. There is a sense of oneness, of community, like blades of grass as part of a lawn – we can compare an orchestra and the audience. *Kirtan* is so accessible, its highest expression is *ras lila*. Group petition is higher than individual petition. (I am reminded of the evocative book by K. Klostermaier, *Hindu and Christian in Vrindaban.*[17])

I was welcomed to this meeting by **Hari Prasad Das/Hari Weiss**, and I had been pointed in his direction by Rukmini. I include here his conversion story. He is a young man of Jewish background, from Long Island. He was an agnostic, and quoted to me Kierkegaard – about how he felt a 'sickness unto death'. At the age of 22, he took up a course on Existentialism and Phenomenology, at New York University. He had not encountered any intelligent religious leaders or lay people before. But Kierkegaard, he felt, wrote intelligently about God, and was more satisfying than Freud or anyone else, and had an intellectual rigour when speaking of God. Hari had a very profound experience, as he learned of his need for God. For four days he wrestled with these ideas. He had a real mystical experience with Kierkegaard, and surrendered to him, reading more and more of his books.

He became vegetarian, encouraged by a very committed vegetarian girlfriend. He came to an ISKCON group to learn this type of cooking, and went back week by week as he developed friendships with the young monks. 'It was cool to live on the East Side with a monk friend,' he told his friends. He found that Hare Krishna people had qualities that none of his other friends had. He met a guru called Radhanath Swami in New York City – and experienced 'being in a room with an angel'. He was now 28/29. He got closer to his parents, and they even came and participated in workshops he was now leading. He was helped by this middle-aged guru, became his student, and decided that monastic life was possible. Today, he keeps his options open about marriage in the future. Along with two others he has developed an extensive educational programme focusing on the Gita, yoga and the Enneagram, a tool for analysing personality, linked originally with Sufi spirituality and now used widely across faiths and beyond.

Indian temples

I visited very major temples in Chicago and New York. These were South Indian dominated, and can stand for many others. I visited also a North Indian temple in Flushing, New York, where indeed I went to seven temples, all in the same Bowne Street vicinity. Gujaratis predominate in New Jersey, though their influence was also in these other temples to a lesser degree. They of course find a major outlet in the Swaminarayan temples, which are mainly Gujarati.

The Hindu Temple of Greater Chicago

In outer Chicago, where temples are mainly on the edge of the city and beyond, I went to the major Venkateswara temple, known as the Temple of Greater Chicago. This was crowded with devotees, and had a range of shrines and deities, a Sanatan temple, but was dominated by South Indians. People of all ages had come there, including one or two American women, clearly in mixed marriages to South Indians. Also, a young boy was chanting, in an unembarrassed way, through an amplifier, displaying his knowledge of the *bhajan* concerned. This all seemed a different world from the Vedanta Center nearby.

I met **Rama Raja Yalavarthi**, a trustee of the temple for 25 years. His story is fairly representative of journeys taken, from being non-practising in India, or even secular in outlook, to becoming much involved as a Hindu devotee. Rama first came to the USA in the 1950s, beginning in California. He came from Guntur in Andhra, and did not come with a religious background. He attended temples occasionally with his parents for cultural reasons. They were middle caste and class, and were rationalists, more like Ram Mohan Roy.[18]

But when Rama settled in the USA and was quite isolated in those days, he developed a craving for Indian music and arts – Bollywood was not enough. He began to long for the Hindu culture, when the only shrines that could be seen were in Indian homes. Now there are 18 Hindu temples in Chicago, mostly based on different devotional emphases, or linguistic background – but not on caste. For example, there are two Sai Baba temples, inclusive of people of all backgrounds. There are few Dalits here, but some white Americans now come for devotion, or out of interest; there are many school and student groups, for example. One white woman comes every weekend, though she has never been to India; her questions show how fascinated she is. The local mayor visits regularly. Overall, about 40 per cent who come are Tamils, and 50 per cent Telegus, as in the great shrine in Tirupati, Andhra, on which this temple is based. A group of Tamil women devote themselves to the worship of Parvathi. But the main gods of North India are also there, creating a very inclusive feel.

The temple was built mainly in 1985–6. Opposition at the time was strong, both to idol worship and to the traffic that would be generated. The Mayor gave important support, attending major functions and supporting fundraising, and now there is no opposition at all. In Minnesota, the idols had been attacked and damaged, but not here. The temple has become part of the establishment. There are 12 priests from India, the majority from Tirupati. They have learned English well, and one has been there for 17 years. They also interact well, which is important because the young devotees often do not speak their local language. Some devotees come from a long way away for functions such as first hair-cutting, for example from Jamaica or Hawaii, and also for annual festivals.

The smooth development and organization of the temple has been much helped by the fact that nearly all trustees have been professionals. They are part of the Council of Hindu Temples of the USA, with headquarters in New York. Rama himself has had a close relationship with Catholic Christians, because he was a doctor in a hospital run by the Sisters of St Francis. Franciscan values are strong here, and he has been to Assisi, financed by the hospital. He often attends churches 'as a spectator'. What makes for ease of community relations are mixed marriages; of the ten in his family, five have been mixed. There are now very few arranged marriages. He cites as a mixed marriage also his daughter marrying a Gujarati young man. There are Hindu–Muslim marriages occasionally; parents are shocked, but they soon get over them. Less and less frequently is there any trouble about marriage. He is also not fussed about conversion questions. He considers there is a kind of paranoia about this, being used to unite Hindus.

Overall, he feels that this and other temples are fulfilling their main purpose: to enable the second and third generations to identify with their culture and faith. Children often have to be dragged to the temple, but now they go freely at university, and nurture their own children. Every two weeks there are classes, on Sundays, and people are enabled to learn local languages and Sanskrit, helping to keep those languages alive.

BAPS (Swaminarayan) Temple

Another vast temple I visited in Chicago is the BAPS (Swaminarayan) Temple (see Chapter 6). It was completed in August 2004, and is one of now so many similar temples in Western countries, part of this major branch of Swaminarayan in the West. According to an ABC News broadcast, this is the largest Hindu temple in the USA. It was built primarily for American Indians, Illinois having one of the largest such concentrations in North America. This, and the following information, was from a DVD presentation, very slickly done, offered to us as distinguished visitors.

The main values of this organization are love for all individuals, respect for all faiths, family harmony and team work. The *mandirs* (temples) are to nurture such traditions, as a celebration of Hindu culture. Members have now also enabled walkathons in 47 cities in the USA, and health farms in 28 cities. They have had clinics for blood and bone marrow transplant drives; also disaster and relief collections, for example for Haiti, and for Louisiana.

The local Mayor of Bartlett has said this temple is a remarkable addition to the community. It hosts art exhibitions, dance programmes, many devotional festivals, and classical Indian music concerts.

Here, joys and sorrows are listened to, peace of mind is given, strength is offered in adversity, and faith and devotion to God is at the centre of everything, says their presentation. We were shown round very courteously by one of the many volunteers in the Mandir, one trained in receiving visitors like us. He is a retired professional, and clearly is devoted to the Mandir and his sense of *seva* (service) given in this way. As usual, with such persons in Swaminarayan temples, he does not talk about theological matters, or his own story, but referred me to a monk who lives in New Jersey as the right person. I found when I got to New York that it was difficult to agree on an appointment time.

The Hindu Mandir of Lake County

A third temple in the Chicago area is the Hindu Mandir of Lake County. I give an account here of **Bindu Shroff** and her temple involvement, which illustrates the important role that can be taken by a woman. It also illustrates how Vedanta influence can permeate well beyond the movement's centres.

Bindu came to the USA in 1971, to study to become an engineer. She came from near Lucknow, and six or seven families came from her village to be doctors or engineers in the USA. As children, they had no exposure to Hinduism. And in the USA there was little need for integration. They were very educated, and gained 'green cards' within a couple of years. They wanted their children to learn of Hinduism, but only church Sunday schools were available. So they joined with other parents in starting a Hindu Sunday school, for adults and children. The Vivekananda Society sent a teacher, the American Swami above. All this was inspired by Christian Sunday schools.

A doctor and his wife had the idea of founding the Indian Cultural Association. They met in a library, but were then removed because they were introducing Hindu religion under the guise of culture. Then they went to halls and schools. They met 15 miles south of Chicago, in an area where there were Catholics and Jews, who were willing to accept them. The Swami expounded the Gita. More came and then more left, since they could not understand the philosophy. Food became important, with a communal lunch cooked at home, and brought. They eventually bought a plot of land in 'Lincolnshire', south-west of Chicago. The group numbers went up and down, but the Swami came loyally. It was 60 miles × 2 to go and get him and take him back.

Bindu's husband sometimes taught; he had been to a Vivekananda school in India. She had been to a convent school. In Lucknow, Muslim influence was very strong and Sanskrit was hardly known. The first phase of the temple lasted seven to eight years and was tough. They began to have festivals in the park – Holi and Diwali. The integration of Gita and festivals, and the fact that Swami was not Indian, was respected by the young. Their daughter was in a school class with just two Indians, in 1991, and only six in the whole school. The teacher said, 'I hope you are not speaking Indian at home!'

In 1984/5, they bought land, but then had to sell it again, since there were not enough funds, and the local community was not accepting them. They sold the land for a profit. There were five original trustees/patrons. One was a nuclear physicist. He had bought land for a factory, but decided to give it to the community for a temple, at a nominal price. Doctors tried to control the deal, and marginalize people like her husband. The doctors could do a lot, but were not good managers. In 2003 a friend with business sense offered to take over, which he did, and things moved forward.

Sunday worship began in 2007, and the new Mandir was opened. It took time, getting builders to come out of Chicago. Bindu does not like the hierarchical structure of BAPS. In her own temple, gods and goddesses are present and all equal. That is what a Sanatan temple is. Bindu herself carried on with the Vedanta Center, and also went for retreats to Ganges, their rural centre. They began camps for their children. They struggled for volunteers, not like Chinmaya Mission or the Vedic Centers, or Ramakrishna Mission. They collected money to pay the Vedanta Center for their Swami visits. The Chinmaya Mission wanted them to combine, but they said 'No, because you worship a guru as God.' For Bindu, Rama is her special god, because he is so important in North India. The Ramayana was their scripture, and they only learned of the Gita when they came to the USA. Most of the North Indians came to India only after partition. But they wanted to make South Indians feel welcome, so they dedicated a very big Siva Linga. Radha-Krishna was also there, and Balaji. The South Indians manage these shrines, though North Indians are the trustees. She does not take to ISKCON, where she feels she does not really belong and there is too much focus on Krishna. She remains a pluralist; she even loves St Francis in Italy.

The website indicates an enormous amount of activity and organization. The *puja* on Sundays is to Ganesh, on Monday to Ahiva, on Tuesday to Rama, on Wednesdays to Krishna, on Thursdays to Saravadev, on Fridays to Devi, on Saturdays to Venkateswara (Vishnu, as at Tirupati, Andhra).

The Hindu Temple of Greater New York

This temple is in the heart of Flushing, Queens, New York, and I mention two key people.

Dr Uma Mysorekar As president of the temple, Uma says that people come to the temple for spiritual reasons, to get energy, to keep in touch with India, to help people feel they were in India. They come from New York State, Connecticut and New Jersey, mainly at weekends. She believes in the cleanliness of the temple – no point in being dirty and worshipping the Lord. Surroundings must be good. She won a battle after seven years – when the supreme court decided in her favour – to be president, as a woman. Many were jealous of her. She is a trained debater on inter-faith matters and social concerns.

Uma believes strongly that Brahmins are Brahmins by birth, not through character. But caste is a dying question, since most marriages are now not arranged. We try to help so-called Dalits, but focusing on caste makes the situation worse. She believes in 'learn and earn', and hates the idea that achieving 30 per cent exam marks in India is enough to be a doctor, if someone is from the lowest castes. The Hindu American Foundation brought up caste as a human rights issue. She comments on the then controversial chief minister of Gujarat, Narendra Modi, and now prime minister, that he is a very special politician, and not corrupt. We can note here how, in many of the Gujarati temples, free papers advertise Modi's good economic activities, and list several venues for broadcasting his talks from India, since he has not been given a visa to enter the USA after the killings of between 1,000 and 2,000 Muslims in 2002, which have never been properly investigated. (This ban has now been lifted, since the 2014 election.)

Uma respects Christianity; the problem is Christians. She hates conversion, and sees them as inducing conversions among the low caste on many occasions.

Mohan Rameswami He is one of the 11 trustees, four of whom are women, and he started the temple outreach programme. This reaches out to seniors and youth, and offers religious and cultural education. The members care for Sri Lankan refugees, who found a home in the temple, and the god Murugan was introduced for them (see Chapter 4). The temple dance-teacher is a Sri Lankan Tamil.

Mohan was brought up in Calcutta, and came to USA at the age of 22. Here he studied and became a chartered accountant, getting his green card 37 years ago. He married a Tamil from Chennai, a Vaishnava Brahmin. The marriage was arranged and he talked with her for just 30 minutes before marriage. His wife writes many religious articles in English. Everything in the temple is in Sanskrit, except for the Murugan devotion, which is in Tamil. For 20 years she has taught Tamil to 12–17-year-olds, most coming from a radius of ten miles.

He is connected with the Interfaith Center of New York, and organizes the Queens Inter Faith Walk, around Bowne Street in Flushing. The road is named after John Bowne, who was a fighter for religious freedom in the nineteenth century. But that is not linked with the temples coming here!

He is a graduate of St Xavier's College, and so has good relationship with Christians. He retired ten years early in order to work for the temple. He engages with local temples, and community meetings with the police, and with Christians. His son married a Christian woman. A Christian teaches yoga in the Saraswati Hall opposite. It is a kind of Hindu yoga, and this has gone on for 40 years. Mohan has also promoted a health clinic. This happens once a year, but if there was more involvement by younger doctors it could happen once a week. He joins with Christians in a soup kitchen locally, and much more charity is needed.

As for evangelical Christians, 'They come, we listen politely, and then send them on their way.' Koreans and Chinese come to eat food in the temple, and come to the big Ganesh *puja*. But Muslims will not come into the temple. 'We leave them alone. They only have two holidays a year, and we respect those days.' Mohan also celebrates Ash Wednesday, when he puts on ash (*vibuthi*) for Siva in solidarity. He himself is 100 per cent

Vaishnavite, with Venkateswara as his *ishta devata*. He has images of the various incarnations of Vishnu in his house. He calls himself a monotheist Unitarian, and follows the teaching of Swami Dayananda in his classes, which he learned from his ashram.[19]

He is totally against conversions in India. He believes too in *suddhi* (the reconversion ceremony for Indian Christians) and does not like a Roman Catholic like Sonia Gandhi having so much power.

Mohan is an Indian in the heart, but an American in practice. He plans like a Westerner, and executes like an Indian. He thinks it is too soon to have a training college for priests in the USA. Hinduism should change and adapt, relying less on rituals, and more on the internet. There is now live streaming of the *puja* from this temple to 15 countries. The compassionate side of Hinduism should be emphasized, which youngsters can get involved in. Anyone who knows the Vedas should be able to become a priest. This will happen before Hindus have women priests.

Other Hindu temples in Greater New York

I visited four more temples nearby in Flushing:

- *The Temple of Amasai.* Here there is a Brahmin priest from Canada, and the temple is largely used by Afghan Indian refugees.
- *Swaminarayan (BAPS) Temple.* As usual, it was difficult to get much information, but I was told there are 350 monks in training, 45 from the USA, and they are centred on one village in Gujarat.
- *Sai Baba Temple.* I talked with a senior, with a young person, and with a very jolly Telegu priest. There has not been much reduction in interest after the death of Sai Baba, though a new Sai Baba has not yet come forward. As usual, there was much belief in miracles among these sophisticated professionals.
- *North Indian Sanatan Temple.* So many deities here, and a priest with little English who gave me *prasad* of sweets and coconut, as a way of communicating.

Nearby, there also several Korean churches, a Jewish project and a Sikh gurdwara. I met a group of Koreans holding up a banner at a junction, indicating that this was a prayer station for those who had prayer requests.

Rather different in Queens are *the 60 Caribbean temples*. I learned of these through **Naidoo**, the leader of the Guyanese Indian Hindus. He described the great racial divide that was there under Prime Minister and then President Forbes, between 1965 and 1985, leading to so much emigration from Guyana.

Naidoo worships Kali, and supports Sanatan temples. A focus in the year is on the Holi festival, when 30,000 people walk in procession with a cavalcade of carts, ending in a park in Richmond Hill. Animals are also offered in such festivals. Queens has 60 Caribbean temples, and their centre is Richmond Hill. Just under 100,000 Hindus from Guyana reside in New York, of 300,000 Guyanese in the USA. About 760,000 remain in Guyana. Their centres are in the Bronx and Queens. Also there is a new Guyanese settlement in Upper State New York in a town called Schenectady. It had been a ghost town, as a major company closed. The Mayor came from Albany to recruit workers. It is now thriving, since Queens is getting too expensive. In Schenectady you can rent a house for 200 dollars a month.

Naidoo is general secretary of Bhavanee Maa Mandirs, secretary of the Federation of Hindu Mandirs, and general secretary of its Parades and Festivals Committee. Anand Rambachan came as a speaker at the Hindu Caribbean Conference. Naidoo is also a senior member of a Caribbean Hindu organization that covers 89 countries.

The great hostility found in Guyana between Asians and blacks is much reduced here. There is still some racism, but mainly they united against the early suffering they experienced in the USA. Naidoo quotes a verse from Sankara Archarya: 'Thou art my only refuge, O great Bhavanee Maa.' She is the goddess who protected the Guyanese.

There is a good relationship with the local Catholic church, looking after each other's property. But there are no joint festivals.

Interfaith initiatives and reflections

The Interfaith Center of New York

This centre is well established, and has an Anglican director and a Muslim responsible for programmes. Both are women.

Sarah Sayeed told me that the Center is primarily about interfaith and civic engagement – helping immigrant communities feel at home in society. It is the Christians who want to have dialogue about faith. A New York Muslim–Catholic dialogue programme started, but it is harder to sell to the Christians than to Muslims. As time goes on, Muslims are engaging well, because they realize that interaction with Caucasians gives access to power. The average New Yorker does not distinguish between other faiths, and much education is needed.

Arundinitta is a major volunteer at the Interfaith Center. She is a Brahmin from Calcutta, Bengal, and attended a Catholic school there, until she came to the USA for marriage when she was 25 years old. She attends a Bengali temple, with Ganesh and Kali as deities. Her father was a doctor and very open. She was given a book to read: 100 Bible and Krishna stories. Celebrations in Calcutta were on the street. Here she finds Christmas, as celebrated in the USA, dull compared with festivities in India, and so she taught Christian songs to her daughter. She has a rosary, given by a nun.

Arundinitta is very committed to the Interfaith Center, and is responsible for liaison with Christian clergy and with Hindu priests. This is a difficult task because they are so different. She also liaises with the Police Department, and is on the Hindu committee of the Interfaith Center.

She connects with the Vedanta Society/Ramakrishna Society. The swamis have a different role from priests. Many Indians attend, and many Bengalis, and this is a place she can meet them. Ramakrishna was a Kali devotee, and very inclusive. Different paths and one destination, heaven. She is involved with CONNECT, a not-for-profit organization. This is to do with preventing extremism, education, free courses, going into the community and doing workshops. Arundinitta finds it easier to work with Christians, because of the defined role of the priest and the fact that they are readers. It is difficult to engage with temples. But she does not believe in conversion; most Indians believe the same, and do not like mission.

Individuals involved in interfaith work

The Revd Christopher Solomon was the only Indian Christian parish priest I met in New York. He was a candidate for the bishopric in Chennai. Having not been appointed there, he settled here in New York. In the Bronx, he has a mixed congregation, mainly Hindu men and Christian women, Guyanans and Trinidadians, with names like Gayathri. There are very few conversions because of concerns about burials, and who will carry out traditional Hindu burials. He has another congregation in New Jersey, of mixed Indians, and more professional. He himself knows few Hindus.

Wesley Ariarajah is Sri Lankan, and the former Secretary for Interfaith Dialogue of the World Council of Churches. He is Professor Emeritus at Drew, a liberal arts college, where there are few Hindus. His engagement consists in small conversations with students on a Friday afternoon, followed by *puja*, *prasadam* and *arati*. Options are given as whether to participate, but people are told they should not stay only to observe. Koreans and African Americans normally say no, while white Americans participate, as does Wesley himself. They struggle as they reflect on the experience – is this real religious experience? Hindus in the USA, Wesley finds, are not interested much in dialogue. This means Hindu–Christian dialogue has no prominence, but only dialogue within Abrahamic faiths.

John Thatamanil, tutor at Union Seminary, has pioneered a training programme in dialogue and interfaith understanding. He is tutor in comparative and religious pluralism. There are very few such appointments in other seminaries and undergraduate institutions. He has trained 60 persons, over three years, on a part-time programme. They have one week together, then a project, meeting mid-year for another day, and in the second year they have another week together. They produce articles and book projects, leading to a journal for comparative theology. Then he has a workshop for producing training programmes in their own institutions, helping tutors to make connections within their own discipline. Each year, there are different focuses. Last year, some Jews enrolled, and two white Hindus.

Frank Clooney SJ is Professor of the Harvard Divinity School and Director of the Center for the Study of World Religions in Harvard.[20] He feels that overall there is little Hindu–Christian dialogue, since Christians are only interested in Abrahamic faiths. Hinduism is seen as far too confusing, and not causing a problem, and so it is best to avoid it. Religious Studies is a Christian-based discipline which avoids polemic and keeps an academic distance. There is a Society for Hindu–Christian Studies and a journal, started by Howard Coward, and this has given 20 years of productive interaction – but this is exceptional. There is a chair in the University of Los Angeles (Tracey Tiemeier) but no posts elsewhere.

An attempt was made to have a Hindu–Catholic dialogue, involving mixed families, in the twin cities (Minneapolis/St Paul), initiated by Anant Rambachan and Frank Clooney. It failed because the Catholics did not follow it up, since it was not felt to be a priority.

Christian yoga is very prevalent. Some Hindus feel that it has been stolen from them. In Harvard, in Clooney's course on yoga, the majority are Buddhists, though none are Asian Buddhists. Spiritual seekers mainly are Buddhists. Hindus are mainly Indian and cultural. It is difficult to become a Hindu. Most Christians know Hindus through their doctor or business associate, not through a religious meeting.

Diana Eck's Pluralism Project has discovered a great variety of interfaith projects, with various names – Dinner Dialogues in Houston, for example, Habitat for Humanity, Building Bridges for Dialogue, and various Festivals of Faiths. City profiles of American cities and Inter Faith Realities are on the Pluralism Project website. These include an amazing Faiths Dinner Dialogue, on the web.

Vaneet As Hindu chaplain at Princeton (see above), Vaneet's experience is that Hindu–Christian dialogue can best be held with Vaishnavites, as led by Anuttama. In Princeton he has started two dialogues, one with evangelical Christians, part of a local Christian fellowship, and their affiliated chaplains were involved. A second was with the more liberal Presbyterian church. This was much easier, but the first achieved more. On one occasion a couple of students, Hindus, heard the evangelical students saying, 'We don't mind dialogue, but we are really about "saving".' They heard of a handout on evangelizing Hindus, how to convert them. Also a Post-it™ notice about praying for their salvation was seen on the board: 'Allegra, leading student, ex-Christian, is to be prayed for, that she may find her way back.' Allegra was the first non-Indian president of the Hindu students. Vaneet was sad because he thought it was going well, but the group had to be suspended. The second dialogue, with the liberal Christians, is like preaching to the converted, as is the Vaishnavite dialogue. There are also weekly chats over tea in the café, without a formal agenda, involving Vaneet and a female chaplain.

Anuttama Kenneth Cracknell guided me to visit his great friend Anuttama (see above in the 'ISKCON' section), just outside Washington. He presented me with a special edition of the *Journal of Vaishnava Studies*,[21] which contains 24 articles by leading participants: Catholic, Protestant, Orthodox and Vaishnavite, mainly ISKCON members. In the dialogues he includes scholars, but also practitioners. Key are people like Frank Clooney and Kenneth Cracknell. The articles are a mixture of reflections after 16 years of meetings, and keynote addresses on some of the key topics tackled, such as consideration of the soul and its destiny, the nature of self, the person of Jesus and the Word made flesh, along with some paintings of Christ's crucifixion and the Rasa Mandala, as two great symbols of divine love (this is an interpretation of a beautiful modern painting of Krishna's dance of divine love). God is worshipped in different ways, and we have to engage with that assumption. A worship or prayer service is fundamental to meetings. Anuttama sets up one table with Christian ikons, and another with Hindu ikons, and each experiences the other in turn. This sustained Vaishnava–Christian dialogue has involved, along with several Christian scholars and practitioners, Hindus of various traditions and now younger

American scholars. Sometimes, Kenneth comments, it felt as though Christians had to fit into their framework.

Anil Yesudas Anil is very different from any of the above, and I write about him at some length. He calls himself a 'Hindu follower of Christ', and what this means is clear through this interview.

Anil is from Kerala, aged 44, and he came to Chicago in 1999. He is a Christian of Brethren background. The challenge for him is: why is there a communication gap between Hindus and Indian Christians? He believes that common culture can be the bridge. But Indian Christians so often seem to communicate as Westerners.

He comes from an important Kerala family, with M. E. Cherian and T. A. Kurien as his relatives. The latter, his grandfather, wrote an epic – 17,000 lines of poetry – a kind of Christian Ramayana. His father, George David, was also vocal about practising faith in an Indian way, in Indian garb.

As a Brethren member, Anil had to become a missionary. There is no hierarchy; every local church is independent. In 2004 he was commended in the USA (like being ordained). He was a pharmacist as well as a religious worker. He decided to focus on Hindus – and the challenge of getting closer to them. He used to go to a Hindu temple and sit in the parking lot till the worshippers came at 6 p.m. He then went to the door, and tried to engage by smiling, though he did not enter. After four weeks he went in – to where the shoes were taken off. Then after some time, he decided to remove his shoes, praying that he would not worship idols, and would sit at the back of the temple. This continued for 18 months; then he used to sit at the front, though taking care not to face the idols. It was a Sanatan temple, with Indian trustees.

The president and his wife became friendly. Anil asked for five days in which to tell stories of Christ. They agreed on two days at Christmas, and two days at Easter. He told stories of Jesus, with the idols behind him. After two years he resigned his job, and called himself now an interfaith worker. It was then agreed he could lead a Christ-centred *satsang* (musical service with Indian *bhajans*) every week. He did this for two years, mainly with Indian Christians, with a couple of Hindus coming. He also went to the Ganges retreat centre, where he was well received, every Monday for two and a half years. A Swami from Chicago then stopped him, and asked him to pray silently. Local people said, 'Please, continue', but he refused, not wishing to embarrass them.

Anil's criterion is the Bible. If Hindu scriptures are compatible, he is happy to endorse them; if not, he just leaves them aside. He moved to

Devana, 'the Little India of Chicago'. He does *satsang* every Thursday for about 25 people, some Hindus. He also celebrates a kind of Eucharist each week – called Maha Mrityon Jaya, 'victory over death'. He has *arati* in his house every day, from 12.30 till 1 p.m., and *kirtan* every month, telling the stories of Jesus. An American works with him, from Christa Mission, which also is connected with Leicester. I attended the midday *arati*, which I found moving. It is in a chapel 'temple' in his house, with prayers offered to Jesus, and the style reminded me of Shantivanam. Anil himself wears simple saffron robes every day.

He has tried to run interfaith groups, making clear that we should not throw out our own faith when coming to such meetings. The groups meet every month with up to ten people, since they try to avoid having too many Christians. They choose one narrow topic; for example, an ethical area, eschatology, symbols, the concept of God. They always open with prayer. Sometimes they agree, sometimes not. The moderator is of one faith; prayer is led by a person of another faith. During prayer, members are to sit in deep respect, but there is no need to say 'Amen, Amen'. The Bahai community is a very good bridge. This is a way of making Hindus think, and sit peacefully. If a Hindu says, 'We have Jesus as one of the gods', we should not denigrate them. When an opponent comes at you, do not confront him violently. This is counterproductive, like in akkaido. Explaining the uniqueness of Christ can come later, not at the beginning. He knows also there can be secret Christians.

Anil calls his organization Sanatan Samaj, 'The eternal community'. It is a community of *Jesu Bhakters*, and he aims to have a mixture of persons, theologians, different languages and different church backgrounds. He thinks that internal dialogue can then lead to external dialogue. It all takes time. His own thinking is that a Hindu bows down before a god, and he does not blame them. They long to see God – this is *darshan*. He longs for Jesus to come to them, as he did to Ramakrishna. He talks of Gandhi, and how Jesus says that faith as small as a grain of mustard seed can be seen by God (Luke 17.6). God is a just judge. All can be saved, except those who actively reject God.[22] We can note, in Chapter 5, reference to *Jesu Bhakters*, and Kumar in particular.

World Parliament of Religions

The ongoing centre for this project is in Chicago, as is natural, since the original parliament was here in 1893. I attended a meeting where each delegate offered his or her thoughts about dialogue. It was very extended, because different Christian denominations all had a place, and different strands within other faiths, including pagans and various New Age groups. Most said similar things, and it is noteworthy that there was only one Muslim present, though he was the chair of the organization. It was a long, and to my thinking, disappointing meeting, full of inclusivist and pluralist thoughts that seemed like slogans. The goodwill there was immense, but it left me wondering where this movement is going, important as its history has been, and also whether those at the meeting were overclaiming what this movement can do today.

9

Three geographical studies: 3. Sweden

I choose Sweden, not because it is the most obvious country to write about, and not because it has very large numbers of Hindus. In Europe, outside the UK, that would be Holland, which has around 150,000 Hindus, and like the UK has a colonial heritage. But Sweden can stand as having a smaller Hindu community, which is the case in most other European countries. If we are considering Hindus in the diaspora, and go beyond USA and the UK, we can learn here about one country where Hindus are present in considerable diversity. The total population of Sweden is under ten million people; Hindu figures are hard to come by with accuracy, since there is no 'religion' question in the Swedish census, though there is an 'ethnic origin' question, which gives a clear indication at least of those of Indian origin, though these will include Sikhs, Indian Christians and other smaller groups such as Jains, and Muslims of Indian origin. In addition there are considerable numbers of Sri Lankan Tamil Hindus, and of course indigenous Swedish people. I was given a maximum figure of 20,000–25,000 Hindus in total, and we can go roughly by this.

The *Brill Encyclopaedia of Hinduism*, published in 2013, has a chapter on Sweden, written by Ferdinando Sardella. This gives figures in 2011 of 18,622 persons born in India (perhaps 80 per cent Hindus), 6,790 born in Sri Lanka (maybe Christians, Buddhists or Muslims included), 6,530 in Bangladesh (mainly Muslims but some Hindus) and 747 from Nepal.

Another and primary reason for choosing Sweden is that I have spent a considerable time there in recent years in several places, and was well placed to meet Hindus in context and consider also their relationship with Christians. I give thanks here to those clergy from the Church of Sweden that I have worked with in interfaith relations and who have directly assisted in my research on Hindus in Sweden; among others I name Marika Palmdahl from Gothenburg, Katarina Wandahl and Maria Bard from Norrkoping, and Kajsa Ahlstrand and Helene Egnell at the national level. On the Hindu side, I thank Ferdinando Sardella (see p. 210 n. 1).

Overview

Gautham (see interview below) at the Swedish Foreign Office, a Brahmin Bengali, gave the following estimates and breakdown to communities, which generally are quite compatible with the *Encyclopaedia*.

Gautham's father came to Sweden 60 years ago. There were 11 Indians in Sweden at that time. Now there are 20,000–25,000. Half are temporary residents – students, IT contract workers and so on. They come and go in rotation, staying between one and five years.

Then there are around 10,000 Swedish Indians, who have been here for 20–50 years. There are 2,000–4,000 South Indians Tamils, or Sri Lankan Tamils. Two thousand have origins in East Africa (see interview with Harilal below). There are a few Nepalese and Indonesians, and 300–500 Indian Bengalis or Bangladeshis. Sikhs overlap through mixed marriages but feel nearer to Hindus than Muslims, though clearly distinctive. Hare Krishna devotees number 200–500, a figure which goes up and down. Many are Swedes, and they are the public face of Hinduism in Sweden. Hindu-linked Swedes and other Europeans living in Sweden may come to up to 1,000 people.

I will now describe my encounters with Hindus in Sweden, and the interviews I conducted. These accounts focus on the ISKCON movement in Sweden, the East African Hindus (easily compared with those in the Leicester chapter), the temple groups in Stockholm, a number of engaging individuals, with varying influence, and an overview of the yoga movement as found in Sweden. Finally, I examine what impact, if at all, this has had on the churches, interfaith structures and Christian thought.

ISKCON in Sweden

There are ISKCON centres around restaurants in Malmo, Gothenburg and Stockholm, and two communities in the south of Stockholm, one on a farm and the other as a publishing centre. Except for Malmo, I visited all of these, and I give an account here of those I met in leadership. This section can be read in conjunction with the specific chapter on ISKCON in the UK (Chapter 3) and sections in the USA journal. I visited each place with a colleague from the Church of Sweden.

The first place is at **Korsnas**, south of Stockholm. This is a kind of ashram and community. Our informant was Ishvara Krishna (initiated name), Ingemar (Swedish name), who first translated the Bhagavadgita from English to Swedish. Today there are about 20–30 persons living permanently at

Korsnas, and there is a temple in the heart of this centre. Chanting there lasts the normal two hours a day for the movement, focusing on Krishna. Krishna/Ingemar is the only Swede there today; the rest come from Germany, Finland, Russia, Estonia, Latvia, Croatia, Canada, Uzbekistan, Mexico and Bulgaria.

Korsnas is the place for book production, not just for Sweden but also more widely. It is called Bhaktivedanta Book Trust (BBT), and Korsnas covers northern Europe and beyond. In the 1990s there were about 150–200 persons living there (from 26 nationalities), but since the internet developed, residential numbers have decreased. The director of book production is now in Germany. We heard of the ISKCON movement in Russia, and a temple even in Uzbekistan.

Another ISKCON community is in nearby **Almvik**. This has farming but not sufficient for all. About 60–70 persons live there and half of the population are children. They may try to restart a free school which used to be there.

At Korsnas there is only one Indian man (aged 70) living. In ISKCON Stockholm there are many more Indian people coming to the temple and Centre, to what is a much more central place.

In 1977 Ingemar became a devotee of ISKCON. His parents are Baptists, but he never felt at home among them, and when he did not have to join his parents he rejected this path. An older friend showed him different scriptures, and he liked a book in Swedish which explained the meaning of life through an Indian mind. For him the Bhagavadgita was the best philosophy he had encountered, and he travelled to India in the 1970s for a month, before becoming ill and returning to Sweden.

Ingemar has been married and he has a 37-year-old daughter. His parents were terrified when he joined ISKCON, but when they saw Ingemar living a healthy life and seemingly happy, they gradually came to an acceptance that there was nothing to fear.

We also met a devotee from Bulgaria, **Tridi Mara**, whose background was as a communist. He became a Hindu in 1989, with the fall of the Iron Curtain. He began asking whether there might be something more than this materialist world.

As a boy, he liked to be in a church. His brother started to read Christian books, but this got him into trouble with their father. In a way he feels he has continued where his brother stopped. His brother joined the army, but then died after some time, very likely killed by the KGB. He had been put in prison because practising one's own religion was not allowed. It was when Tridi Mara went to the funeral that he decided to join the

ISKCON movement. This had to be done in secret, and there was no temple in Bulgaria.

After 1989 it was easier to join the movement and he did not have any problems with the authorities. He came to Korsnas in 1991 and returns once a year to Bulgaria. He says, 'I am happy and it gives me peace and is like my family. The life outside takes energy from Krishna; here it is easy to be relaxed.'

ISKCON Stockholm

We met various Hare Krishna devotees at Govindas, a very popular ISKCON vegetarian restaurant in central Stockholm, where there is also a temple and a shop selling many different resources connected with the movement.

Our informant was **Tapasa Dasa**. He has been in Stockholm for 15 years, as manager, priest and lecturer. He is married and is now 57 years old, having been a monk earlier.

In Stockholm many members of the congregation are ethnically Swedes; some are immigrants, and not so many from India. They may be students, or project workers who stay in Sweden for a couple of months. The proportion of immigrants is as the population in Stockholm.

ISKCON was seen as a sect, and if an Indian participates, this causes no difficulties, but for Swedes there are stumbling blocks. It requires courage to be an active member. There are about 100 members and 50 are immigrants. Indians tend to come, not because it is ISKCON, but because at the Centre there is a temple. But the Swedes who are members are stable and committed, and the movement is viewed as less of a sect than it used to be.

In the 1970s it was mostly young people who joined the movement, and they were seen by wider society as having been indoctrinated. A rescue organization was formed: FRI Föreningen Rädda Individen, 'Foundation for Rescuing the Individual', and it made 70 kidnappings. But today ISKCON is well organized, and has a better reputation after several investigations.

The neighbouring Norway movement has not been very stable. Today Pragosh, who is Irish, is responsible for the Nordic countries and the UK – rather like an archbishop – and his area includes Sweden. Tapasa himself came from Norway. He was 25 when he joined the movement, having had his interest raised by hearing George Harrison when he was 15. He came from a wealthy family in Bergen, Norway, and could have inherited his father's business, but he had not found the meaning of life.

He got a religious belief in school through a good teacher, and took part in biblical dramas. In gymnasium (high school) he became an intellectual and thought he knew a lot about life. But the realities of life came through, and he became humble and started to search. Tapasa started to read the Bible again and met a person who gave him the Bhagavadgita.

In 1981 he started the movement in Bergen, but moved to Korsnas after six months. There he deepened his understanding of philosophy, and this was a good place because of the number of new members there. One thing he realized was that a person's spiritual story started in former lives. He became Tapasa Das in 1981. He was based in Bergen and then in Oslo, but there were problems, and he moved to Stockholm in the 1990s. Today there is a small temple in Oslo.

In Stockholm, ISKCON owns a building and apartments. Those who rent are not allowed to cook meat or drink alcohol. There are many activities in the evenings and on Sundays (40–50 persons), and a feast is held once a month, with about 100 people attending. Members often stay for a while and then move on. Tapasa commented, 'We are not so much involved in getting members. Quality is more important than quantity.' The members are clearly concerned about education of the wider public, as groups visit from schools, colleges and elsewhere, and learn of the Hindu world view, as well as the movement.

ISKCON Gothenburg

This again is a combination of restaurant and temple, and it is much visited for educational purposes.

The informant here is **Julia**, a tall 35-year-old. She dresses in characteristic ISKCON garb. I met her in Gothenburg, but she comes from Stockholm. Her parents are atheists. She read the Bible in school, and used to attend church at the end of semesters, as was the practice (this has now been stopped, which she regrets and sees as the influence of the USA – and an ideology of multiculturalism). She was confirmed, but had not been very serious about her faith. She never found answers in Christianity, though she was always inspired by Lord Jesus. Rather, she found the truth in Vedanta, in Varanasi. Here she was centred on Siva devotion. At the age of 19, she went travelling to India and spent a year in Goa. There she met an Indian guru, and began meditating before many deities, including the moon god and sun god, and also used the Gayathri Mantra.

From India, she returned to Stockholm, but felt lost there. She ended up going to the ISKCON temple. She felt she just had to go. There she talked for an hour with a friend about Vaishnavism. She gradually realized that she had been looking on the other side of the world to find her soul and for salvation – and there it was, 100 metres from her home. She worked now at shifting from being self-centred to God-centred. She has learned that she can realize herself by being a servant of all. Happiness is found more in serving than being served.

Julia began training in Stockholm. She went to the temple for one to three hours a day – for listening, chanting, learning and eating sanctified food. She did not feel called to become a nun, but went to Chaitanya's birthplace for two years, for several months at a time. Central to this journeying was chanting God's name.

She was then sent to Gothenburg, by Tapasa, to consolidate the work there. She would rather have gone back to India, but feels that wherever Krishna's name is chanted, there is a holy place. She receives school classes in the temple/restaurant in Gothenburg, and preaches to the congregation on Tuesdays and Sundays. Between five and 30 people attend, with 100 people there on Krishna's birthday. Often foreigners come on Sundays, from Europe and the Middle East. She also represents Hindus in the Interreligious Council, and found herself elected to the Board. Her central task has been to bring religious life back to Govinda Temple.

She also attends another Vaishnavite temple which is part of the Vrinda group, a split from main ISKCON, who have their Swami in Germany and have 55 temples in South America. There are several who attend both groups, and there is no attempt to evangelize the other group. They follow an 'etiquette of balance' and both wear the same *tilak* mark. Julia herself has not yet taken initiation; she will get an indication when this can be from her guru in India. It is immensely serious, she feels, like a marriage.

In general, it is not politically correct to be religious in Sweden, and people think you are less intelligent if you are. Her father was very disturbed when she began attending the ISKCON temple, particularly as they lived next door. Some parents think this is worse than a child becoming a drug addict! But gradually, Father has accepted things, letting her go her own way, and has even been for an ice cream at Govinda's! Overall, he agrees with the opinions of Julia's brother, who is humanist and a sceptic. Julia has been hurt by this conflict in the family. Her sister is more sympathetic to Christianity, having met a priest in Uganda, and 'chants' in a gospel choir, something that Julia respects as part of God's plan. Julia believes in soft evangelism: we should never force God on anyone, nor does God force himself. But he never gives up on us.

Julia is inspired by some ideas in Christianity, such as the church as the body of Christ, and the concept of servanthood – to be like Jesus in this, and to stop complaining, which leads to so much self-inflicted suffering.

Other Hindu temples

Stockholm Sanatan Mandir

Our informant here was **Dr Narendra Yamdagni.** He arrived in Sweden in 1963 when he came to study in Uppsala, and has lived here for 50 years. He is married and has two daughters who are married to non-Indians.

There were about five families at the same time who came from India. There was an Indian Association in Stockholm even before there was a temple. The Mandir was started in 1988, and Dr Yamdagni became president of the temple and member of the board. This is not the case any longer.

The weekly programme includes recitation on Tuesdays and on Sundays, with worshippers eating together at 3 p.m. Different families donate each week. At festivals, up to 300 people may come, for example to celebrate Diwali. Staff from the Indian Embassy come on Indian Independence Day. The younger generation of Hindus is interested in Indian politics, but also Swedish politics and cricket.

Their priest, from India, has been here for three years, but his family is in India and the temple cannot afford to pay for his family members to stay in Sweden. The priest goes to India once a year and stays for a month.

In Sweden it is a rule that every immigrant child has the right to learn the mother's tongue, and by that they also receive the language of religion, whether Gujarati or Hindi or Tamil.

The Ganesh Tamil temple is for those who come from South India and Sri Lanka, and is in Farsta (south of Stockholm). This Mandir temple has contact with a couple of thousand people. But is not necessary for a Hindu to visit any temple. For Dr Yamdagni, it is important to create a spiritual context for religion, focusing on emotions and relationships as well as rituals. His philosophy is that there are many ways to reach the same goal, and if you argue that your way is the right one you will have a conflict with others. It is important to understand that God is One, with various attributes and forms.

Stockholm Ganesh Temple

We visited here on a Friday evening, which is the weekly *puja* time. This temple is in a building rented from the Church of Sweden, next to a second-hand retail shop. Inside it is a typical Tamil temple, with Ganesh in the centre and Murugan in a side altar, a Siva shrine, and several other deities, including one peculiar to Sri Lanka. The priest is South Indian and is part time, having to work also in a travel business. He was very welcoming as he showed us round, and invited us to witness the *abisheham* (washing) of Ganesh, which comes before the main *arati*. He did this in a very elaborate way, using much milk, and flowers and fruits and water etc. This took about 15 minutes, and was done with loving care, as devotees stood round, chanting.

Numbers began to grow before the main worship, and this was to be followed by a meal, as happens every week. We were not able to stay, but were there about 100 attending, both South Indian, Sri Lankan and North Indian. There were a group of Tamil women from Sri Lanka, leading the *bhajan* singing. We talked at some length with the members of a family who had come from Hyderabad, Andhra Pradesh; the father is an IT worker on a contract for some years, seconded by his company in Cyber City there. This was clearly an important thing for them to do, to show their young son – a toddler – a temple, and what went on there.

We met one of the trustees, who are mainly Sri Lankan, but I was told he was not an Eelam Tamil (a Tamil seeking independence for Tamils in Sri Lanka).

Mariestad, mid-Sweden: Sanatan and Swaminarayan temples

Members of this community, like those in Leicester, were originally from India and were taken to Uganda by the British colonial administration. They were sent out by Idi Amin in 1972, and came to Sweden via a refugee camp in Austria. This was a group of people who did not have British passports. About 200 came to a refugee camp near Malmo, where they remained for three and a half months, until Christmas 1972. They were stateless when they left Uganda, with very little time to prepare. They were mostly business people, with servants in their large houses. They had a temple for worshipping in. They are now in Stockholm and Gothenburg, and in various centres in western Sweden – Mariestad, Jonkoping, Boras, Trollhattan – places with much industry at that time. Most are Gujaratis and of the same background as so many Leicester East African Hindus (see Chapter 7).

I met **Harilal Raja** first in Mariestad, and then again in Leicester when he came for a wedding. There seems to be much such coming and going. He came to Sweden with his wife and a baby boy just two weeks old. His business had been importing and selling matches and Primus stoves, and newsprint from Sweden. So he applied for entry to Sweden, which he was happy to consider, since it was the country with the best reputation for equality within Europe. The Hindus did not practise caste distinctions in Uganda, and have not done so in Sweden, even related to weddings, though they faced some pressures from the elders of their caste.

In Malmo, everyone was friendly, and Harilal joined a group of refugees who were allocated to Mariestad, where there was a large Electrolux factory that was looking for labour. It was the middle of the winter, and very cold, but they were put up in a hotel owned by a Ugandan Swedish earlier immigrant. Early days were tough because they were not used to labouring work, and the women had to work also.

The church in Malmo welcomed them on arrival, and at the Christmas Eve service. The refugees found the same welcome in Mariestad. The Christians welcomed them as fellow human beings and religious people, but they did not try to convert them. They had had some interaction with Christians in Uganda, through having teachers from the UK and Goan Roman Catholics as customers. Nowadays there is no direct relationship, though students come from schools and colleges to look round the temple and learn of Hinduism.

Thirty families came together to Mariestad, and there are 45 families there today. There is a Sanatan temple in a block of flats which I visited. There is no resident priest, and the *puja* is led by women of the community. They managed it from the beginning also, and on a Saturday they do *arati*. The language used is Gujarati, with *slokas* in Sanskrit, written in Gujarati. They read the Gita in Gujarati, and the children learn Hinduism intentionally.

Preachers and teachers come from India for occasional teaching programmes. Also there is a Swaminarayan group of 30 families which meets in a former church of the Jehovah's Witnesses; they come mainly from the district of Kuch in Gujarat. This leaves only 15 families in the original Sanatan temple. Harilal is a trustee of both temples. The name is now a combined one – Sri Sanatan Swaminarayan Temple, an ecumenical name, suggested by a visiting guru from India, Sankaracharya.

Most of the younger members of these families marry out, into Stockholm or overseas. They make an effort to come back for Navaratri and Diwali. Harilal even dreams of moving to Stockholm now that he is retired, but his wife is not yet keen. They fear lack of social networks in Stockholm.

There are 12 Muslim families in Mariestad, with a small mosque, and the Hindus have a good relationship with them. He highlighted 20 Hindu families like this in Boras, 45 families in Jonkoping where there is a well-maintained temple in a flat, which I visited, and 20 families in Trollhattan.

These are all industrial cities. There are also 30 families in Gothenburg. In Stockholm there are ten families from Uganda, but 600 Punjabi families connected with the Sanatan temple.

Harilal is pious in his Hindu practices. His *ishta devata* is Radha-Krishna. He also venerates Jalaram, for him not a god but a saint, and the family guru. I met Harilal in the Jalaram Temple in Leicester when he was on a visit to that city (see Chapter 7 on Leicester). He venerates also his family ancestors, Raghu/Vanshi.

As a summary of this story, I was able to see, in Harilal's house, three flags standing on his mantelpiece. The Indian flag, representing his origins and heritage; the Ugandan flag, for the country where he was brought up; and the flag of Sweden, where he found safety and a future. It is noteworthy that the Swedish flag was the largest!

Four individual informants in Stockholm

Willy Pfandtner (Ajit Das) and Stig Lundgren (Shiva Shankar)

This dialogue was conducted with these two together. They clearly admire each other, but are very different in their approaches. Stig is coming at this from a very religious and practising perspective, while Willy is looking from a philosophical and academic background.

Willy was one of the first to bring ISKCON to Sweden. He had been a hippie in Australia, met some earlier followers there, and moved into a temple in Sydney in 1970. Prabhupada came in 1971 and Willy was inspired, and initiated by him. He came back to his native Sweden and began the movement in a travelling van with a few others. He started in Stockholm in 1973. He was one of two main leaders of the movement in Sweden until the mid-1980s. They parted company with the main movement then, when they had considerable differences with the then leader of ISKCON in northern Europe, an American.

Stig was on a spiritual quest, searching here and there, but not part of any Westernized organizations such as different yoga schools, or New Age-inspired *satsang* groups. But he eventually discovered Advaita Vedanta, not by going to India or the USA, but by reading books and scriptures. He was already a vegetarian at the age of 16, and had taken up meditation. He has never been an alcohol drinker. He eventually found a guru in Bangalore and developed links with an ashram 350 miles north of there, the mainly Advaita Vedanta centre called Sringeri Sharada Peetham. He found their inspiration a guiding light, and considers himself a follower of their lineage of gurus.

He was never a backpacker, but came to this through study. He is not a member of a temple even now, though he attends the Ganesh temple sometimes, liking to be part of a worshipping group with a Hindu feel. Here the Indian people are much more accessible, in his experience, than the Sri Lankans. And there are many enquiring Indian students also. But his practice does not depend on this temple culture at all. At home, he does one and a half hours of worship on average each day, in a Vedantic way. He has been accepted as a Brahmin, and was given the sacred thread at the age of 34! All agreed, even in South India, that he could be such an honorary Brahmin. Anyway, these days, many Brahmin young people only put on the thread before marriage.

Willy is a lecturer in the study of religion and the philosophy of religion. He wanted to improve his 'dialogical' abilities by improving his academic perspective. He remains 'religious', but not strict in his practice. He left the movement in the 1980s after Prabhupada died. Or rather he was sent out, because he was too much going his own way, and wanted the movement to integrate in Sweden. He had his own group of intellectuals, acceptable within the wider movement but not locally, and they formed the Bhaktivedanta Society. They cooperated with the ethnographic museum in Stockholm and conducted daily services there as part of an Indian exhibition. He engaged much in dialogue with Christians, for example in Stockholm Cathedral when a radical dean let the devotees chant in the cathedral. This was highly divisive within the church, and became a cause célèbre. The Dean was quoted as saying, 'At least the Hare Krishnas wanted to talk to me about God, which the congregation never do!' Stig recited the Vedas in Uppsala Cathedral later, as part of a festival of ecology, and this was not so controversial.

At this time Bede Griffiths came to stay with them. This was at the invitation of the Gnosis movement and magazine they were involved with – a kind of post-secular religious revival movement. It had a small ashram where people could come and stay.

Willy's group eventually disintegrated, and he transferred to studying Western theology and philosophy at Uppsala, subjects of which he knew little. He finished in 2005 and now teaches at Sodertorn University. He still says he is a Hindu if anything, and is a strict vegetarian, but unlike strict Hare Krishna devotees, drinks coffee!

Generally, he says, he theorizes about dialogue rather than practising it. He is now respected again by ISKCON leaders, and has close friends who are Christians with whom he talks informally.

Stig is an almost permanent doctoral student in philosophy of religion. He works as he studies, as is normal in Sweden. This includes giving small early-morning talks on the radio quite often, from a confessional perspective. He is to speak on the symbolism of light this week – for Hannukkah and for other religious festivals, including Diwali.

Stig now has one follower who provides him some Vedantic support. He is more interested in Hinduism than in India. He is not part of any organization, and relies on books, the internet, Skype and so on. Many are generally interested here, but there is no community context like in India, or even in the UK. He feels compelled to go to the very source of things. He reflects on Vedanta societies in the USA; some are very authentic, while others are very watered down and Westernized. He corresponds a little with individuals there. At some point in the future, he might go and live in an ashram, when he is free of family obligations. He does feel somewhat isolated.

What is the future for Hinduism in Sweden? They believe this depends on a few like themselves. There is not much teaching for the next generation of Indians – a vital need, but materials are not there in Swedish. And the parents would find it very difficult to explore Hinduism in Swedish. They are not organized, and so do not get financial support from the government. Hindu culture and religion is very decentralized, so does not fit the model of other religions. Hindus follow local traditions. It is difficult to get them together, yet alone to have substantive dialogue with them.

School texts are gradually improving. The problem is that those who are qualified to write are in universities, and not interested to do this.

In general, Hinduism is a very anonymous religion in Sweden.

Stig is a member of the Board of the Swedish Indian Association, a kind of cultural London Nehru Centre type organization, where he gives talks. Vishva Hindu Parishad (VHP) – of which a few North Indians are followers – is more cultural than political in Sweden. *Willy* does not like the way it tries to simplify Hinduism. Its members try to centralize an essentially decentralized faith.

Their views on conversion? It is OK, if it is done in a Gandhian way.

Sudhagar

Sudhagar is employed as a youth coordinator with the Fryshuset youth project in Stockholm. He introduced himself as Sanatan Dharma, not simply Hindu. One grandfather was a Saiva Hindu, while his grandmother on the other side was Vaishnavite. They were from Tirunelveli, Tamil Nadu.

He was brought up in Stockholm, and as a teenager linked with ISKCON. He then took *diksha* from a guru in Vrindavan, in the Gaudiya Vaishnavite tradition. He studied religious studies in Stockholm University, and became a high-school teacher.

In 2010 Sudhagar founded the Stockholm Young Dharmist and Zoroastrian Association (there are 20 Zoroastrians in Sweden, he estimates). He has one Syrian Orthodox Christian supporter, who encouraged him to start his venture. The organization consists of five Zoroastrian youths, ten Hindus, two Jains and two Buddhists (one Sri Lankan and one Thai). The Hindus include Sri Lankan Tamils, and Hindus from Bangladesh. The organization also includes 300 people on Facebook. They meet once in a month, or every other month. There are now three Sikhs cooperating, though they did not at first; Sikhs, if having to choose, always go with Hindus rather than Muslims. Sudhagar felt that the Abrahamic faiths have many organizations, and he wanted an alternative network.

He wants to support young people who are caught between two societies, and gives lectures on themes such as the history of India, individual religions, and different approaches to marriages, as interpreted for Sweden (many still bring marriage partners from India).

He himself is a Dalit (a Pariayar). Many of his family members in India have married Christian Dalits. Even in Sweden, most Sri Lankan Hindus marry according to caste, though such caste traditions are declining among other groups. In his own family, his sister married an adopted Indian from Maharashtra, and was sent out from the family for quite a time by his father. She had a traditional Hindu wedding, but that was not enough.

'From India,' he says, 'we get the values of respect for elders, for religion, for family, for knowledge. From Sweden, we get respect for democratic values, freedom of faith, liberal values.' He was sent home to Chennai for schooling from the age of 12 to 16, where he stayed with his sister and mother. His father was a lifelong supporter of DMK, the Dravidian party, and he wanted this kind of Tamil inculturation for his son.

Sudhagar values the way Hindu customs were before the coming of Islam and Christianity – when, for example, Hijras (transgender or transsexual people) were not persecuted or stoned to death. In his area of Tamil Nadu, many Christians are turning to Pentecostalism.

At Fryshuset, he is coordinator of 20–25 youths of different faiths, aged 16–25. The emphasis is on interfaith leadership training. Twice a year he also leads big seminars, for example on interfaith dialogue, or against racism.

The wider society has very little understanding of Hindus or of dharmic teaching. So Sudhagar took part in the writing of an important schools study book. His strong emphasis is on what he sees as the monotheism of Hinduism in all its forms, whichever god is put first. He mentions a new word to me: 'Kaumara' Hindus – Tamil worshippers of Murugan, the Tamil god, second son of Siva and brother of Ganesh. He emphasizes that the stereotype of Hindus as cow worshippers is not true.

He observes that most 'ritualistic Hindus', temple Hindus, do not want to build bridges with other Hindus. And priests rarely have any theological background. Some conventional Hindus see him as a threat. Particularly he mentions the Ganesh Tamil temple committee, whose opposition is perhaps for caste reasons, as it is Sri Lankan dominated. He finds Sri Lankan Buddhists want to cooperate, but not Eelam Tamils, as they used to call themselves. As for Hill Tamils, he knows of just two. He has good contact with North Indian and Bangladeshi Hindus.

Gautham

Gautham is a Bengali Hindu whose father came to Sweden 60 years ago (see above). He finds Sweden to be a very individualized society, and in religion also. The handing on of the Hindu faith occurs through families, but this is difficult with the pull of secularism. Swedish and Hindu youth culture are similar; their trends are the same. But new immigrants are usually more conservative, as in all societies.

He has Hindu deities in the house, though it is totally cultural for him. Most Hindus have these, but only some use the shrines religiously. The next generation may be culturally Hindu, but not ritualistically. New immigrants coming from India do continue to refresh the tradition, but they come to raise their place in society, rather than to be faithful Hindus. The temple culture only appeals to a minority. The majority never go to temples. Marrying another Hindu cannot be insisted on, unless you bring a spouse from the USA, from India or from the UK.

Hindu society has little professional leadership in religion. Priests in the North Indian temple are on six-month contracts only; their families remain in India, and they do not know Swedish.

Gautham's views on Sudhagar are that his ambitions are too broad, and so he has limited success. Stig is someone he is close to. Stig is the Vedanta Society!

When asked about the relationship between the Swedish media and Hinduism, he responds that it is now the internet that is central. People are free to write extreme articles. Newspapers are now limited in power. Hindus do not feature in that media at all.

As for dialogue with Abrahamic faiths, we can meet as human beings, but not as religions or theologically. And who is to represent Hindus in such dialogues? There are no mandates. The critical mass too small; Holland is OK – it has 150,000 Hindus.

Hindus in Sweden have had few concrete practical problems, such as with authorities, or with freedom of religion. Ashes of the deceased can be scattered in any lake or sea. His father's he scattered half in the Ganges, and half in Sweden, representing the two halves of his life.

It is difficult for anything traditional to survive in this ultra-modern society, he says. (I disagree – Sweden has many traditional customs!) Emphasis is on the individual and the state, not on the family.

Concerning his own belief, Gautham describes himself as a dharmic Hindu, following many thousand years of heritage. It is a way of looking at the world. He is pantheistic, and does not believe in a personal God. He is not a follower of 'a' god, but believes in reincarnation. Reading scriptures is a way of connecting to his forefathers. He is a Brahmin, but eats some meats. He is a priestly family Brahmin, and went back to Calcutta to put on the sacred thread. Some Westerners like Stig have also done this.

Hinduism is like a large ship – all know if they are on it in some way. Hare Krishna devotees are at one extreme, Stig at the other!

Yoga in Sweden

As in many European countries, yoga in various guises has become more and more popular in recent years, and in particular in the last decade, as the country has become more secular as a whole. It is reckoned that 400,000 Swedes engage in some form of yoga, out of a total population of under 10 million. This is a very high percentage. For most this has little or no religious connotation, and participants take it up from a number of directions. The majority are people who are not part of the Church at all.

Some take up yoga as pure physical training, where exercise is to the fore. Another group sees it primarily as psychological, a training of the mind, in concentration and stillness, with a vaguely spiritual aspect. A third group start for medical reasons, and it is even recommended and prescribed in certain hospitals. I interviewed three Swedish people about their involvement. One saw yoga as primarily a way into meditation in general. She practises *kundalini* yoga, which emphasizes the channelling of energy, and meditation with the help of a mantra. She sees it as linked in some way to Buddhism, and she has become more interested in Buddhism through doing yoga. She did know much about its origins within Hinduism, though she has a strong wish to visit India. The other strand, for her, was to do Chinese meditation, and she describes how yoga came out of that. She finds she needs others to do it with her at least occasionally, through a class or with friends. But the class is not primarily a place to make friends, not primarily a social occasion, but a serious time for yoga. She only says 'Hi' and 'Bye' to those practising with her. The important thing is to do it on a daily basis. She is seeking to begin an open class in the hall of a local church, though her first attempt failed because of lack of takers. When questioned, she is, like many Westerners, interested in the concept of reincarnation.

A second person I had discussion with said she has a husband who does yoga every day early in the morning. He says he is doing it as a gymnastic exercise, with no religious or spiritual motivation. He is tired of all the talk about yoga in Sweden for the last 40 years since he has been practising it. But she thinks there is nevertheless a hidden mystical side also.

My informant began doing yoga occasionally as early as the 1970s, before she visited India and went to an ashram, in the north, which had a Sikh background; here yoga was a means of entering into deep meditation. This for her was important spiritually – it was about India, rather than the rituals of formal Hinduism. Yoga was part of the alternative movement of those times, and a kind of movement against the Church. But now it is no longer alternative; in fact it has become fashionable, part of self-development and growth to wholeness. Some who practise, for example, *kundalini* yoga chant mantras as they practise, though they have little idea of the background within Hinduism, or of Sanskrit. It is just a way of focusing the mind, leading to more awareness and capacity to reflect.

Yoga originally came more from the Hindu background, she feels, while Buddhism undergirds the mindfulness movement, and stress management, and yoga practised with that aim in mind. Swedish people are very interested in evidence, and how there is some research suggesting that yoga is effective in this area. But yoga from whichever source can also work at the subconscious level, and meet certain spiritual needs.

A third person I interviewed is a Church of Sweden pastor in Gothenburg. She took up yoga prior to becoming a priest 20 years ago. She was self-taught, encouraged by her sister who is a dancer. She went to New York City, and there began to take it more seriously. This was while she was dipping into all kinds of religions and spiritual practices. She had left the Church of Sweden when she was 18. Her grandfather had been a priest, while her father was an atheist.

Her yoga practice was not because of any supposed link with Hinduism; she did not understand this religion, though she has tried. She does not like yoga just being seen as a kind of gym practice, totally unspiritual, and often there accompanied by music. The essence of it is to help us to feel one: body, soul and spirit.

On her return to Sweden after some years, she became a regular church-goer and eventually trained as a theologian, and was ordained. She now practises in a multicultural context. She has had two vicars to whom she has been answerable. The first was relaxed about her yoga. The second was very anxious, and asked, 'Should we not, as Christians, look to our own traditions to include taking care of our bodies – just as Muslim prayer is also bodily prayer?' She puts the yoga practice on her CV, but it is rarely discussed.

Her mission is to those many in Sweden, ex-members of the Church, whose spiritual needs are very confused. How can we help them find a link with the Church, and normal sacramental life? People wonder: 'If yoga is my primary focus, can I also come to church?' Her mission is not to convert people, but to build bridges. Though she has conducted yoga in the basement of her church, and once in the church itself, she has concentrated on helping lead retreats. She has done this for two years, with a yoga teacher. This has created a lot of interest, mainly among women. People call and ask her to come, including fellow female priests in the Church. One retreat centre said she could not come any more, blocked by the Board there. Yoga can be controversial.

Does she see its roots as more Hindu or Buddhist? Hindu, she replies, though she still knows little. Buddhism leads to meditation and non-violent movements. She has still never been to India.

She is to appear in an article in a national church paper in January 2014, and perhaps yoga will be even more controversial after that.

Summary

The Church in Sweden has been giving increasing attention to Muslims. This is the result of the large influx of Muslims, many from traumatized parts of the world, since Sweden has admitted refugees in a fairly generous way. In addition, there are large numbers of Orthodox Christians from countries like Iraq, Egypt and Syria. For obvious reasons, the latter have increased sharply in very recent years. Enabling these two groups to accept each other is no small task, in view of the reasons for their having come to Sweden. This, and the lack of colonial links with India, explains to a large extent why there has been little attention paid to Hinduism and to Hindus. They remain hard to understand, and rather exotic, for those from the churches, as well as those from society in general. The fragmentation seen above in this chapter makes relating to them difficult also. This explains why the restaurants of ISKCON have been vital to provide some links, not least because of their vegetarian menus which are followed by a significant minority of Swedes. Yoga is the other main link, consciously or unconsciously. Hinduism remains a low-profile faith, as Hindus are a low-profile people. Numbers are also key to this. This may change in the future, hence the inclusion of this chapter, representing the various smaller communities in Europe, as explained above.[1]

10

Two examples of Hindu–Christian forums in the UK: Leicester and national – difficulties and possibilities

These forums are few and far between. Leicester has been one of the few examples, and has had a limited life. The national forum has been able to continue with some ups and downs, and one of its stated purposes is to encourage local dialogues, which it has done with limited success. More positively, Hindus have played a major part in Councils of Faiths locally, in the Inter Faith Network UK, and in Inter Faith Week local events held throughout the country in November. We consider here the two examples, in both of which I have been closely involved. I have gone into considerable detail about the national group, as well as gathering the comments of the two present chairpersons. This is so that readers can see both the opportunities and pitfalls that can enable or hinder progress in such a journey together. What is encouraging from all this is that this journey continues after more than ten years – and dialogue is about building long-term trust, and not finding quick answers. I thank here Richard Atkinson, former Archdeacon of Leicester, now Bishop of Bedford, and Ramesh Pattni, from the Chinmaya Mission – and now studying for a doctorate of Oxford University through the Oxford Centre for Hindu Studies – for the ready way they took on leadership of the Forum when I went to Sweden, and the way they have taken it forward, as well as their support to me in this book project.

Leicester Hindu–Christian Forum

This began in 2002, following on from a very successful Muslim–Christian group set up in 2000, which continued for 13 years. The Hindu–Christian group was to be a balance to this, involving the other major faith in Leicester, and it was open to all who had an interest in meeting 'the other'. An example of agendas, in 2004, was: living across faiths, how to use our scriptures, our faith pilgrimages, the concept of sainthood. It was decided eventually to meet always in the same Hindu temple. Hospitality was normally better in temples, and Christians would more readily go to temples than vice versa. Attendance was varied, and in 2005 an attempt was made to ask people to sign up to the group, involving commitment to attend five meetings a year. It was decided to tackle tough themes intentionally in 2005/6: terrorism, conversion and mission, caste and class, reincarnation and resurrection, religion, culture and citizenship – a fine and daring agenda.

Memorably, Israel Selvanayagam was a speaker when we held an evening comparing the birth of Jesus and the birth of Krishna, a topic where his depth of insight was much appreciated, and this was one of the best meetings of the Forum. It also looked at ikons and deities – we viewed deities in a temple, and ikons on slides – and at mixed-faith marriage and families, for which the speaker was a member of the clergy, married to a Hindu. We considered common ethical values, with special reference to non-violence and ecology; living in contemporary society, and issues of secularism. This meeting was held in a church, and I remember that a Hindu friend said, 'How wonderful to be in such a holy place!' We said compline at the end of the evening. A group of Hindus began to attend the midnight mass at Christmas, and these became dozens. They hesitated whether to take their shoes off in church, on this most holy of nights.

Plans were also made to have outings, to St Albans Abbey, and to Bhaktivedanta Manor. But want of organizing capacity prevented this happening. The Teape Foundation in Cambridge gave modest support to the group at this time, which was a great encouragement. The St Philip's Centre for Study and Engagement in a Multi Faith Society, of which I was the founding director, drew up a fundraising proposal for a Hindu staff member to be sought, at least part time, but funds were never forthcoming.

Eventually the Forum declined and is not now operating for lack of leadership in both communities. The Christian expertise is now lacking. The Hindu leadership was also affected when its key person lost his place as secretary of a leading temple where we used to meet. Hopefully, there can be a second coming of this group, since my research now has shown me how much was done, and how promising it had been.

Hindu–Christian national forum

It was in late 2000 that the then National Inter Faith Adviser for the Church of England, Michael Ipgrave (now Bishop of Woolwich), approached me to join a small group of Hindus and Christians, to meet as an informal forum, with the agenda first of all of getting to know each other and then to see whether we could initiate a national Hindu–Christian forum. We were an interest group, handpicked by Michael with his wide networks. Before long Michael asked me to become joint chair with a prominent Hindu leader, Dr Bhan, a vice-president of the Inter Faith Network, and chair of the Vishwa Hindu Parishad, a powerful Hindu organization in India linked with the BJP, the ruling party at that time, and the militant activist movement, the RSS. I agreed to this, and we proceeded step by step.

The context of the Forum

The Council of Christians and Jews (CCJ) was formed at the time of the Holocaust (1942) to enable reconciliation and a new beginning in Christian–Jewish relations. A Christian–Muslim Forum was formed in 2004, after an extensive listening exercise, and it is now a settled part of English religious and public life.

The third religion of the UK, and indeed of the world, is Hinduism, with a global population of around one billion, and British numbers, in 2001, of 559,000, equal to the population of Sheffield (which has risen considerably since then, with the coming of large numbers of Sri Lankan Tamils, the majority Hindu). The fast-growing importance of India economically, the significance of the Indian diaspora to life in the UK, and the great contribution made at local and national level of Hindus to Councils of Faiths, and bodies such as the Inter Faith Network UK, made it obvious that the next bilateral forum to be considered should be that of Christians and Hindus. Another fact was the geographical spread of Hindus, and their professional and educational contribution. So many UK citizens had experienced Hindus as doctors, nurses, teachers, shopkeepers and academics.

The early years of the Forum

There was no formal establishment of the Forum. The group called together by Michael Ipgrave included Anglicans, Roman Catholics, Methodist, United Reformed and Indian Christians. Later a Baptist participated. Hindus who participated were members of ISKCON (Hare Krishna), Swaminarayan, the British Hindu Council, the British Hindu Forum, Vishwa Hindu Parishad and the National Council of Hindu Temples. There were never more than 25 included. By far the majority were men, and on the Hindu side almost exclusively. On the Christian side, most of the members had a fair knowledge of Hinduism, and some a lifetime experience of it. The Hindus usually had a working knowledge of Christianity, though few were scholars in dialogue. A first agenda was set to consider the nature of the Hindu community in the UK, conversion issues, media representations and secularizing atheism in the UK.

Three or four meetings a year were held from 2001 until 2007. They were alternatively in Hindu and in Christian premises, in Leicester or in London, and lasted several hours on a Saturday. Topics for discussion varied between the theological and the practical. There was a degree of coming together, but also some hesitancy and suspicion pervading the atmosphere at times. Fear of Christian mission, and the dominance of conversion questions, overshadowed meetings and hindered progress. It became clear also that there was an unseen third party in the room, with considerable feelings, usually unexpressed but sometimes coming out openly, that relating to Muslims was the primary Christian agenda and that, because Hindus did not cause disturbance, they could be largely ignored, or treated as of secondary importance.

A major issue from the beginning was whether questions related to India could be addressed in the Forum. The general understanding was that India should not be the primary focus of attention, and that the Forum was about the UK. However, it was understood, from the Christian side at least, that what happens in India does impact upon Hindu–Christian relations in the UK, and that the distinction neither could nor should be made absolute. A parallel is what we experienced in Leicester with a Jewish–Christian Forum. This had to be suspended for several months when misunderstandings arose about Israel–Palestine. It was agreed that the Forum would continue but avoid questions of the Holy Land. This was artificial, but was the only way forward.

Some fruitful meetings were held in these years. Memorable was the warmth of welcome at Bhaktivedanta Manor, Watford, and discussions about the ISKCON document on dialogue, a model of its kind. ISKCON's willingness to be seen as a missionary organization was often helpful in our dialogues, particularly about mission and conversion. Excellent day discussions were held on Grace, Prayer, and Suffering.

A very significant meeting was held in the Sanatan Mandir in Leicester. This was within a day visit by Dr Rowan Williams, Archbishop of Canterbury, in 2003. At the beginning of this day, the Archbishop was shown round the temple by a local Hindu, and he showed great attention as he always does. He presented an ikon to the temple, and the temple presented a statue of dancing Siva to the Archbishop. There was a major meal for large numbers of local people, and he was led through to the dining hall under a dedicated arch of flowers. I asked why they were putting so much effort and money into the day and its detailed preparations. The answer was moving: that they wished to honour a living saint. There then followed a meeting of the Forum.

At the beginning, the Archbishop said how important it was to ask questions in critical encounter. He spoke about how he hoped the forum would address issues of spirituality, theology and Scripture, since this is what had happened in India at its best, and we now had an opportunity here. He spoke of Father Bede Griffiths as an example. He endorsed the request that Hindus should have people included when the House of Lords is reformed (still in process now nine years later!), and he said he would be happy to consider their issues with sympathy meanwhile. Discussion followed on some of the media reporting of the killing of Graham Staines in Orissa, and assumptions of its being linked with Hindu extremists. The Archbishop also offered to consider issues related to attacks on temples, such as the recent incident in Wembley, within a concern for the protection of all religious buildings. At this point, Israel Selvanayagam, an Indian Christian theologian working in the UK at the time, raised further questions related to India, including questions of religious freedom in Gujarat and a regulation of conversion bill in Tamil Nadu. This was indeed a highlight of the story of the forum, and of the Archbishop's engagement with Hinduism.

This was followed by two open sessions, one where Hindus spoke of their faith journey, and the other built around Christian stories. Hindu emphases varied. Bimal Krishna Das of ISKCON said he was concerned about truth, and questions such as: who are we, where do we come from, what is the purpose of life, what is before birth and after life? Others looked at caste and class, at the origin of Hindu ethics, at what makes a Brahmin, at the concept of the guru, the one who helps others to move from darkness to life. Concern was expressed about chaplains of Roman Catholic or Muslim faith who acted exclusively in their prisons.

Another meeting looked at stereotypes of each faith, and the danger of using these in the absence of people of the faith being stereotyped, and the need for members of the group to show an example by countering such stereotyping.

The most significant achievement by the Forum was 'An Agreed Statement of Goodwill'. I quote this here in full:

1 We respect one another's faiths as sources of spirituality and of ethics, while acknowledging our differences of belief and practice.

2 We affirm the importance for both our communities of religious freedom:

(a) Freedom to worship according to the practices of one's own faith.

(b) Freedom to teach the tenets of either faith.

(c) Freedom for those who wish themselves to change their belief after due deliberation and thought, and as an expression of genuine spiritual commitment.

(d) Freedom for those who do not wish to change their faith to be left alone to practise either religion without further intrusion.

We recognize that the balancing of one another's interests in the exercise of these freedoms can be a sensitive matter. There is a fine line between laudable enthusiasm and destructive fanaticism, and anyone can cross that line, whether deliberately or unintentionally.

3 We believe that it is necessary to repudiate strategies for conversion which are coercive or manipulative. In particular:

(a) Medical, educational and social welfare services must not be misused to facilitate conversions.

(b) Conversions must not be sought through force, fraud, threat, illicit means, grant of financial or other aid, or exploiting a person's poverty, ill health, mental weakness or without due consideration.

(c) The methods employed to propagate either religion should be explicit and acceptable to the two communities. They must not be of such a kind as to encroach on the freedom of religion of citizens.

(d) Persons contemplating to change their faith should be advised to consider carefully the impact their decision may have on themselves, their family, and their community.

4 We unequivocally condemn all attacks on places of worship and on members of religious groups; we disown individuals or organizations responsible for such attacks, and we urge responsible and accurate reporting of these events by the media. We believe it is very important that Christians and Hindus should meet together to listen to one another's concerns and to affirm their respect for one another, and we invite our fellow believers of both faiths to engage together in dialogue, mutual learning, and service of the community.

Full agreement is here reached about full condemnation of attacks on places of worship and members of religious groups. This became very pertinent afterwards, with the attacks upon churches and Christians in Orissa, Karnataka and Gujarat. It became a grey area, since it was in India, but unequivocal voices of condemnation were few and far between from the UK. Much of the statement about conversion is perhaps more directly applicable in India than in the UK.

The comment in the statement about the media is also pertinent. Hindu members feel the media does not give them a fair hearing, unlike, in their view, Christians or Muslims. Examples are issues related to sacred cows in the UK falling ill, and clashes with the RSPCA who insist they should be slaughtered – which happened in Bhaktivedanta Manor, Watford, and in a temple in Wales.

What lacked clarity was who was bound by the statement. Was it just the individuals of the forum? What of their parent bodies? It was clear, for example, with the VHP, that this could not bind the Indian VHP. It was unclear how far British organizations had agreed. And what of our churches?

The statement never came to official circles, nor was it ever published.

Weaknesses The Forum never had any money, and hence depended entirely on the goodwill and voluntary labour of its members. There was no money even for travel expenses, and members had to bear this themselves, or draw down funds from their sponsoring organizations. Nor was there any paid administration, and dependence here was on the organizations employing the leaders. This limited the number of meetings that could be held, and activities that could be initiated. Ideas were not lacking, but the means to implement them. The leaders themselves were involved as an add-on to everything else they were doing, and members attended by grace.

Commitment to the idea of the Forum was strong from some individuals, who kept things going. Others were only nominally members, and they were distinguished by their non-attendance. But there was no mechanism for dropping people, unless they so agreed. Women and young people were conspicuous by their absence.

The Indian Christian question Indian Christians are 30 million, and there are growing numbers in the UK. As joint chair, I involved them from the beginning with two representatives. Robin Thomson brought in Sivagopalan Kumar, a Baptist minister and Brahmin convert, who calls himself a *Jesu Bhakter*. Robin and I had also served as missionaries in India. My co-chair was not happy with an article I wrote on Hindutva, and I had a two-hour meeting with him, which was very useful from both sides in bringing clarification, if not agreement. This helped the knowledge of Hinduism in the group, but increased the suspicion, I am told, of hidden agendas, in view of the extreme sensitivities on conversion issues. Also we were clear that caste has not gone away, either in India or in the UK. Softening does not mean abolition. This made someone of Israel's background uncomfortable at times in the Forum, I felt.

Strengths The strong feeling was that there was a need for this forum, and this was one of the fruits of these early years. It became clear that it was not about whether to go forward but how to go forward. There was also a growing commitment from the Inter Faith Network, and then the Department of Communities and Local Government (DCLG), that they wished to support and undergird a forum of some kind. Important topics were discussed.

These included the report *Connecting British Hindus*, published in 2006, introduced by Ramesh Kallidai of the Hindu Forum, now a major player among Hindus. He made the significant observation that 85 per cent of respondents did not like to be named 'Asian'. They split 50:50 on being called 'Hindu' or 'Indian'. Respondents say there are multiple ways of expressing their identity, including British/Hindu/Indian/Asian. This is typical of diaspora communities. Dialogue was held at the Home Office in 2006 on the Incitement to Religious Hatred Bill. The resulting bill was seen as a damp squib, and Israel quoted the words of St Paul, about 'speaking the truth in love' (Ephesians 4.15), and said that there needs to be more of a cutting edge in the legislation. Israel also took part in an open dialogue invited by South Asia Concern about their website. This is an evangelical organization, and Israel suggested a sentence should be added about a commitment to good interfaith relations, and the need for Asian Christians to be educated to take part in dialogue. Gauri Das, an ISKCON representative, said clarity about commitment to Christ should not be seen as negative by Hindus, as long as this did not mean being derogatory about Hindus, something understandably they are very sensitive about.

Israel was one of three Christians who spoke of his faith journey at a meeting in 2004. He told how he had been brought up to feel himself superior to Hindus, as a Christian brought up in a remote village. But he had much broadened in his faith, as he helped to liberate his co-villagers from various oppressions, while studying to the highest level. On coming to the UK in the 1990s he had been shocked by the lack of spiritual maturity of Christians here. His own faith centres on the love of God, which only comes alive when God shares in his suffering, as a mother cries with her child. He now feels his Christ-centred spirituality is integrated and inclusive.

I reported on two European conferences, one of the WCC in Rome about conversion, where I had drawn attention to the goodwill statement; and one major conference of the European Churches in Romania, where my efforts to get Hinduism included on the agenda, as well as Abrahamic faiths, failed.

Provision of chaplaincy was another area we were involved in, and this meant expressing the need for Hindu as well as Muslim chaplains in a range of institutions. We raised the question with the Home Office of visa requirements for Hindu priests, in the light of increased English-language requirements for imams and others. At that stage (January 2006), they were not included because their duties did not include counselling or preaching, or house visiting. *Pujaris* (temple priests) chant the rituals in Sanskrit.

The saga of the listening exercise

In 2006, the decision was made to initiate a listening exercise, modelled on the Muslim–Christian exercise above. It was felt that the Forum needed some more energy, and to be more representative. It was decided to focus upon Leicester, London and Lancashire. Visits were to take place in 2007, to be undertaken by members of the group, and were to be organized by a steering group which was to meet at Lambeth Palace, at the invitation of Guy Wilkinson, Archbishop's Officer for Inter Faith Relations. There was some hope of getting a civil servant seconded to take the role that Julian Bond had taken most effectively in the Muslim–Christian exercise. This was a hopeful period, and the minutes of the time record how plans were to be made for a national conference to be held in 2008, which would be addressed by the Archbishop of Canterbury.

Things had progressed by April 2007, and there was now a grant from the Community Development Foundation to help with finances. Guy Wilkinson commented, 'We need to do everything we can to demonstrate to the wider world that relationships between the faith communities are not the source of conflict that they are too widely perceived to be.'

However, all juddered to a halt in April 2007. To the amazement of Guy Wilkinson and all the four Christians on the steering group, the four concerned Hindus withdrew from the listening exercise unilaterally. They were from the Hindu Forum, Hindu Council, VHP and National Council of Hindu Temples. This took place in a two-line email sent by Jay Lakhani of the Hindu Council. A press release was promised about the reasons, though that was never published. It took several weeks for me to find out from my co-chair, Dr Bahn, himself not on the listening exercise group, what were the stated reasons. These were two: that the Archbishop had received at Lambeth a delegation of Dalits, through the Christian Solidarity Forum, and was felt to have implicitly endorsed their demands, including the inclusion of the caste issue within the equalities legislation in the UK (an error of fact); and that research had shown that Christian organizations in India were involved in inappropriate methods of mission and inducing conversion, as reported in a document written by Anusha Prasad, of the Hindu Forum (later a report that was disowned by the chair of the Forum, and of dubious academic validity). It was later clear also that there were rivalries and lack of trust among Hindu organizations involved.

Next stages

It was decided to leave a gap for all to take stock, and then to try again. There was a conviction from both Christians and Hindus that to have this forum was important. This was encouraged by the interest now shown by the Inter Faith Network, which was concerned about what had happened between two of its most significant members. With the Network's encouragement, it was decided to go to the Department of Communities and Local Government (of the then Labour government), to seek funding for a listening exercise to be facilitated by a paid academic from a recognized university. At the same time, it was agreed to continue with meetings of the Forum, as before, making sure that all the main Hindu organizations were represented, as above. Meetings continued in a peaceful way, around largely theological and spiritual themes. This felt like a holding time. And DCLG eventually came up with an adequate grant, which needed to be supplemented by small amounts from different churches and Hindu organizations. A researcher recognized in this field was engaged, from De Montfort University, and she worked hard in preparing a presentation about how she intended to go about the work, following the guidelines as drawn up for the previous aborted attempt.

It was then discovered that DCLG could only pay the money to a recognized charity known to them, and their suggestion was that the grant should be made to St Philip's Centre. This would be an in–out transaction, and the exercise was ready to go, and dates pencilled. However, things foundered again, because the Hindu group overseeing the listening exercise said they were not happy for the money to go through an explicitly Christian organization. There was a long further delay, and meanwhile the engaged researcher had moved to the far north of England, and her new employer did not agree to her secondment for this work. It should also be noted that St Philip's trustees were not happy with the complicated quasi-legal memorandum, drawn up by Hindu members, which they would be expected to sign. DCLG kindly did not impose a strict deadline, but allowed time for this latest stumbling block to be overcome.

The comment of this first researcher is pertinent as a summary of the problems she met: 'I do not fully understand the complexities underlying such difficulties – though it seems to be that there could be issues around history, ownership, risk management, conflict of interest, communication, representation and trust.' Trust was very fragile, and the only way to overcome this was to form a new sub-company to run the listening exercise. It engaged the Oxford Centre for Hindu Studies, and a researcher employed by them, Jessica Frazier.

Newly launched Forum

The resulting research report is titled *Bridges and Barriers to Hindu–Christian Relations*. It was released in June 2011, and given a high profile at Lambeth Palace, with the Archbishop and the head of Bhaktivedanta Manor making significant speeches, at what was a relaunch of the Forum. This seemed to many like a first launch, but the above narrative shows how much had already been done over the years, by a committed group from the two faiths, and this should not be overshadowed by the problems around the listening exercise.

There is no space here to summarize the well-researched and balanced report. I feel it underestimates the problems, but maybe this is a healthy balance after the three immediately preceding years. I just highlight one of the consequential aims of the Forum: to research models of good practice in local dialogue and shared service to the community. The Leicester Forum above shows there can be good models, if they can be sustained. Encouragement from a national body would be very helpful, and clusters of local models can be formed and sustained. What is important is that these are not about one-off events, but building up a group together.

In 2009 I had handed over the chairmanship to the Archdeacon of Leicester, Richard Atkinson, who has recently become Bishop of Bedford. Dr Bhan had ceased to be co-chair at the same time, and Ramesh Pattni took over, someone deeply committed to the vision of a forum. Some funds have been accessed from the Near Neighbours Fund of the Church

Urban Fund, for conducting one-off events, such as a dialogue programme held in Leicester and a dance programme in Neasden Temple. But finance is still lacking for a paid worker, which I would see as essential for the work of the forum to develop as might be hoped. Various plans were made earlier which could not be implemented for various reasons, among them lack of staffing. Two examples were plans for a major residential conference, with Rowan Williams booked to give a keynote address, which would have involved academics and practitioners. Another was for a scriptural workshop, on the lines of the Muslim–Christian Building Bridges seminars, which was to lead to a publication. I drew up the plan with Bimal Krishna Das in early 2005 – but he was then transferred to India, and the initiative went no further.

Another key need is in the training area. There are few clergy with adequate knowledge, and above all experience of Hinduism or Hindus. For this, some experience of India is not just desirable, but I feel essential. Perhaps Israel, now back in South India, could play a role here. Abrahamic faiths dominate the learning agenda in theological colleges and in local contexts. So also Hindus have focused on developing their structures and temples in our cities. Here the Oxford Centre has been a very helpful development. As British Hindus grow in their knowledge of their faith, hopefully they can grow also in what it can contribute in dialogue with Christians and others. This means they need to know something of these faiths. So mutual education should be a major focus of an ongoing forum.

Hindu response from Ramesh Pattni, at Oxford University through the Centre for Hindu Studies, joint chair of the Hindu–Christian Forum UK[1]

The HCF in its conception and development has gone through the classic stages of formation of many groups, stages of 'forming, storming, norming and performing'. The added dimensions of a long history of Hindu–Christian interactions and relations on the subcontinent of India, and the backgrounds, experiences, hopes and aspirations of the participants, sometimes made it a challenging and difficult journey. There were times when the storms of complex views and positions made the Forum dysfunctional, and periods when we seem to making substantial progress. In particular for the Hindu members, the topic of conversion seemed to lurk in the background as the 'ultimate Christian agenda', and at other times was openly being discussed as a barrier to all Hindu–Christian relations. There were periods when the Hindu mistrust of Christian personal and organizational agendas made things come to a standstill, and other occasions when there was a feeling of understanding, camaraderie and a deeper understanding of each other as individuals and as the 'other'. The turning point came when, through the shifting membership of the organization, the appropriate people, energies and commitment came together to make the HCF a performing group that went on to commission the *Bridges and Barriers* report. This well-researched project by the Oxford Centre for Hindu Studies gave us the focus and objective to direct our energies. Not only did the report give us the context and the goals within which to work, but it also made the Forum a 'performing' entity which now has a vision and a programme, including a conference on yoga, plans for further interactions of the members and communities through the Near Neighbours Programme, and setting up networks of Hindu–Christian groups through the country to create a network feeding into the national forum. Challenges and difficulties, especially funding, lie ahead, but the HCF has at least the energy, commitment and inner resources to move forward within the framework of deeper sincere relationships, resilient and sincere friendships, and working within the communities to share our theologies and actions for the mutual benefit of the Hindu and Christian communities.

The Hindu–Christian Forum since 2010

I include here also the reflections from Richard Atkinson, now Bishop of Bedford, who became joint chair after me. Written at the beginning of 2014, this brings the story up to date (almost!).

Bridges and barriers to Hindu–Christian relations The *Bridges and Barriers* report is important not just for its overview of Hindu–Christian relations in the UK today, but because it set the agenda for the HCF for the coming years:

- Develop a positive dialogue between Hindus and Christians;
- Explore each other's theology and spirituality, including scriptural study;
- Address issues of concern through honest and open discussion;
- Strengthen the contribution of faiths in the public square;
- Encourage and develop joint educational and other activities;
- Develop and provide resources for Hindu and Christian groups to engage with each other;
- Research models of good practice in local dialogue and shared service of the community;

- Monitor the media and respond to inaccurate presentation of Hindus and Christians and where necessary provide a credible point of contact for the media on Hindu–Christian relations;
- Liaise with national bodies and policy makers to represent and profile Hindu–Christian relations.

To a very large extent, not least because of the continued challenges of funding and resources, this remains aspirational, but it provides a focus and direction for HCF.

Near Neighbours The government-financed Near Neighbours programme included within the £5 million grant to the Church Urban Fund a modest three-year commitment to enable HCF to be one of the bilateral partners in Near Neighbours delivery. Initially the proposal was made to run two significant residential events in Leicester and London, followed by further such events in subsequent years. Hindu and Christian invitees would spend time together sharing their faith journeys and exploring how they might work together for the good of their neighbourhoods. The plan was then for participants to work together on a Near Neighbours project before returning for a follow-up day.

Although a good residential meeting was held at Launde Abbey in Leicestershire and a similar day in east London, it became clear that this was not an effective way of developing Hindu–Christian relations. Eventually it was decided to employ Paresh Solanki on a part-time basis to develop a series of one-off events, which have been much more successful. These include the grass-roots 'Comparing Notes' conversations and a shared visit to temples and churches in Leicester.

The Near Neighbours programme has been an opportunity for HCF to extend its work, including the development of an effective website. If phase two happens there will not be the same funding provision, although HCF will be able to be involved with some of the faith-leader development work and in other local events. Near Neighbours has caused tensions for HCF in that it has tended to drive the agenda and made it harder to find time both for some of the other priorities highlighted in *Bridges and Barriers* and for opportunities to mutually explore the faith traditions.

Inter Faith Week The offer of a grant from DCLG to provide an event for Inter Faith Week in 2011 resulted in an evening of reflection, food and music at BAPS Swaminarayan Mandir and The Swaminarayan School, London. In 2013 HCF shared in the organization of an event at the

Zoroastrian centre in Harrow to celebrate the one hundred and fiftieth anniversary of the birth of Swami Vivekananda. At this event the Rt Revd Richard Atkinson gave the keynote speech.

Lambeth Palace Alternating between Hindu and Christian venues has been an important emphasis for HCF with either the ISKCON Mandir off London's Oxford Street or BAPS Swaminarayan Mandir being the main Hindu venues. In 2012 a memorable Christmas meeting, with vegetarian Christmas lunch, was held at the Bhaktivedanta Manor, Watford.

The main Christian venue has been Lambeth Palace, which has a wider significance as a place of meeting and dialogue for faith communities. Not only was it the venue for the launch of the present Forum, but earlier in 2011 Archbishop Rowan Williams invited Hindus to hear his reflections on his visit to India and his dialogue with the Swamis. Equally welcome was an initial meeting of HCF with Archbishop Justin Welby in December 2013 with his offer of shared work on prayer, mission and reconciliation.

The contributions of successive Inter Faith Advisers at Lambeth, Canon Guy Wilkinson and Canon Toby Howarth, have been crucial to the development of HCF, as was the work of Kate Wharton, whose specialist interest in Hinduism was of particular value to the Forum.

Events Although Near Neighbours events have driven the agenda recently, HCF has continued to make space for occasions that allow for dialogue and understanding. In November 2012 Forum members used the Niland Retreat Centre in Hertfordshire for a day meeting which included the opportunity for each person to share a text with particular significance for him or her, as well as time for silent reflection. 'The Concept of God in the Bhagavad-Gita: Hindu Views and Christian Responses' was an event held in both Birmingham and London at which Ramesh Pattni and Kate Wharton were the speakers.

Challenges Recent years have seen a growth in trust and friendship among Forum members. Central to this was the completion of the *Bridges and Barriers* project, along with a growing readiness to listen to each other when the inevitable challenges and harder issues arise. The well-publicized personal comments of an Italian Roman Catholic priest on the evils of yoga resulted in a statement from HCF and, more significantly, was the prompt for the successful day conference on yoga held at Heythrop College, London. More recently, the inclusion of 'Caste' as a category within the Equalities Legislation has led to much challenging conversation, as well as shared concerns about aspects of what is proposed, not least the underlying research. The ability to talk about the hard issues is a sign of maturity for interfaith relations.

Organization HCF continues to reflect on its structure and membership. There is awareness that most of the members live in London and there is a commitment to address the gender imbalance. However, the current structure of six Hindu and six Christian representatives (the Hindus being representatives of the British Hindu Council, British Hindu Forum, Vishwa Hindu Parishad, National Council of Hindu Temples, ISKCON and Swaminarayan; the Christians drawn from the Church of England, Baptist Church, United Reform Church, Methodist Church, Roman Catholic Church and South Asia Concern) continues to be the preferred structure.

The future The year 2014 will see further Near Neighbours events, the continued development of the website, and work to encourage shared action by Hindus and Christians. The opportunity to work with staff at Lambeth Palace will be taken forward, as will the priorities from *Bridges and Barriers*. The need to raise funds to continue the employment of a development consultant is a priority.

Final reflection on the story, in the light of the four acknowledged Principles of Inter Faith Dialogue[2]

- *Dialogue begins when people meet people.* This certainly happened over these years, and there was a consistent commitment from a small group of people to stick together. But we never quite got beyond the language of 'two sides'.
- *Dialogue depends upon mutual understanding and trust.* As Ramesh Pattni said above, this came and went and came again, but was never secure. This was because there was a willingness to tackle difficult subjects, but we remained at the mercy of those who were not members of the Forum who did not trust its validity, and of what happened in India. Different views of conversion could never be really reconciled, in spite of the goodwill statement.
- *Dialogue leads to common service in the community.* We had a wish to do something here, but never the capacity. It would have made much difference if we could have isolated a project and done it together, not just giving mutual solidarity to each other when one or other suffers.

- *Dialogue is a means of authentic witness.* We were able to share our faith journeys quite effectively at times, without any hidden agendas. We were each able to respect the other. I have found this in educational work with theological students involving dialogue with Hindu leaders such as Ramesh Pattni. There will always be a difference about fundamentals, but if these are acknowledged it is perfectly possible to go forward, following the title of my book, *Celebrating Difference, Staying Faithful.*[3]

11

Theological, spiritual and missiological challenges

The meeting between Hindus and Christians in the West is not just a practical challenge, how to enable these two communities to work with each other to contribute together to the common good. It is also a profound theological encounter, with spiritual and missiological implications. It is crossing a divide far more radical than that between Christians and Muslims, or Christians and Jews. The Abrahamic faiths represent one world view, whatever the differences between them. They come out of the same cradle of the Middle East. They are in linear sequence one after the other. They have a dateable history, and clear scriptural markers by which they can be assessed, and the changes one from the other, be measured. It is standard to suggest that 'there are very few differences between Muslims and Christians'. This is true at one level, though of course those differences are immense in implication. So also between Jews and Christians. Those differences especially concern the person of Jesus, the question of cross and resurrection, and the nature of God as Trinity.

But the list of challenges becomes both wider and deeper as we turn to the Eastern faiths, and in particular to the relationship to Hinduism. This can be seen as I list and comment on the issues involved. But there is also the prior question of the diversity of Hinduism and of Hindus. There are certain boundaries to what makes a Muslim or a Christian. This is because they are credal religions, and adhere around books/ Scriptures which are fundamental to those creeds. There is vast diversity within both, the result of long histories, and contextual differences as they have fulfilled the challenge of their founders to become global religions. There are a limited number of profound splits – between Christianity East and West, between post-Reformation protestant churches and Catholic churches based on Rome; and in more recent times, between traditional denominations and churches of the Spirit, both Pentecostal and indigenous. Within Islam, there is not just the Sunni–Shia divide, but also that with Sufism, and wide divisions within Sunni Islam between Wahabis and others. But theological differences are comparatively small compared with what we now consider, that between Hindus and Christians. Here, the very diversity of Hinduism is difficult for Christians to relate to, not so much practically and spiritually, but theologically. What are some of the main challenges for Christians in understanding Hinduism, yet alone relating to it?

The question of God/gods

This is an immensely confusing question for Christians to address as they relate to Hindus: do they worship one God, many gods? Are they polytheists, or monotheists, or panentheists, or pantheists (worshippers of many Gods, or one God, or believers that God is in all things, or everything is God)? At one extreme are those who are insistent that there is only one God, who is termed normally Brahman, but can also be Krishna or Swaminarayan (see other chapters) or whoever. Other gods are manifestations of this one God (see next section on idols). Others are clear that there is one God for them, their *ishta devata*, the one they choose, be it a family god, their village god, or one who has especially helped them. Other gods are respected, but this is the one that has pride of place in their house, and whose temple they go to visit when they return to India. For others, there are truly many gods with different characteristics, and they go to one or another, depending on their need of the moment. These are the classic gods. But there are also the countless village gods, those worshipped under banyan trees, or in ant hills, or in crude local temples, with a range of local practices which can involve animal sacrifice. These are the kinds of gods recorded in William Dalrymple's book, *Nine Lives*.[1] Some are quite fearsome, Kali-style deities. What is clear all over is that female balances with male in how gods are seen, with the one being worshipped alongside the other. Everything is potentially God, and this is why the normal greeting of *Namaste* (Gujarati, Hindi), or *Vanakkam* (Tamil), means 'May the God in you be blessed'). If this applies to human beings, and because of the belief in reincarnation all life is potentially one, then God can be found in all living things. The challenge then is to think: what is the God beyond? If there is none, then this is pantheism.

The further problem for Christians in relating to this variety of possibilities is that every Hindu may give a different answer to the question: how many gods, do Hindus worship one God, and whom do you worship? This is the attraction of Hinduism – there are so many possibilities. It is also the great puzzle for the Western mind. Something should be this or that (the Aristotelian law of the excluded middle); it cannot be both this and that – both many gods and one God, both male and female, both in all things and beyond all things.

But this complexity is also very attractive. It is noteworthy how many Indian Muslims go to Hindu festivals, or worship at tombs of saints in a Hindu-type way. These are converts of many generations, but still they overlap in the villages. So also Indian Christians, who in the village context engage in a mixture of practices; see P. Luke and J. Carman's *Village Christians in Hindu Culture.*[2] Both groups, Christians more than Muslims, engage in practices that they should not be doing, so strong is the pull of their heritage. This natural religiosity can be found also in popular Catholicism, particularly in Latin contexts and in Ireland as it used to be, and in Poland. When does a saint become de facto a god?

The question of 'idols'

A Western Christian going into a temple will see a whole range of gods. A Hindu guide will tell what are their names, and what are the stories associated with them. The guide will speak of them using a variety of words. He or she may call them 'idols', or 'deities', most commonly. The guide will not realize probably that the word used will have an effect on the Christian listener. **Idol** is the least appealing, since there is so much material in the Old Testament deeply condemning of idol worship, including the fourth of the Ten Commandments.

The term **image** may also be used. Here a bridge can be considered, since in the book of Genesis human beings are created in the 'image' of God. And in the Epistle to the Colossians, Paul calls Jesus the 'image of the invisible God' (1.15), and we are called to put on the new self, and to be 'renewed' after the image of the Creator, where 'there is no Greek or Jew . . . slave or free . . . but Christ is all, and is in all' (3.11).

Rowan Williams writes in depth about ikons in the Eastern Orthodox tradition, in his book *Lost Ikons:*[3]

> The traditional ikon . . . is never meant to be a reproduction of the realities you see around you; it is not even meant to show what these realities will ever look like.
>
> The point of the ikon is to give us a window into an alien frame of reference that is at the same time the structure that will make definitive sense of the world we inhabit. It is sometimes described as a channel for the 'energies' of that other frame of reference to be transmitted to the viewer.

Could this be likened to the interaction between the pious Hindu devotee and the image in front of him or her, as the worshipper lies prostrate or sits in quiet meditation? Is this very different from the sight of an Orthodox Russian woman in St Petersburg, queuing patiently for the chance to touch a beloved ikon of Mary or of Jesus Christ? The Hindu talks of receiving *darshan*, grace from being in touch with a favoured deity, and probably receiving materially *prasadam*, blessed food.

Rowan Williams goes on to say:

> The Church that commissioned and used such images knew perfectly well that God and heaven don't 'look like' anything, and that divine reality can't be rendered exhaustively in material terms. The image gives directions, it essays a way of bringing you into a new place and a new perception.[4]

Can similar be said of an image of Krishna, or of Lakshmi? Of course, there is all the difference in the world between Krishna and Jesus, yes, but the act of devotion may have similar connotations.

Another word that can be used is **symbol**. A flag symbolizes what lies behind it; so does the Olympic torch. This has great power, beyond just being a piece of cloth or a burning flame. The insulting of a flag is considered a desecration of what lies behind it. Hence the symbolic power of the decision in 2012 to stop flying the Union Flag every day from Belfast Town Hall. This led to days of rioting from Unionists who saw it as an insult to their commitment to the unity of the United Kingdom. So a deity can be a kind of symbol of what lies behind that image. For example, the goddess Lakshmi is a symbol of the understanding that all wealth is a gift of God: 'Everything comes from you, and we have given you only what comes from your hand' (see 1 Chronicles 29.14). Saraswati is the goddess of learning, so all learning is a gift of God, and she is a symbol of this.

Another word can be **sacrament**. In the Anglican catechism, as it used to be learned by confirmation candidates, a sacrament is 'an outward and visible sign of an inward and spiritual grace'. The cleansing water of baptism, or the oil of healing, is an example of this, or the signing of the cross in absolution of sins. Water, oil or the hand making the sign of the cross are not in themselves powerful. What is powerful is what they signify, the inward and spiritual grace that they offer. So it can be with the image of a Hindu god or goddess – in itself just a stone or wooden figure, or a picture. But what is powerful is what energy these images can release, as they point beyond. The sign is sacred, is a sacrament, because of what it points towards. Roger Hooker wrote a short but powerful book, called *What Is Idolatry?*[5] This considers the different ways that the Hindu devotee may see an idol, compared with how the Christian may consider the blessed sacrament of the bread and wine, especially the reserved sacrament. This may be taken as literally the body and blood of Christ. Or it may be a sign of this. For other Christians, to sit before the blessed sacrament can seem, or even be described as, idolatrous. The consecration of bread and wine at the altar may be a literal transformation, or a sign of the real presence of Christ, or a memory of the last supper, helping to create faith in the eyes of the believers, which is where the real presence is found. So with the different ways a Hindu image may be seen or experienced. And as with the Eucharist, or mass, so here it depends where one is coming from, and it is not necessarily that one way is more acceptable than another. The key question again is: whose image is this a symbol of?

I am reminded of the story of the French village priest who used to go into his church each morning, and he observed an old woman kneeling before a crucifix and staring at Jesus. She was always there, and one day he asked her what she was doing. She replied, 'I look at him, and he looks at me, and we are happy.' This could describe Hindu devotion at its most appealing. But of course, so much is not like this. I believe that the Holy Spirit is a gift to help us to discern what is good and wholesome in another faith, particularly one which is so complex as Hinduism, and what should and must be avoided by a Christian. I think of a visit in 2011 to a village temple near Madurai, Tamil Nadu. It is a place where animal sacrifice takes place every Friday, to the god Pandi. It has surprisingly grown more popular over the years I have known it, with its devotees now coming out from the city, and coming from all castes, including Brahmins.

On this occasion, I talked to a devotee, an intelligent young woman who was training to be an airline pilot. She had come to get the god's blessing for her studies. She was very clear that this village god – probably originally a local hero raised up to deity status – has real power, and also that he is a separate deity, one of many, but a most powerful one. Clearly she is a polytheist. But when we went into the various small temples around, there was, as I found it, an unhealthy atmosphere. One god was receiving 'beedis', the local cigar, for that was what he smokes. Babies were brought to another, and ash was put in their ears. More disturbingly, there was a group of women – all women – shouting in tongues and running round ecstatically. Around each there were four or five women, and an interpreter, giving meaning to her shouting, and seeing it as prophetic. Money changed hands as an offering for her divine guidance. Then there took place something I found deeply disturbing. I made the mistake of trying to take a photo, using a camera on which I had forgotten to switch off the flash. My purpose was to take an unusual photo to help me in teaching about the whole of Hinduism. As the camera flashed, the woman hissed, and ran at me, throwing her hands around and attempting to hit me, and also most notably, throwing *vibuthi*, sacred ash, at me. I ran away, protected by the two Tamil friends who had brought me. On returning to the road, my colleague who had come with me, and already withdrawn, suggested we said the Lord's Prayer: 'Deliver us from evil'. Could it be that somehow the possessed woman recognized the presence of Christ with us, and wanted to ward such an influence away?

I tell this story at length, lest the reader thinks I can see only the positive in Hindu devotion.

Two other descriptions I have heard appear a little strange, but have been used to enable groups of Christians to understand what is meant by the deities. One is that they are like **angels**. The one God, Brahman, is beyond, and beyond description. But the divine communicates through the visible gods as in the images. So the Jewish or Muslim God communicates through angels. The guardian angel of the individual is the chosen god, the one seen in the shrine in a house, or in the village of origin. This is 'God with us'. Another explanation is that the gods are like **government ministers** – those who have their own departments and do the direct work on behalf of the Prime Minister (Brahman again).

All the above descriptions are part of the sincere effort to communicate to the onlooker the heart of Hindu practice. But some will then add that no deity, image, idol is ultimately necessary. We can go beyond these into direct communication with the divine. This requires a lifetime of practice, prayer and meditation. It is a question of moving through popular *bhakti* practice into the practice of yogic meditation, which requires no image. But as such, this will never be a normal practice, any more than was the way of prayer recorded in the practice of Abhishiktananda, in his various books, and in his remarkable biography as recorded in his letters written when he went up to Rishikesh and lived alone. Here he even left the mass behind, as he realized the kind of oneness outlined in the philosophy of Sankara, and in the central Advaita philosophy. This may attract some Christians in theory, but few can follow it in practice.

The area of grace: works and the link with *karma*

This is an area of historical division among Christians. Superficially, the Reformation hinged upon whether justification/salvation was through good works, or through faith in Christ. The Epistle of James superficially seemed to tend towards the first, Paul's epistles, particularly the Epistle to the Romans, towards the second. Luther reacted very strongly against the ritual practices of his Catholic Church, which when misused were means of ensuring salvation or reductions from purgatory for the believer or for his or her departed relatives. Multiple masses and payment of indulgencies were at the fore in this dispute. But James says clearly that, though faith without works is dead, faith is still to the fore. What is required is good works flowing from faith, otherwise faith becomes another work.

On engaging in discussion with Hindus, we soon enter this area. How much do works of devotion give the devotee good *karma*? So also good works shown in helping the neighbour, the poor, the blind and so on. The benefit may come during this life, or be carried through to the next life. So comes the link with *reincarnation*. We reap what we sow. At the other end, we inherit what came before. Moreover, how far is faith a matter of gift, or a matter of hard work and spiritual practice that we build up? Hindus vary greatly in their response to this area, as many others. There is a philosophy connected with the Saivite side of Hinduism, and with Tamil Hinduism in particular. I took part in a major seminar at the Tamil Nadu Theological Seminary, which was published as *Grace and Saiva Siddhanta*. From the Catholic perspective, a vast study was done: *Grace in Saiva Siddhantham and in St Paul*, by Joseph Jaswant Raj.[6] These books draw on the works of the two great Tamil poets, Thiruvalluvar and Manikkavasagar. There is clearly also a major experience and concept of grace in the Vaishnavite tradition.

Where then the place of *karma*?

The uniqueness of Christ and the cross

The issues here relate, not to the person of Christ or to the cross in itself, but to their uniqueness and universality. Most Hindus have no issue with Christians holding Christ as the centre of their faith as Christians, nor that the cross is inextricably linked with salvation for Christians. The problems, however, are two. Christ can be both god and human; that is not a difficulty. The Hindu may have more difficulty with the humanity of Jesus than his divinity – that Jesus wept, that he was tempted, that he suffered and truly died. Is this what happens to gods? But more significantly, how can Christ be the only way? Does this not diminish the divine, to have only this one vehicle of the divine being with us? What about Rama and Krishna and the Buddha, all the *avataras*? Are they nothing, or are they lesser? The Jalaram Temple in Leicester has a beautiful painting on the roof, in the centre of the temple, with five figures portrayed: Jesus, Mahavira, Gandhi, Guru Nanak, the Buddha. This in pictorial fashion shows the normal Hindu understanding, where the gods or holy figures are equally ranked. The Hindu view can be summarized in the words of Gandhi:

> God did not bear the cross only 1900 years ago, but he bears it today, and he dies and is resurrected from day to day. It would be poor comfort to the world if it had to depend on a historical God who died 2000 years ago. Do not then preach the God of history, but show him as he lives today through you.[7]

> I have never been interested in the historical Jesus. I should not care if it was proved that the man called Jesus never lived, and that what was narrated in the gospels was a figment of the writer's imagination. For the Sermon on the Mount would still be true for me.[8]

> I regard Jesus as a great teacher of humanity, but I do not regard him as the only begotten son of God. That epithet in its material interpretation is quite unacceptable. Metaphorically we are all begotten sons of God, but for each of us there may be different begotten sons of God in a special sense . . .[9]

Here there is clearly a dialogue to be had on the theology of the cross. The Hindu view is consonant with some theories of the atonement, notably the subjective theory propounded by Abelard, that the cross is a supreme example of love in action, and to be responded to in those terms. This is what became known as the 'exemplary' theory of the cross. If one supreme example, why not more? But other understandings are grouped under an objective understanding: on the cross, or in cross and resurrection, something unrepeatable happened, in whatever way it is reflected upon: 'once, only once and once for all, his precious life he gave . . . and what he never can repeat, he shows forth day by day.'[10] Whether it is to redeem the sins of humanity, to be victorious over the last enemy, death, or to give his life as a ransom for many (Mark 10.45), the cross will be a stumbling block for Jews, and foolishness for Greeks. We can add, in that it has a potentially exclusivist feel, abhorrent to Hindus.

Nevertheless, there is a very fruitful area for dialogue. Jesus giving his life for others, as he had washed the feet of his followers – this self-giving love is enormously attractive to a Hindu. It is a special example of *bhakti*, love for God in action.

The challenge of certain ideas

Ahimsa – 'non-violence'

This is primarily a central tenet of Jainism. It is often associated with Hinduism because of Gandhi's commitment to it. It is found in certain ascetic traditions whose followers have renounced the world, and also associated with some traditions within Buddhism. But the majority of traditions within Hinduism do not make 'non-violence' central. And we can see in the Gita that the whole story is based upon the willingness and indeed requirement of the Pandayas to fight and if necessary to kill their relatives. This can be spiritualized away, but remains at the heart of the beautiful and central poem. Hindu stories are full of violence involving the deities as well as human beings. But because of Gandhi and the inspiration he acknowledges from the Sermon on the Mount and the person of Jesus as a model of non-violence, this is a fruitful area for discussion.

Nishkama karma marga

This is one of the many attractive ideas within the Gita. It is the idea that we are to do works of mercy and compassion, but without seeking the fruits of such actions. We should be indifferent to whether we are praised or blamed, but do what is right. If benefit comes to us, we should accept that without being carried away by it; if it does not, then that is fine also. This is a clear concept that provides a challenge to Christians. Our works of compassion should not be to get a good name, but should be done for their own sake. 'Do not let your left hand know what your right hand is doing' (see Matthew 6.3). A clear example is that of the parable of the sheep and the goats in Matthew 25.31–46. Those who have cared for the prisoners, the hungry, the thirsty, the homeless – the 'little ones' – are astonished when they are received into the kingdom of heaven. For they did these things for their own sake, not to get to heaven, or to be seen to be so acting. This is duty for duty's sake, compassion for humanity's sake.

In both faiths, the motivation for helping the one in need is purely because he or she is in need. It is not to get a good name for the giver. This is the same whether it is donating money to a new church or temple, or making a charitable donation to tsunami relief or to Christian Aid. So with giving to a person who is homeless in the streets of London, or on the pavements of Delhi. If we do this to let others see how kind we are, then this is what is condemned, or nullified in terms of *karma*.

The wholeness of life/reincarnation/vegetarianism

Hindus are clear that all life is one. There is no great gulf fixed between humankind and animals. The belief in rebirth means that I may potentially be reborn, in my soul, downwards or upwards in the chain of life. This applies within humanity, and the caste I may take on. But it applies also that I may be reborn as an animal. Vegetarianism is recognizing this, and that I am not to kill an animal for human consumption because I am liable to be killing a fellow soul. Brahman, God, is in all beings (panentheism). Very strict vegetarianism arose under the influence of Jainism and Buddhism in the sixth century BCE, and the animal sacrifice that is enjoined in the Vedas died out. Fruit and flowers and coconuts became the normal offering, though animal sacrifice continued in villages. Different practices are found in different castes. Most Brahmins are vegetarian, though not in Bengal or Kashmir, where they can eat fish. The lower down the caste system you go, the more meat is allowed. But not beef eating, which happens only among outcastes, and of course normally among Muslims and Christians.

Cows are considered sacred animals, and worshipped as such, particularly in Vaishnavism. This is partly because Krishna was a dairyman's son, and he lived among the cows and grazed them in the fields. In all societies, cows are sources of milk and dairy products. They symbolize maternity, endurance and service. The bull is linked also with Siva, as his vehicle. Protection of the cow has become a major Hindu concern. Gandhi considered this had got out of proportion. In 1924, he chastised Hindus who were rioting about cows slaughtered by Muslims. He said this was an insane waste of effort, when they did not worry when the British killed cows.

Dialogue with Hindus in these areas can be very fruitful, and throw Christians back to the challenge of how we care for Creation rather than exploit it for our corporate benefit, something which has caused the enormous ecological crisis we are all in. A symbol of a different attitude has been shown in the Chipko movement in the Himalayan forests. Here tribal women tied themselves to trees which they embraced. To cut the trees down, so important ecologically, would be to cut them down. They embraced them as sacred, and were quite successful in their campaign, which was religious as well as ecological. We can mention also the *Bhumi* ecological project recently developed at the Oxford Centre for Hindu Studies, which has already been active in India and the UK, and aims to become a worldwide movement.

The four stages of life

These are, I think, a very attractive side of the Hindu *dharma*. For each of these stages the *dharma* is different, and of course, there are caste differences. But here is the general pattern. The first stage is that of *bhamacharya*, when the focus is on being a student, and the primary task is that of learning, pushing out the boundaries, being a good student in religion and in life, following a guru or teacher. The second stage is that of the householder (*grihastha*). This is the time of family life, after marriage, and of building up the house and the career. The aim is to make as much progress in these areas and also to enable children to be married well. The third stage is *vanaprastha*, the time when in theory, and occasionally in practice, the Hindu would leave the comfort of home and go into the forest, retiring from his or her career. This is a time when the focus can be on religious devotion, and serving the temple or community. It can involve sexual abstinence, in the famous or infamous case of Gandhi. The fourth stage is that of *sannyasi*, that of renunciation and preparing for death. These are by no means universal, and it is also possible to stay in one stage and make that the place to stay, particularly the second stage.

For Christians, this can be a useful challenge to reflect on our own journeys. Do we focus on the wrong priority when we are worried about not having enough young people in church? Should they not be focusing on exploring the nature of life, and doing their studies well? And the second stage – perhaps too often churches put pressure on parents to be involved in running churches, to the neglect of their main priorities at this stage: bringing up their family well, taking their own career forward, and making the money that will provide security for themselves and their children as they grow older. The third stage is a kind of 'third age' time, when individuals, perhaps a couple, can downsize their house and give up trying to get to the top of their professions; they have come far enough. It is a time to offer themselves to the Church, using all their accumulated experience, and also to focus on their own spiritual journey. The last stage comes to us all, but we often prefer to ignore that death is coming, and to think we will live for ever. It is a time of renunciation, and preparation to go through death to new life (for a Hindu, reincarnation; for a Christian, new resurrected life in Christ).

The nature of salvation and ways to salvation

Classic Advaita understanding of salvation is that this consists of reaching the point where dualism or semi-dualism ends, and we reach a oneness with Brahman, or the divine. We become absorbed into the ocean of the divine, like a river entering the ocean, or a grain of salt being absorbed into the sea. This is *moksha*, or *mukti*. The individual soul is freed, not only from the chains of this world and of perpetual reincarnation, but also from the body and the flesh. In the classical phrase, this is the realization, 'that art thou'. This may be available only to twice-born castes (those in the higher three, of four, caste groups) or be available to all. But the goal is clear, that of absorption in the divine.

This kind of monism is not the only vision. In Ramanujam, and other teachers, there remain two. *Moksha* here means entering into a perfect relationship with the divine, a profound devotional relationship but not one of total absorption. This is much closer to the normal Christian understanding that the Christian hope is about being in the deepest personal relationship with God, which is found in Christ and through his Spirit. How this will be remains unclear, but what is clear is that this is about relationship, and not absorption. St Paul puts it clearly:

> now we see through a glass, darkly; but then face to face: now I know in part; but then shall I know even as also I am known
>
> (1 Corinthians 13.12 AV)

> neither the present nor the future, nor any powers, neither height nor depth, nor anything else in all creation, will be able to separate us from the love of God that is in Christ Jesus our Lord. (Romans 8.38–39)

St John has the vision that eternal life is being with Christ, a foretaste of which we can have while on this earth. In the Synoptic Gospels, salvation is around realizing the kingdom of God, in terms of concrete actions for justice, compassion and peace; that is salvation, and Christ is both the proclaimer of this and also himself the actor who brings in the signs of the kingdom.

What then are the Hindu ways towards salvation? Here the Gita is our primary guide. Here are outlined the three *margas*, three ways. And these are not exclusive. Each is a way, and we will all have a part in each, though for individuals the emphasis will vary. For some, probably the majority, the way of *bhakti* is the main way. This is the way of devotion, of charismatic engagement with the deity or deities, with the *ishta devata*. This may be focused on being in a temple, in daily devotion or in a festival time. It may be found in the Hinduism of the home and the daily devotion in the home shrine. A second way is *karma marga* – the way of good works, works of compassion. These need to be done, not to get a big name, but flowing from faith, and to be done without drawing attention to the doer.

The third is *jnana marga*; this is the way of knowledge, not in an academic sense, but in a deep understanding of the ways of God. And one of the ways to reach this is through *yoga marga*, detachment and concentration on the divine, what Christians call 'contemplation'. This is emptying the mind of distractions, and focusing on God.

It should be emphasized that these three ways are not hierarchical, nor one superior to the other. And individuals will find one or other is more natural for them – and this may change during different stages of their lives.

This is a fruitful area for dialogue with Christians. All these three *margas* are in Christian tradition and practice. And there are those in all our congregations who are more ready to do good works; others are more charismatic and devotional, and others are more contemplative. Each needs the other. Charismatic worship without practical action is frothy. Practical action without prayer makes for a busyness that becomes self-absorbing, and debilitating to others. Contemplation can be world-denying, and Christianity is very much a religion of the world, and the kingdom of God is about concrete actions for the betterment of the world, especially the poor. But it is very fruitful to reflect on these concepts through dialogue with Hindus and with the Gita.

Of course, a big difference is that salvation for Christians is in the end about faith, and its relationship to Christ and to good works. It is what St Paul calls justification by faith. Good works are still important, but they should flow from faith. They should not be done to secure salvation, as this would mean salvation by one's own efforts and not through Christ, and Christ would have died in vain. The cross and resurrection are central to a Christian understanding of salvation. Interesting here is the parable of the sheep and the goats in Matthew 25.31–46. This comes close to *nishkama karma*. The sheep are those who do the works of compassion and justice, without knowing they are thereby serving Christ who is in the 'little ones'. They are not doing these things to get salvation.

Scriptural dialogue

This is an enormous area and one that cannot be addressed here except to signpost it. Much work has related to comparisons with the Gita, often with St John's Gospel. Catherine Cornille, whom I met in Boston, has recently compiled a collection of such commentaries.[11] It is also good to dip into Hindu commentaries on the Gita. I mention here just two. A comprehensive recent Hindu commentary, by Sri Sri Yogananda, is subtitled

God Talks with Arjuna. He died in 1952, and this is a spiritual classic, published in 2002 by the Yogoda Satsanga Society of India. Another classic is that by Gandhi.[12] Gandhi wrote memorably:

> When doubts haunt me, when disappointments stare me in the face and I see not one ray of light on the horizon, I turn to the Bhagavad Gita and find a verse to comfort me; and I immediately begin to smile in the midst of overwhelming sorrow.[13]

There are so many Hindu scriptures and stories, and of course, prayers that can be reflected upon. But probably the Gita is the simplest place to start a dialogue, if we have a Hindu dialogue partner who can help us interpret it. And from the Christian side, it is best to begin with the Gospels – John, but also places like the Sermon on the Mount, so loved by Gandhi that he read from it every day, and the parables, stories of Jesus' life, and the cross and resurrection. The possibilities are endless, and without fear of offending, in relating to such a diverse faith as Hinduism. Even such an *apparently* exclusive text as John 14.6 – 'I am the way and the truth and the life. No one comes to the Father except through me' – can be interpreted inclusively (see the interview with Ramesh Majithia in Chapter 7, on Leicester).

Hindu–Christian groups

I am here adapting this section from my earlier book, now reprinted three times, *Celebrating Difference, Staying Faithful: How to Live in a Multi-Faith World*.[14] See also Chapter 10 on the national Hindu–Christian Forum.

Hindus do not divide life into segments; their faith is truly a way of life. Adjusting to life in the UK and Europe, so far from the homeland with which their faith is umbilically connected, has caused a certain amount of strain. However, gradually, as they work out what it is to be British and Hindu, their faith community is gaining in confidence, and those who have experienced it in both India and the UK will notice both difference and similarity.

Young people often live in two worlds: that of their family and that of their peer group. The elders are very concerned about this, and seek to involve young people at all levels. They have instituted classes to learn about the faith and mother-tongues, and there have also been youth camps to foster a sense of identity. Hindus will therefore be keen to involve young people in dialogue programmes, though it may be difficult to get them to see the point. The difficulty is often to bring in practising Christian young people, who are often very suspicious of other faith adherents, since they are likely to be involved with churches concerned primarily with evangelism.

Most Hindus are very suspicious about becoming targets for Christian mission, a feeling stemming from experiences in India, as well as from encounters from particular groups in the UK. They do not wish to convert others, and fear losing their own youth, either through secularization or conversion out of the faith. That someone should wish to do this is inexplicable to them, since there are many ways to God, and they do not see any reason why anyone would need to leave his or her own path, culture and family deities. This area can either be bypassed or confronted in a dialogue group. The first option is by far the easier one; the second is hard work, but it may prove worth the effort.

It is easy to have dialogue with someone from the ISKCON/Hare Krishna movement, as we have seen in Chapter 3. Also with other *bhakti* groups such as Sai Baba groups. His shrine will usually include a picture of Jesus, and his followers often meet in church halls or schools. Devotees regarded Sai Baba as a living incarnation of God, until he died recently, and believe that he had miraculous powers, including his breathing out sacred ash (*vibuthi*). Such faith may seem alien to Christians, and certainly his opulent style of life in his home near Bangalore cannot be compared with that of a Galilean peasant. But it is easy to see how his devotees can be also devoted to Jesus. We can see the devotional following in someone like Manjula Sood (see pages 87–90).

Another group is that of followers of Sri Sri Ravi Shankar who hold devotional meetings all over the world, and study the Gita. They follow their deceased guru, Dadaji, and non-Hindus are very welcome at their meetings.

An important issue related to Hindu groups is *caste*. Naturally, it is a subject that always comes up, and it makes Hindus defensive, expecting, from their experience, that they will come under heavy criticism. This has become even more difficult since the bill brought to the House of Lords by Lord Harris, retired Bishop of Oxford, wanting to add caste to the list of illegal discriminations, along with gender, race, sexuality and so on. Most Hindu organizations disagree profoundly with this move, seeing it as scapegoating their religion, and even being racist itself. They are most unhappy that this has come about through the lobbying of Dalit organizations.

The general view of Hindus is that caste no longer exists in the UK. It has certainly weakened, but most marriages still take place on caste lines. This is not in itself illegal, of course, but reinforces ongoing divisions. Love marriages weaken caste bonds, and they are increasingly frequent. Another reality is that Dalits may worship in any temple, but in practice do not have power in the management of those temples, and find such a place in a temple such as that of Guru Ravidas, venerated by both Sikh and Hindu lower castes. There is one such temple in Leicester.

I often hear it asserted that today anyone who has 'priest-like qualities' can become a priest, and does not need to be a Brahmin. This may be so, but in practice nearly all priests in significant temples are Brahmins.

Another response is that caste was not part of the original Hinduism but was imposed from outside, or that it is purely cultural and about division of labour. It is gradually weakening with the rapid urbanization of India, and anyway, it is no worse than the class system which India experienced from Victorian England.

It is tempting to challenge these claims, particularly when Indian Christians have faced many difficulties in recent years. Indian Christians who visit the UK – the majority of Dalit background – wonder why we do not raise more questions. However, it is important to bear in mind that there are also many negatives that can be thrown at Christians – 'caste' divisions also remain in Christianity. And the kind of extensive and aggressive mission practices encouraged by the American right make Indian Christianity vulnerable to attack. So it is wise to build up trust for some time before raising these controversial areas. There can be almost an obsession with this subject both ways round. I heard a good lecture recently by an academic from the Oxford Centre for Hindu Studies, about the doctrine of God in different Hindu Vedantic traditions. Afterwards, over the refreshments, I saw a group of Gujarati Hindus engaged in an animated way with the learned speaker. But I found they were accosting her, not about her speech, but about the caste legislation question in the UK House of Lords, and what had the Centre done to oppose it!

Opportunities

For all these cautions, there are real opportunities for dialogue between Christians and Hindus. Their hospitality makes their temples easy to visit, and on any evening there are normally tasty and varied refreshments on offer. It is not easy to reciprocate when most churches only rise to a cup of tea and a biscuit! In the group, Hindus will softly sing devotional prayers and occasionally bring a display of dance. It is good that Christians also be ready to sing, and offer a simple liturgy. Hindus will find it easy to join in whatever prayer Christians offer. They will also respond to church buildings, and will express their feeling of being at home in a place of holiness and prayer. The Hindu community is one that is easy to relate to at all kinds of levels, and we should rejoice at their generosity of spirit and readiness to share the best of their faith and culture, in a way that often puts us to shame.

Over the years I have taken countless groups of Christians or students to Hindu temples. The response is almost without exception positive. Those who may object to what they find there usually opt out from going. I record here, as I often do, one word to express the feelings of visitors – in this case second-year medical students from several faiths or none, after going on an ordinary Monday morning, when maybe 50 elders, women and men, were singing and praying. These are the descriptive words given: 'Peaceful, confused, content, musically uplifted, warm, felt good, surprised, sense of celebration, calm, intrigued, serene, fascinated, spiritual, involved, strong community involvement.' Nearly all positive, unlike the response usually found after a group has been to a mosque. And what of entering the church as outsiders?

I ask a second question: 'What do you particularly notice or see, or hear?' The answers from the same group:

> Statues of gods; separation of men and women, but in same hall; men ringing the bells; colours; repetition, meditation and entering a trance; woman making flower garlands; use of varied musical instruments; the ceiling painted in rainbow colours; a nice smell; active involvement in worship; style of singing prayers; lots of activity; the priest throwing liquid over the worshippers; worshipping of each god separately; involvement of everyone; different kinds of bells.

Again, what would be the comments on going into church worship? Invitations should be offered to Hindus, not only to see the building, but to attend worship. Colourful times like Harvest, Christingle, and of course Christmas, are great opportunities. A visit together to a meditation centre such as a retreat house can be powerful in its effect. Even better is a joint pilgrimage to a Christian holy place and a Hindu place of meditation. This could include a possibility of a joint visit to holy places in India, Christian as well as Hindu – though this is a long-term ambition, difficult to organize, and practical issues such as diet will become very important.

Dialogue topics Many of the subjects in this chapter can be included. This is a list of possible topics: the understanding of God; *karma*, free will and grace; the nature of salvation; the place of images and ikons; idol/image worship; the nature and practice of prayer and spirituality; non-violence and other ethical issues; the nature and meaning of key festivals; saints and gurus and what makes them; the family life-cycle events; birth, death, reincarnation and resurrection; the nature and purpose of suffering; the person of Jesus; the Incarnation and cross; approaches to meditation; scriptural studies; living as Hindus and Christians in the UK today.

Action together What can be done locally for poor or marginalized communities, including asylum seekers? Are there advocacy issues we can take up together? Education or health issues? What can we do together as two faiths; what can be done with other faiths?

Learning about some great historical figures from our two faiths Gandhi (known as Gandhiji by Hindus, and most Indians) is an obvious place to start. His statue can be visited if geography allows. Two examples are that in Bloomsbury Park, near Euston, and that in Leicester, on the Golden Mile, the place of Hindu shops, in the north of the city. This created some controversy when erected by the city council a few years ago, with letters to the local paper asking why we should honour an Indian who had campaigned to remove the British from his country. The answer was that he is a world figure as well as father of the Indian nation, and Leicester has so many Indian-background people. There was fear of damage to the statue, but that had never to my knowledge happened, until June 2014 when graffiti were written on its plinth, saying 'Remember 1984', the year of the massacre of 400 Sikhs in the storming of the 'Golden Temple' in Amritsar. Preparation for learning can also be through seeing the *Gandhi* film together, or separately.[15]

Gandhi can be discussed from many angles: learning about his life in South Africa as well as India and how his hatred of racism developed in South Africa. His friendship with C. F. Andrews, the Anglican priest.[16] His political philosophy, and his deep commitment to an India united across faiths and languages and cultures, for which in the end he gave his life, killed in the street by an extremist from his own religion because he would not support the idea of a Hindu-exclusive India. His methods of *ahimsa*, non-violence, learned from Jains and from Jesus and the Sermon on the Mount. His understanding of caste, where untouchables are renamed Harijans and their work is given dignity, but caste remains as part of the way society should be organized. His economic philosophy, that 'small is beautiful', and the village is the best unit of production, including handloom weaving. His educational dream, of village schools nurturing students in practical skills and not in an academic direction. His Hindu faith, as shown in his autobiography. How he saw Jesus. How he saw missionaries. How he has influenced the non-violent movement throughout the world. And so on.

And then critical questions: is Gandhi still relevant in an India which is a nuclear power? Does India pay lip service to Gandhi but not much more? And his attitude to women, with his giving up sexual activity beyond a certain age, even with his wife. What is that about?

Other figures who could be discussed: Ambedkar, for example, a contemporary of Gandhi, a top lawyer who drafted the egalitarian constitution of India, and was a Dalit. He, rather than Gandhi, is the guru and hero of the Dalit movement. Ambedkar is memorably recorded as saying, as early as 1935, that though born a Hindu, he would not die as a Hindu. As an Untouchable, he felt there was no future for him in Hinduism. He saw that both Christianity and Islam were good and egalitarian religions, but they were not Indian. Sikhism was egalitarian, but Punjabi. So he came to Buddhism, which he embraced, along with thousands of his followers, in Maharashtra in 1956. They had no monks, because Buddhism had been removed from its native soil in India, by Brahminic persecution. So he brought monks from Sri Lanka. And many more have followed over the decades since. This conversion movement may not be liked by caste Hindus, but at least it is within the Indian fold. Studying Ambedkar and his life and philosophy can provide a background for discussion around a number of critical issues.

Other Hindus can be introduced, and we just list them here: Sri Aurobindo (whose ashram is in Pondicherry); Ramana Maharshi (whose ashram is in Tiruvanamalai, Tamil Nadu), Rabindranath Tagore (from Bengal); Ramanjam, Chaitanya (Vaishnavites), and so we can go on.

From the Christian side, it is good to look at great Indian Christians such as, most obviously, Sadhu Sunder Singh, Pandita Ramabai, Mother Teresa, Father Bede Griffiths and many others.[17]

Conversion and mission

These issues are clearly one stumbling block to smooth dialogue (see Chapter 10 on the national forum). This is often linked with discussion of Hindutva, and political Hinduism. Both these two topics are referred to often in this book. But I end this chapter with showing how wide the polarization can be, by means of two stories that have come to me recently. I do not suggest these are at all the norm, but they illustrate where extremes can lead us.

The first is that I went to preach at All Saints, the Asian Christian Anglican church in Leicester. It is situated across the road from the new and beautiful Swaminarayan Temple (see Chapter 6 on the Swaminarayan movement). After my sermon, a charismatic woman was called out to lead the intercessions. She came to the front with a ram's horn, as used traditionally among Orthodox Jews, and she proceeded to blow it loudly in all directions, and especially in the direction of the walls of the temple. She prayed loudly that they might all fall down, as had happened to the walls of Jericho when Joshua's people blew their horns. She called for the end of idol worship. It was the time of Diwali, and she shouted that Hindus claim to celebrate the coming of light, but that they remain in perpetual darkness unless they find the light of Christ. The presiding minister was embarrassed, but I reflected that any Hindus hearing this would feel all their opinions of Christians were just reinforced – that they are to be 'conversion targets' and nothing more.

A second concerns Hindutva. At the time of writing, I received a round-robin link message – as a message addressed to 'All Indians'. It was clear from the article that 'All Indians' meant 'All Hindus'. It was alerting readers to a bill called Prevention of Communal and Targeted Violence Bill, being brought by the Congress government. It was inspired by an analysis by Dr Subramaniam Swamy (see also page 122). The commentary says that this is to protect minorities, including Muslims and Christians, who can then, without redress, file cases against Hindus, 'the majority of whom are working and business class'. If they do not stop this anti-Hindu, anti-Bharat, bill and remove from power the party bringing it forward, then Hindus will be left with only three options, as in Pakistan, Bangladesh and Kashmir: to convert, to flee, or suffer their whole life. This, of course, came before the 2014 election of Narendra Modi, and the fall of the Congress government.

Of course, these two stories represent two extreme positions. But they only encourage us who work for understanding between Christians and Hindus to work all the harder to highlight the positive engagement, of which there is so much. The pursuit of dialogue and mutual education may be hard work and long term, but this only shows how essential it is.

12

Afterword: the meeting of opposites?

The reader has met many people, Hindus and Christians, in the pages of this book. There are many others who do not appear here, but who have shown great interest in this project. In general, both groups have been intrigued by the title – what do I mean by this, and in what sense can Hinduism and Christianity be seen as opposites? Can they also be seen as 'closest in affection', as the Qur'an says of Christians in relationship to Muslims?[1] And we need of course to clarify whether we are thinking of Hindus or Hinduism, Christians or Christianity. The answer may depend on which of these we choose.

Above all, whichever of these two we choose, the answer will depend on which Hinduism, which Christianity, which Hindus, which Christians we ask. For some Christians, the answer will be that these two religions are irrevocably opposites, however close the adherents may be to each other. For those who do not follow Christ and see him as their Lord and Saviour, they are inevitably opposites as Hindus, and may ultimately be lost. Added to this, there is then polarization brought about by the way Hindus, however devout, seem at least to worship images, idols, multiple deities.

From the other side, many Hindus feel a sense of superiority because they accept all religions; Christianity is bound to be inferior and lacking in such generosity of spirit, tied as it is to one historical figure, and his death on a cross. Hinduism is inclusive of all; Christianity is exclusive, and so inferior. Moreover, such a verdict will extend to Islam also, another Abrahamic faith with a unique scripture, and an understanding that this scripture is the 'last testament' and so envelops all others. It is only Hinduism that displays the openness to all.

But there are many nuanced positions in between. In doctrine, in teaching, Christianity may be opposite to Hinduism. But in spirituality, it may well be much closer, and we have seen this often in these pages. Moreover, there are some Christians who are very close to some Hindus, and vice versa. This applies particularly and most obviously to those in *bhakti* traditions, and Christians in charismatic practice. Theologically they may be far apart, but devotionally can come close. So also those who go deepest into contemplation, and so can relate to Advaita Vedanta; they may be fewer in number, but such persons can come close. And similarly those who practise yoga from a spiritual perspective, as seen in the examples from Sweden, but found throughout Europe, and much more in the USA.

Perhaps most often, Christians and Hindus live in two worlds. They do not think much about each other religiously and spiritually – they are two cultures, with two histories. They can get on perfectly well side by side, but do not really need to meet. And so there is no need to confront this question, whether they meet from opposite perspectives. In India maybe they have to encounter each other, as the minority Christians are surrounded by the vast populations of Hindus on all sides. But in the West, they may live in two separate worlds religiously – church and temple. This has become more difficult, as religion has become politicized in recent decades, and being a Hindu and being a loyal Indian have become for many identical. So on the other side, being a Christian means being identified with what has often been seen as a 'Western' and 'colonial' religion, which does not encourage a meeting of equals.

In the West, Hindus, in the USA and UK in particular, have grown more and more confident and sure of their place in society. This means 'meeting' as equals becomes much more possible. The chapters in this book on dialogue initiatives, and on theological, missiological and spiritual issues (Chapters 10 and 11), are where we can look for some clues as to how to move forward. They are written on the assumption that such a meeting can be possible, at the four levels of dialogue indicated on pages 178–9.

Perhaps what is fundamental is that we meet, not primarily as Hindus and Christians, but as human beings. We meet as created in God's image, in Christian or Jewish terms. And we are called to meet as we live together in society, and are called to love our neighbours as ourselves, whether Hindu or Sikh, Muslim or Jew or Christian. This book is written to encourage readers to do this, as fellow human beings, fellow citizens, fellow religious and spiritual friends. Without such meeting, life will be very much the poorer; with this meeting, each of our faiths can be much enriched, while remaining faithful to its core.

Glossary of terms

Advaita literally means 'non-duality'; cf. Advaita Vedanta philosophy where Brahman, the supreme being, is identified with the *atman* (soul). This unity is the one source of reality

arati the camphor flame that a priest raises to each deity and then offers to the devotees, who wave their hands over it, and then over their heads, as sign of receiving *darshan* from the deity

Arya Samaj a nineteenth-century reform movement founded by Swami Dayananda Saraswati; monotheistic faith, based solely on the Vedas, that came into conflict with traditional Hindus and with Christians, and is still around today

ashram an abode of ascetics, a kind of monastery

atman the 'soul' or inmost being of a person, or just 'oneself'

avatara (or avatar) literally means 'descent'; normally used of the 'descents' to earth of the gracious god Vishnu; there were ten of these, but the most important were Rama and Krishna

bhajans devotional songs in praise of a deity; usually sung congregationally (same root as *bhakti*)

bhakti loving devotion to a personal god or goddess, usually expressed in poetry, music and song, which have a profoundly emotional flavour; one of the three ways of obtaining release from the round of birth and rebirth (as in the Gita)

Bharat Sanskrit word for 'India', or 'Mother India'

Brahma the God responsible for creating the universe; sometimes said to have uttered the Vedas at the beginning

Brahman the final ground of all that is, identified in Advaita with the *atman* (soul)

Chattriya the second of the four main caste divisions – warriors or local lords

darshan 'to catch sight of'; to visit a holy site and view the deity; to receive spiritual blessings, by extension, by meeting a holy person

dharma literally, 'that which is established or firm', hence: law, custom, duty, righteousness, morality, prescribed conduct

diksha initiation to become a disciple

Diwali the most celebrated of Hindu festivals in the UK, held in October or November. It means literally 'a row of lights'. It is known as the festival of lights, light overcoming darkness, good overcoming evil. The goddess Lakshmi, the goddess of good fortune and wealth, is particularly celebrated, and Diwali represents the beginning of the new financial year, with appropriate prayers. Leicester has the biggest Diwali festival outside India

dosai a rice pancake, often eaten for breakfast in Tamil Nadu; now becoming common in South Indian restaurants in the UK

Durga one of the many names of the great goddess; in this case, the name emphasizes her terrible aspect – as Kali also

Gayathri Mantra the most important prayer in Hinduism. Brahmins are expected to recite it three times a day

Hindutva the political ideology that claims India as the homeland of Hindus, and is working towards that goal. At its widest, this includes all the old British India. Non-Hindus are either to be tolerated or to be second-class citizens. This applies particularly to Muslims and Christians, foreign religions and predatory religions. Jains, Sikhs and Buddhists are seen as really Hindu, part of the Hindu *dharma*. This is a major part of the ideology behind the Bharatiya Janata Party (BJP) and its activist wing

Holi North Indian festival, involving throwing coloured chalk/paint over friends. It is held in February/March and is a joyful time, recalling the playfulness of Krishna and his consort Radha

ishta devata the preferred or chosen deity – maybe for family reasons, or by conscious choice about who to be devoted to

karma an action which produces inevitable consequences leading to rebirth; also 'fate', some misfortune which is seen as the consequence of unremembered actions in a past life

kirtan chant, song

mandalas symbolic images used as a basis for meditation; may be found on the floor

mandir temple

maya illusion, trick; a key word in Vedantic thinking, where it is used to refer to the deceptive nature of experience based on the senses

moksha, mukti release from the continuing round of rebirths, and therefore the final goal in all Hindu spiritual devotion. It can be interpreted as 'salvation', but should not be linked with the use of that word in Christianity, which is very different

murthis deities, images

Navaratri a festival of nine nights, in September/October, pre-Diwali. It is devoted to the many forms of the great mother goddess Devi, including Durga. Both fasting and night dancing in temples form part of the celebration

prasad/prasadam gift of divine grace, often received through the gift of dedicated or blessed food

puja homage shown to a chosen deity, and then to other gods. Traditionally, it consisted in 16 actions, accompanied by songs and mantras. In the house, a domestic *puja* will essentially be the lighting of an oil lamp, making offerings of flowers and saying a prayer, including the reciting of mantras. In the temple, the priest will offer more elaborate actions and prayers

ras lila dance of divine love, as imitating Krishna. *Ras lila* festivals have now been developed

sadhu holy person, worthy person; 'one who is straight and without defect'

Sai Baba a great saint of Maharashtra, who illustrates a very integrative spirituality; led to a vast and diversified religious movement, 'the Sai Baba movement'. Active from the village of Shirdi, from 1858 until 1918, Sai Baba was revered as a holy man, a miracle worker, and for many God incarnate. The living embodiment of Sai Baba – Sai Baba of Puttaparthi – was based in Karnataka and had a vast following. He died in 2012, but the movement lives on wherever the followers are spread throughout the Indian diaspora. There have been many Western followers, particularly in Bangalore, and his movement remains very inclusive

Sanatan temple a generic temple, where many deities are displayed, which will normally include Radha and Krishna, Rama and Sita, Vishnu and Lakshmi, and many lesser deities

Sankara (also Sankarachrya) the most famous interpreter, through his many commentaries, of Advaita Vedanta, and generally recognized as India's greatest philosophical thinker; lived probably around 788 CE until 838 CE

sannyasi 'one who renounces'; may be a wandering monk, or someone who enters the final stage of life; normally wears a saffron robe of unstitched cloth

seva service

Shakti 'energy' depicted as mother goddess, the consort of Siva

Sita faithful wife of Rama. She insisted on accompanying her husband during his 14-year exile, but was abducted by the demon king Ravana, and taken to Sri Lanka. She was rescued by Hanuman, king of the monkeys, and brought back unspoiled by her captivity

Siva Linga a symbol that may look phallic, arising from the female symbol of the *yoni*, the vulva, but the faithful do not associate it with these erotic ideas. It represents the supreme Lord, a symbol of divine infinitude, and a god who manifests himself to save the faithful. Usually milk is offered to it, and in some temples this is a continuous flow

Sloka double verses, based on the Vedas, with a metric rhythm

Sudra (Shudra) a member of the lowest of the four caste groups, and so a manual labourer. So-called 'untouchables', or Dalits, are outcastes and so even lower

tabla small upright drum, played with the hand, and ubiquitous in Indian music

tilak mark on the forehead, with spiritual meaning

Vanaprastha third stage of life – 'life in the forest' – the stage of life prior to the complete renunciation stage of Sannyasa, which a sannyasi undertakes

Venkateswara, Tirupati temple to Vishnu in southern Andhra Pradesh, on the top of a hill, said to be the richest temple in India, and one of the most visited

Yogeswari very popular female spiritual yoga teacher, based in New York, who travels the world

Notes

1 Today Islam, tomorrow Hinduism? Challenges for Christians in the West

1 Geoff Oddie, *Reimagining Hinduism: British Protestant Missionary Constructions of Hinduism, 1793–1900*, New Delhi and London, Sage, 2006.

2 The Huntington Thesis in essence: 'It is my hypothesis that the fundamental source of conflict in this new world will not be primarily ideological or primarily economic. The great divisions among humankind and the dominating source of conflict will be cultural. Nation states will remain the most powerful actors in world affairs, but the principal global conflicts will occur between nations and groups of different civilizations. The clash of civilizations will dominate global politics. The fault lines between civilizations will be the battle lines of the future.' This became famous because of the focus on the conflict between Islam and the West, leading to George Bush's linking this thesis with the War on Terrorism after the attack on the Twin Towers on September 11, 2001 and the invasions of Afghanistan (2001) and Iraq (2003). Samuel Huntington, *The Clash of Civilizations and the Remaking of the World Order*, New York, Simon & Schuster, 1997. See preceding article, Samuel Huntington, 'The Clash of Civilizations?' *Foreign Affairs*, Summer 1993, pp. 22 and 39, where the phrase is first used.

3 Huntington, *Clash of Civilizations*, p. 258.

4 Dilwar Hussein, in *Emel*, July/August 2004, p. 16.

5 Tariq Ramadan, *What I Believe*, Oxford, Oxford University Press, 2009, p. 20. See also his many other works.

2 Christian–Hindu encounter in India: From the beginnings of Christianity in Kerala to the present day

1 We will be writing about Dalits frequently in this book. For those who are unfamiliar with this term, it is a name adopted by a group of castes at the bottom of the social system. There are at least 180 million Dalits, and some estimates are higher. They are scattered throughout India, and were known as 'depressed classes' in the British period, and were renamed 'Harijans' by Gandhi, 'people blessed by God'. They were called *scheduled* castes in independent India. These were all names imposed upon them. The word Dalit has been chosen by their leaders, and means 'crushed' or 'bruised' people. They are often associated with tribals, who are again found throughout India, and are also among the scheduled groups.

2 Ambedkar was the foremost lawyer who drafted the Indian constitution. He was a Dalit, and the constitution suggested that caste would wither away in 30 years. He made clear, in a book written in 1938, that he would not die

a Hindu. He chose to become a Buddhist, because other religions, in his view, were foreign religions. Sikhism was too regional, being practised by Punjabis only.

3 For the story of this remarkable priest, see V. Cronin, *A Pearl to India: The Life of Robert di Nobili*, London, Hart-Davies, 1959.

4 C. Mosse, 'Caste, Christianity and Hinduism', unpublished DPhil thesis, Oxford University, 1986.

5 See his various books on prayer, for example *Prayer*, New Delhi, ISPCK, 1967, and *The Further Shore*, New Delhi, ISPCK, 1975.

6 S. Radhakrishnan, *Eastern Religion and Western Thought*, Oxford, Oxford University Press, 1939. See also his small book *The Hindu View of Life*, New York, Macmillan, 1936.

7 Geoffrey Parrinder, *Avatar and Incarnation* London, Faber & Faber, 1970 and New York, Oxford University Press, 1982. Cf. also his *Upanishads, Gita and Bible*, London, Sheldon Press, 1962, 1975.

8 *Docetic* – relating to the heresy of docetism, that Jesus 'appears' to be human.

9 Rashtriya Seva Sangh (RSS) is a right-wing activist movement with some militant elements.

10 P. Luke and J. Carman, *Village Christians and Hindu Culture*, London, Lutterworth, 1959.

11 Robin Boyd, *Introduction to Indian Christian Theology*, Madras, CLS, 1969, and much reprinted.

12 Christine Manohar, *Spirit Christology*, New Delhi, ISPCK, 2009.

13 Kirsteen Kim, *Mission in the Spirit*, New Delhi, ISPCK, 2003.

14 Thomas Thangaraj, *The Crucified Guru*, Nashville, TN, Abingdon, 1994.

15 Detailed in *Religion and Society*, March 1972, pp. 69–90.

16 The Nadars were a backward caste community, some of whom had come up through education and embracing Christianity. They are a major and successful group within the Church in Tamil Nadu.

17 See the book of H. Hoeffer, *The Debate on Mission*, Madras, Gurukul, 1979; and my book *The Church and Conversion*, New Delhi, ISPCK, 1997, ch. 6.

18 A. Ayrookuziel, *The Sacred in Popular Hinduism*, Bangalore, CISRS, 1985.

19 J. Pickett, *Christian Mass Movements in India*, Nashville, TN, Abingdon, 1933.

20 Duncan Forrester, *Caste and Christianity*, London, Curzon, 1980.

21 M. M. Thomas, *The Acknowledged Christ of the Indian Renaissance*, London, SCM Press, 1969.

22 Kenneth Cracknell, *Justice, Courtesy and Love: Theologians and Missionaries Encountering World Religions*, London, Epworth, 1995. Cf. Wesley Ariarajah, *Hindus and Christians: A Century of Protestant Ecumenical Thought*, Grand Rapids, Eerdmans, 1991.

23 J. Farquhar, *The Crown of Hinduism*, Oxford, Oxford University Press, 1913.

24 H. Kraemer, *Christian Message in a Non-Christian World*, Edinburgh, 1938, reprinted in Bangalore in 2009.

25 For studies of Chenchaiah and Chakkarai, see M. M. Thomas, *The Acknowledged Christ of the Indian Renaissance*, and Robin Boyd, *Introduction to Indian Christian Theology* – see 'Further reading' list. These quotations are found there, as well as in their own writings: D. A. Thangasamy, *The Theology of Chenchiah*, Bangalore, CISRS, 1967; P. T. Thomas, *The Theology of Chakkarai*, Bangalore, CISRS, 1968.

26 Raymond Pannikar, *The Unknown Christ of Hinduism*, London, Darton, Longman & Todd, 1964.

27 K. Klostermaier, *Hindu and Christian in Vrindaban*, London, SCM Press, 1969.

28 Such as *One Christ, Many Religions*, New York, Orbis, 1991, and *Between Two Cultures: Ecumenical Ministry in a Pluralistic World*, Geneva, WCC, 1996.

3 Three *bhakti* movements in the UK, and Christianity: 1. ISKCON (Hare Krishna movement)

1 ISKCON – International Society for Krishna Consciousness, known popularly as the Hare Krishna movement, after the distinctive chanting of its members.

2 The Teape lectures are endowed lectures, given in India, normally, but not always, by a British speaker. They have been given for the last 50 years, approximately every other year. There are also Teape seminars given in Cambridge, normally by someone from India, and The Teape Foundation is Cambridge based. The lectures are on themes related to Hindu–Christian dialogue. They began with a focus on Vedanta, but have since become broadened.

3 John Moffitt, *Journey to Gorahkpur: An Encounter with Christ beyond Christianity*, New York, Holt, Rinehart & Winston, 1972, p. 129.

4 Ranchor Prime, *When the Sun Shines: The Dawn of Hare Krishna in Britain*, Watford, Bhaktivedanta Book Trust, 2009. Evocatively he quotes Prabhupada: 'When the sun shines, England is one of the most beautiful places on earth' – hence the title of this book.

5 See Prime, *When the Sun Shines*, pp. 266–8.

6 See the discussion on dialogue forums in this book (Chapter 10).

7 Available on its own website, where all back copies can be easily accessed and read.

8 Sankara is traditionally dated 788–820. He is seen as the founder of Advaita Vedanta. This is called monist, because Brahman is the sole reality, and there is no ultimate duality. The individual soul, *atman*, is ultimately to become one with Brahman, where there will be no two – 'that art thou'. References from this article of Cracknell, and that of Ranchor Dasa that follows, are from the online journal, where there are no page numbers. Both articles are quite short, summary articles.

9 See Chapter 8 on the USA, and references to Cracknell, and especially Anuttama Dasa, in the ISKCON section.

10 Daphne Green, 'A Comparative Study of Krishna Consciousness in ISKCON, and the Practice of the Presence of God in CSMV (the Community of St Mary

the Virgin, with Headquarters in Wantage, Oxfordshire)', Leeds University, 2000, pp. 267–77.

11 The idea of the universe as a playground of the gods. Krishna demonstrates this with his love of dancing and play. The *rasa lila* is Krishna's divine circle-dance with the *gopis* (cowherd maidens). This is what lies behind the devotees dancing in the streets.

4 Three *bhakti* movements in the UK, and Christianity: 2. South Indian *bhakti* movements through temples

1 These are also known as Ambedkar Buddhists. Ambedkar (see Chapter 2) converted to Buddhism in 1956, in Maharashtra, and large numbers of his fellow Dalits ('Harijans' at that time) converted to Buddhism. They had to bring over monks from Sri Lanka, as there were no indigenous monks available. Many more have followed in the ensuing years up to the present time.

2 Joanne Waghorne, *Diaspora of the Gods: Modern Hindu Temples in the Urban Middle-Class World*, Oxford, Oxford University Press, 2004.

3 Frank Clothey, *The Many Faces of Murugan*, The Hague, Mouton, 1978.

4 Waghorne, *Diaspora of the Gods*, p. 131.

5 See R. Burghart (ed.), *Hinduism in Great Britain*, London, Tavistock, 1987, pp. 224–51.

6 Waghorne, *Diaspora of the Gods*, pp. 70ff.

7 The equivalent of interstate highways in the USA.

8 A *kollam* is normally created in the early morning outside a house, on the doorstep or pavement, and is in rice flour or chalk. It may be a sacred pattern or mandala, or symbol. This is ubiquitous in Tamil Nadu, and also found outside many Tamil homes in the UK.

9 The Chettiahs are from the group of castes second to Brahmins, and they focus on making money, through trading or businesses. They have large houses, like palaces, in this area of Ramnad District, and much of the furniture is brought across from Burma, where they have traded a great deal.

10 See further reference to this church in Chapter 5.

5 Three *bhakti* movements in the UK, and Christianity: 3. Hindu conversions to Christianity in the UK; *Jesu Bhakters*

1 Information from Raj Patel, present director (2011). The founder was Pradip Sudra. Raj Patel wrote an article, 'Why Do Christians Wear Ties?', in P. Grant and R. Patel (eds), *A Time to Speak: Perspectives on Black Christians in Britain*, Nottingham, CRRU/ECRJ, 1990.

2 Information from Jagdish, leader of the congregation of All Nations, and from the Revd Richard Espin, vicar of St Luke's, Wolverhampton.

3 Ravidas was a North Indian Guru and mystic and Vaishnavite poet, who lived in the sixteenth century. He was from the *chamar* Dalit caste, and he attacked

the Brahminic dominance, saying the path of God was open to people of all castes. He is venerated in several temples in the UK, by the Dalit communities, both Sikh and Hindu. There is one in Leicester. These temples use a holy book consisting of 240 hymns of Ravidas, and 41 verses are contained in the Sikh holy book, the Guru Granth Sahib.

4 Both are given pseudonyms.

5 Dag Hammarskjöld, *Markings*, London, Faber & Faber, 1964, p. 169.

7 Three geographical studies: 1. Leicester, England

1 *The Independent*, 28 July 2013.

2 The others are in Bradford, east London and east Birmingham. St Philip's is the most developed and diverse of these centres, and Archbishop Rowan Williams was sole patron while Archbishop, and he encouraged Hindu–Christian work. The present Archbishop, Justin Welby, has also become patron.

3 I was at the time a curate in a parish in the West Midlands. The parish prepared two council houses for occupation, as happened in many places. But the settlers hardly stayed any time before going off to Leicester.

4 The Brahmo Samaj was founded by Ram Mohan Roy (see ch. 8, n. 18) in 1828. It promoted a monotheist, reformed Hinduism, with a universal spirit in its worship. Devenranath Tagore, father of the poet Tagore, and Keshab Chandra Sen (1838–84) were other well-known Bengali figures in its later leadership. It has faced splits in the last hundred years, and remains weak, but an important symbol of a reformist, modernist Hinduism.

8 Three geographical studies: 2. The United States

1 Philip Goldberg, *American Veda*, New York, Harmony Books, 2010.

2 Goldberg, *American Veda*, p. 10.

3 See Karen Pechilis (ed.), *The Graceful Guru: Hindu Female Gurus in India and the United States*, Oxford, Oxford University Press, 2004.

4 Goldberg, *American Veda*, p. 9.

5 Diana Eck, *A New Religious America*, New York, HarperCollins, 2001.

6 Eck, *New Religious America*, pp. 80–141.

7 Ramakrishna was a great mystic, from Bengal, who lived from 1836 to 1886. He was devoted to the goddess Kali, and he had many mystical experiences, including one notable one of Christ. His most famous disciple was Swami Vivekananda.

8 See Chapter 2.

9 Pravrajika Vrajaprana, *Vedanta: A Simple Introduction*, Hollywood, CA, Vedanta Press, 1999.

10 Frank Clooney, *Hindu God, Christian God*, Oxford, Oxford University Press, 2001.

11 Subramaniam Swamy, 'How to Wipe Out Islamic Terror', *DNA*, 16 July 2011.

12 Rajiv Maholtra, *Being Different*, Noida, HarperCollins India, 2011. Cf. also his *Breaking India: Western Interventions in Dravidian and Dalit Faultlines*, Princeton, Infinity Foundation, 2011 (with Arvindan Neelakandan). This argues for the build-up of Dravidian and Dalit identity as being a Western construct, in the name of human rights, and to encourage conversion to Christianity.

13 <www.youtube.com/watch?v=4yz6ZL>.

14 Paul Courtright, *Ganeśa: Lord of Obstacles, Lord of Beginnings*, New York, Oxford University Press, 1985, Motilal, 2001. The second edition in particular was seen as pornographic, because of the way Ganesh is depicted on the cover. He is attacked by many Hindus for bringing in a psychoanalytic analysis of the stories of Ganesh.

15 Jeffrey Kripal, *Kali's Child: The Mystical and Erotic Kin. The Life and Teaching of Ramakrishna*, Chicago, University of Chicago Press, 1995, 1998.

16 See his major book, *A Living Theology of Krishna Bhakti: The Essential Teachings of A. C. Bhaktivedanta Swami Prabhupada*, Oxford, Oxford University Press, 2012.

17 K. Klostermaier, *Hindu and Christian in Vrindaban*, London SCM Press, 1969. Klostermaier also wrote the highly recommended *A Survey of Hinduism*, Albany, NY, SUNY Press, 2007, and several other significant books in the field of dialogue.

18 Ram Mohan Roy (1774–1833) was a prominent Bengali reformer. He challenged many Hindu practices, including caste and *sati* (widow burning), and had constructive dialogues with Baptist missionaries in Serampore, near Calcutta. He admired greatly Jesus' Sermon on the Mount. There is a statue in his honour at College Green, Bristol.

19 Swami Dayananda is a distinguished philosopher and teacher of Vedanta, based in his ashram in Rishikesh, North India. He travels much, and founded the Chinmaya Mission. He was born in 1930.

20 Clooney's books are numerous, for example, *Hindu God, Christian God: How Reason Helps Break Down the Boundaries between Religions*, New York, Oxford University Press, 2001 (where Parimal above has written a response). See also *The New Comparative Theology: Interreligious Insights from the Next Generation*, New York, Continuum, 2010.

21 *Journal of Vaishnava Studies*, vol. 20, no. 2, Spring 2012.

22 We can compare Kumar in Chapter 5 on South Asian conversions.

9 Three geographical studies: 3. Sweden

1 I acknowledge here my particular debt to Dr Ferdinando Sardella, both through discussion, and through reading his recent article on Sweden in the *Brill Encyclopaedia of Hinduism*. I am yet to read the publication of his PhD thesis, *Modern Hindu Personalism*, Oxford, Oxford University Press, 2012. A former Roman Catholic, and ISKCON leader, he now describes himself as a Sri Vaishnava devotee.

10 Two examples of Hindu–Christian forums in the UK: Leicester and national – difficulties and possibilities

1 Ramesh Pattni BSc (Hons), MBA, MA, MSt (Oxford) is a doctoral student at the Oxford Centre for Hindu Studies.

2 The Principles of Inter Faith Dialogue were developed from the work of the World Council of Churches.

3 Andrew Wingate, *Celebrating Difference, Staying Faithful: How to Live in a Multi-Faith World*, London: Darton, Longman & Todd, 2005.

11 Theological, spiritual and missiological challenges

1 William Dalrymple, *Nine Lives: In Search of the Sacred in Modern India*, London, Bloomsbury, 2009. This is a brilliant study of a range of individuals from different traditions, from all over India, some of whom, as the cover says, 'live on the farthest extremes of religious ecstasy'.

2 P. Luke and J. Carman, *Village Christians and Hindu Culture: Study of a Rural Church in Andhra Pradesh, South India*, London, Lutterworth, 1968. This was a WCC-sponsored study, and its findings echo what I have seen among village Christians in much of Tamil Nadu also.

3 Rowan Williams, *Lost Icons: Reflections on Cultural Bereavement*, Edinburgh, T. & T. Clark, 2000, p. 2.

4 Williams, *Lost Icons*, p. 182.

5 Roger Hooker was an Anglican priest who lived for many years in North India, and then in Birmingham. He wrote several important books, such as *Journey into Varanasi*, Oxford, CMS, 1978. His major work, entitled *Themes in Hinduism and Christianity*, Frankfurt, Peter Lang, 1989, is hard to get hold of and very expensive. Nearly 400 pages long, the titles of the chapters speak for themselves: 'Myth', 'Time', 'Evil', 'Purity', 'Images' (pp. 192–240), 'Renunciation', 'Woman', 'Journey's End'. It is an ideal resource for the reader who wants to move forward in depth, as a follow-up to this book.

6 *Grace and Saiva Siddhanta*, Madurai, Tamilnadu Theological Seminary, 1975; Joseph Jaswant Raj, *Grace in Saiva Siddhantham and in St Paul*, Madras, South Indian Salesian Society, 1989.

7 *Young India*, 11 August 1927.

8 *Young India*, 31 December 1931.

9 *Harijan*, 17 April 1937.

10 W. Bright, *Hymns Ancient and Modern*, number 298.

11 Catherine Cornille (ed.), *Song Divine: Christian Commentaries on the Bhagavad Gita*, Eugene, OR, Cascade Books, 2007. This covers a period from T. S. Eliot to Bede Griffiths. Some are detailed exegesis; some are spiritual or theological comparisons. Some look at similarities, others at difference. Such themes as detachment, incarnation and eschatology are addressed. Bede Griffiths' commentary is called *River of Compassion*, Springfield, IL, Templegate, 1987,

2001. This was compiled from original talks given at Shantivanam in Tamil Nadu, and is detailed, over 300 pages long.

12 Mahatma Gandhi, *The Bhagavad Gita According to Gandhi*, Berkeley, CA, North Atlantic Books, 2009.

13 *Young India*, 8 June 1925.

14 Andrew Wingate, *Celebrating Difference, Staying Faithful: How to Live in a Multi-Faith World*, London, Darton, Longman and Todd, 2005, pp. 24–8.

15 *Gandhi*, dir. Richard Attenborough, 1982.

16 See the collection of letters, *Gandhi and Charlie: The Story of a Friendship*, edited and narrated by David Gracie, London, SPCK, 1989.

17 See the important book of M. M. Thomas, *The Acknowledged Christ of the Indian Renaissance*, London, SCM Press, 1969. Also P. J. Thomas, *100 Witnesses to Jesus Christ*, Bombay, Tract and Book Society, 1974.

12 Afterword: the meeting of opposites?

1 Surah 5.82.

Further reading

Hinduism in general

Bowen, Paul (ed.), *Themes and Issues in Hinduism*, London and Washington, Cassell, 1998
Copley, Antony (ed.), *Hinduism in Public and Private: Reform, Hindutva, Gender and Sampraday*, New Delhi, Oxford University Press, 2003
Demariaux, Jean-Christophe, *How to Understand Hinduism*, London, SCM Press, 1995
De Smet, R. and J. Neuner, *Religious Hinduism*, Mumbai, St Pauls, 1996
Doniger, Wendy, *The Hindus: An Alternative History*, Oxford, Oxford University Press, 2009
Eck, Diana, *Encountering God: A Spiritual Journey from Bozeman to Banaras*, Boston, Beacon Press, 1993
Flood, Gavin (ed.), *The Blackwell Companion to Hinduism*, Oxford, Blackwell, 2003
Klostermaier, K., *A Survey of Hinduism*, Albany, NY, State University of New York Press, 1995
Knott, Kim, *Hinduism: A Very Short Introduction*, Oxford, Oxford University Press, 2000
Lipner, Julius, *The Hindus: Their Religious Beliefs and Practices*, London and New York, Routledge, 1994
Radhakrishnan, S., *The Hindu View of Life*, New York, Macmillan, 1936
Smith, David, *Hinduism and Modernity*, Oxford, Blackwell, 2003
Sugirtharajah, Sharada, *Imagining Hinduism: A Postcolonial Perspective*, New York, Routledge, 2003
Vertovec, Steven, *The Hindu Diaspora: Comparative Patterns*, New York, Routledge, 2000
Vrajaprana, Pravrajika, *Vedanta: A Simple Introduction*, Hollywood, CA, Vedanta Press, 1999
Zaehner, R. C., *Hinduism*, London, Oxford University Press, 1962 (old, but a classic)

India

Cracknell, Kenneth, *Justice, Courtesy and Love: Theologians and Missionaries Encountering World Religions, 1846–1914*, London, Epworth Press, 1995
Eck, Diana, *India: A Sacred Geography*, New York, Harmony Books, 2012
Felix, Wilfred (ed.), *Leave the Temple: Indian Paths to Human Liberation*, Maryknoll, NY, Orbis, 1992
Fuller, C., *The Camphor Flame: Popular Hinduism and Society in India*, Princeton, NJ, Princeton University Press, 1992

Gracie, David (ed.), *Gandhi and Charlie: The Story of a Friendship*, Cambridge, MA, Cowley, 1989

Hardiman, David, *Gandhi in His Time and Ours*, New Delhi, Permanent Black, 2005

Oddie, Geoff, *Imagined Hinduism: British Protestant Missionary Constructions of Hinduism, 1793–1900*, New Delhi, Sage, 2006

Thomas, M. M., *The Acknowledged Christ of the Indian Renaissance*, London, SCM Press, 1969

Hindu–Christian dialogue

Ariarajah, W., *Hindus and Christians: A Century of Protestant Ecumenical Thought*, Grand Rapids, MI, Eerdmans, 1991

Barnes, Michael, SJ, *God East and West*, London, SPCK, 1991

Brockington, John, *Hinduism and Christianity*, London, Macmillan, 1992

Clooney, Francis, SJ, *Hindu God, Christian God: How Reason Helps Break Down the Boundaries between Religions*, New York, Oxford University Press, 2001, 2010

Clooney, Francis, SJ, *Divine Mother, Blessed Mother: Hindu Goddesses and the Virgin Mary*, New York, Oxford University Press, 2005

Coward, H. (ed.), *Hindu–Christian Dialogue*, Maryknoll, NY, Orbis, 1989

Cox, Harvey, *Many Mansions*, Boston, Beacon Press, 1989 (especially the chapter on Krishna and Christ, pp. 45–73)

Griffiths, Bede, *The Marriage of East and West*, Springfield, IL, Templegate, 1982

Hooker, Roger, *Uncharted Journey*, London, Church Missionary Society, 1973

Hooker, Roger, *Journey into Varanasi*, London, Church Missionary Society, 1978

Hooker, Roger, *Voices of Varanasi*, London, Church Missionary Society, 1979

Hooker, Roger, *What Is Idolatry?* London, British Council of Churches, 1986

Hooker, Roger, *Themes in Hinduism and Christianity*, Frankfurt, Peter Lang, 1989

Journal of Vaishnava Studies (JVS), edition of papers from annual meetings of Vaishnava–Christian Dialogue, vol. 20, no. 2, Spring 2012

Klostermaier, K., *Hindu and Christian in Vrindaban*, London, SCM Press, 1969, 1993

Little, Gwyneth (ed.), *Meeting Hindus*, Leicester, Christians Aware, 2001

Panikkar, Raymond, *The Unknown Christ of Hinduism*, Maryknoll, NY, Orbis/London, Darton, Longman & Todd, 1981

Parrinder, Geoffrey, *Avatar and Incarnation*, New York, Oxford University Press, 1982

Radhakrishnan, S., *Eastern Religions and Western Thought*, Oxford, Oxford University Press, 1939; New Delhi, Oxford University Press, 1989, 1991

Sharpe, Eric, *Faith Meets Faith: Some Christian Attitudes to Hinduism in the Nineteenth and Twentieth Centuries*, London, SCM Press, 1997

Thangaraj, Thomas, *The Crucified Guru*, Nashville, TN, Abingdon Press, 1994

Thatamanil, John J., *The Immanent Divine: God, Creation and the Human Predicament. An East–West Conversation*, Minneapolis, MN, Fortress Press, 2006
Wardell, M. and R. Gidoomal, *Chapatis for Tea: Reaching Your Hindu Neighbour. A Practical Guide*, Guildford, Highland, 1994

Scriptural dialogue

Gandhi, Mahatma, *The Bhagavad Gita According to Gandhi*, Berkeley, CA, North Atlantic Books, 2009
Griffiths, Bede, *River of Compassion*, Springfield, IL, Templegate, 1987, 2001
Griffiths, Bede, *Universal Wisdom*, London, HarperCollins, 1994
Parrinder, Geoffrey, *Upanishads, Gita and Bible*, London, Sheldon Press, 1962, 1975
Yogananda, Sri, Sri Paramahansa, *The Bhagavad Gita: God Talks with Arjuna*, Los Angeles, CA, Yogoda Satsanga Society of India, Self-Realization Fellowship, 2002

The USA

Eck, Diana, *A New Religious America*, New York, HarperCollins, 2001
Goldberg, Philip. *American Veda*, New York, Harmony Books, 2010
Malhotra, Rajiv, *Being Different: An Indian Challenge to Western Universalism*, New Delhi, Infinity Foundation, HarperCollins India, 2011
Pechilis, Karen (ed.), *The Graceful Guru: Hindu Female Gurus in India and the United States*, Oxford, Oxford University Press, 2004
Radhanath Swami, *The Journey Home: The Autobiography of an American Swami*, San Rafael, CA, Mandala, 2010
Ramaswamy, K. et al. (eds), *Invading the Sacred: An Analysis of Hinduism Studies in America*, New Delhi, Rupa and Co., 2007

The UK

National Council of Hindu Temples (UK), *Directory of Hindu Temples in the UK*
Woodhead, Linda and Rebecca Catto, *Religion and Change in Modern Britain*, London, Routledge, 2012 (especially pp. 121–30)

ISKCON (Hare Krishna movement)

Gelberg, Steven J. (ed.), *Hare Krishna, Hare Krishna*, New York, Grove Press, 1983
Goswami, Tamal Krishna, *A Living Theology of Krishna Bhakti: Essential Teachings of A. C. Bhaktivedanta Swami Prabhupada*, New York, Oxford University Press, 2012
Prime, Ranchor, *When the Sun Shines: The Dawn of Hare Krishna in Britain*, Watford, Bhaktivedanta Book Trust, 2009

Swaminarayan Hinduism and other movements

Kim, Hanna, 'Public Engagement and Personal Desires: BAPS Swaminarayan Temples and Their Contribution to the Discourses on Religion', *International Journal of Hindu Studies*, vol. 13, no. 3, 19 February 2010

Kim, Hanna, 'Svaminarayana: Bhakti Yoga and the Aksarabrahman Guru', in Mark Singleton and Ellen Goldberg (eds), *Gurus of Modern Yoga*, Oxford and New York, Oxford University Press, 2014

Patchen, Nancy, *Swami Chinmayananda: Journey of a Master*, Mumbai, Central Chinmaya Mission Trust, 1989

Rigopoulos, Antonia, *The Life and Teaching of Sai Baba of Shirdi*, Albany, NY, State University of New York Press, 1993

Rudert, Angela Carol, 'Inherent Faith and Negotiated Power: Swaminarayan Women in the United States' (thesis presented to the Faculty of Graduate School of Cornell University, 2004)

Williams, Raymond, *An Introduction to Swaminarayan Hinduism*, Cambridge, Cambridge University Press, 2001

Interfaith in general

Cornille, Catherine and Stephanie Corigliano (eds), *Interreligious Dialogue and Cultural Change*, Eugene, OR, Cascade Books, 2012 (especially ch. 8: Swami Tyagananda, 'Hindu Identity in a Multicultural World')

Cornille, Catherine and Glenn Willis (eds), *On Discernment in Interreligious Dialogue*, Eugene, OR, Cascade Books, 2009 (especially ch. 9: Anantanand Rambachan, 'One Goal, Many Paths: The Significance of Advaita Apologetic Norms for Interreligious Dialogue')

Cornille, Catherine and Glenn Willis (eds), *The World Market and Interreligious Dialogue*, Eugene, OR, Cascade Books, 2011 (especially ch. 7)

Coward, H., *Sin and Salvation in the World Religions*, Oxford, One World, 2003 (especially ch. 5)

Lott, Eric, Thomas Thangaraj and Andrew Wingate, *Discipleship and Dialogue: New Frontiers in Interfaith Engagement*, New Delhi, ISPCK, 2013 (20 essays in honour of Dr Israel Selvanayagam, the majority of which concern Hindu–Christian encounter; available from Christians Aware)

Wingate, Andrew, *Celebrating Difference, Staying Faithful: How to Live in a Multi-Faith World*, London, Darton, Longman & Todd, 2005

Conversion and mission issues

Robinson, Rowena and Sathianathan Clarke, *Religious Conversion in India*, New Delhi, Oxford University Press, 2003

Romain, Jonathan, *Your God Shall Be My God: Religious Conversion in Britain Today*, London, SCM Press, 2000

Wingate, Andrew, *The Church and Conversion: A Study of Recent Conversions to and from Christianity in the Tamil Area of South India*, New Delhi, ISPCK, 1997